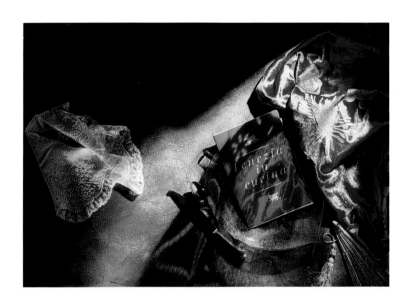

Pino Agostini - Alvise Zorzi

Venice
Tradition and Food

*The history and recipes
of Venetian cuisine*

Potographs by
Luca Steffenoni

arsenale e editrice

First edition 2004

Arsenale Editrice
A division of EBS
Via Monte Comun, 40
I-37057 San Giovanni Lupatoto (Vr)
www.arsenale.it
arsenale@arsenale.it

Photographs
Arsenale archives, Verona
pages 19, 21
Osvaldo Böhm photographic Archive, Venice
pages 8-9, 11, 18
Cameraphoto, Venice
pages 2, 6-7, 15, 32-33, 94, 188
Francesco Turio Böhm, Venice
pages 12-13, 17, 22, 23, 24-25, 26, 29, 31
Fulvio Roieter/Overseas, Milan
page 34

With thanks to
Giuseppe Dominici from Venice for the antiques
Fondaco srl, Venice, for the tapestries
Jesurum and Messrs.Levi Morenos from Venice for the tablecloths and lace
Richard Ginori from Milan for the porcelain
Vetreria Carlo Moretti glassworks of Murano for the crystal

Preparation of the dishes
signora Mirella Terrin Bettio
chef at the *Agli Alboreti* restaurant in Venice
and signor Elia Rizzo
chef at the *Il desco* restaurant in Verona

The editor extends special thanks to
Contessa Maria Pia Ferri
signora Giovanna Giol
signora Silvana Mainardis de Campo
Girolamo Marcello
for allowing us to take photographs inside their homes

as well as to
Bonifazio Brass of the *Locanda Cipriani* in Torcello
Natale Rusconi of the *Hotel Cipriani* at the Giudecca
for their courtesy they afforded out photographer

We finally wish to thank the following for their much-appreciated help
the marchesa Barbara Berlingierei of Venice
signora Anna Linguerri of Venice
signora Paola Marini, director of the Museo di Bassano
(now of the Museo Castelvecchio of Verona)
Carlo Pagnini of the Richard Ginori Milan
Francesco Paolini of Venice
The Atelier Nicolao of Venice
Lugo & Poiesi, antiquarians in Verona

Graphics
Brunhild Kindermann

Translation
William George
Kelly O'Connor

Printed by
EBS - Editoriale Bortolazzi Stei
37057 S. Giovanni Lupatoto (Verona) Italy

© 2004 EBS - Arsenale

ISBN 88-7743-311-6

contents

7

*The great culinary tradition
of the Serenissima Republic of Venice*

8

Venetian life, then and now

12

The origins of Venetian cuisine

22

From the Renaissance to modern times

33

Venetian cuisine

35

Antipasti

53

First courses

95

Meat and game

131

Fish, crustaceans and molluscs

161

Side dishes and eggs

189

Desserts

219

Bibliography

221

Index of recipes

THE GREAT CULINARY TRADITION OF THE SERENISSIMA REPUBLIC OF VENICE

Alvise Zorzi

VENETIAN LIFE, THEN AND NOW

The great masses of tourists arrive tired and out of breath at Saint Mark's Square, the Mercerie, San Salvador and San Bortolomio, rarely venturing beyond these well-trodden venues. What they know of or learn about Venice also goes little further than what could be gleaned, with less effort, from a post-card. Perhaps less. The glittering gold of the Basilica, the studied carelessness of the Palazzo Ducale's brickwork, the bronze-green moors wielding their hammers at the Clock and the majestic columns of San Marco and Tòdaro are wonders hardly glanced at by many; their hunger for the "antique" satisfied by a once-over look at the Bridge of Sighs, a Venetian cliché for the cultured and illiterate alike. The average visitor's knowledge of Venetian life itself is practically non-existent, decimated as this life has been by the mass exodus of the indigenous population on the one hand and the mass invasion of uncontrolled tourism on the other. Local and traditional cuisine has, if possible, been even more neglected, elbowed out by fast-food "restaurants", malodorous micro-waved pizzas and dishes that even in many of the smarter restaurants lack either personality or style. Such places are no longer the haunts of those who know the Venetian traditions. What the tourist demands are the likes of spaghetti with meat sauce or clams, tagliatelle alla bolognese, or tortellini with various creamy sauces. The few restaurateurs who still dedicate themselves to Venetian cuisine, and there are some who do so with praiseworthy enthusiasm, are constantly up against the ignorance of the customer as well as competition from those tempted by "creative" cooking. This latter is a local variant of the *nouvelle cuisine* that, promoted by the great Bocuse, spread throughout France. Nouvelle cuisine then crossed the Alps where many an ancient dish of robust culinary tradition and noble origin fell victim to its philosophy. These dishes had in the past stood out above all for their honest good taste and flavour, only to be sacrificed by "creative" chefs on the altar of a culinary alchemy that had little to do with the pleasures of the palate. All this is not to say that you can no longer eat well, even very well, in Venice and the Veneto region. In the Veneto region itself, rather more than its ancient capital of Venice, there has been an extraordinary and sustained economic boom over the last forty years that has seen the area transformed from one

of poverty and resignation. From being a candidate region for inclusion in the UN's "depressed areas" list, it has become one the most industrialised parts of Italy, with its traditional industries fast developing into big business. The region's small and medium-sized businesses have succeeded in dramatically raising income per head, defeating unemployment and exporting the Veneto brand to those distant lands which previous generations had been forced to go to as immigrants. The area's traditional virtues and culture were channelled into industrial activity. These virtues include an unequalled tenacity, great honesty, pride in one's work, down-to-earth realism and proper self-criticism. A self-criticism that has not extended to its own eating and drinking habits.

Francesco Guardi, *Banchetto per le nozze Polignac* (The Polignac nuptial banquet) watercolour on drawing; Museo Correr, Venice.

This is a civilisation that has all too often suffered food shortages and the pangs of hunger and it is perhaps because of this that its twin vices of the well-laden table and the full glass have developed. It would perhaps be fairer to see them as rewards or compensations rather than vices. These are people who want genuine wines, local flavours and food like Grandma used to make, albeit a little more refined and tastefully presented. These are people who also demand honest and jovial company from the restaurant-owner and as long as these conditions are met their number continues to swell those innumerable restaurants that still today

never fail to pleasantly surprise those who discover them. In Venice itself it is a different story. Since the true Venetians have mostly left, moving out to the likes of Mestre and Marghera, the number of traditional bars with their tasty *rafredi* snacks has dropped dramatically, though mercifully a few remain. Their hard-boiled eggs, *folpeti* (small octopus), *garuso'li* (sea snails), *sardè'le roste* (sardines) and so on were all designed to encourage you to drink more wine and they can still be found under their more recent name of *cicheti*. Meanwhile the genuine Cartizze, and pleasant Prosecco continued to fill the customers' glasses as well as wines such as Raboso, that can still sometimes be found, and Corbinelo, now completely vanished. Sadly the last of the *frito'lini* have disappeared; these were purveyors of enormous polentas and excellent choices of tasty fried fish, as well as cuttle-fish in ink, and from time to time *baca'là mantecato* (see recipe on pages 132-33). As youngsters we used to eat these on oiled paper laid over thicker polenta-yellow paper, all set on large solid wood tables where everyone ate together. Until recently these *frito'lini* were refreshingly classless eating houses where everyone from porters to *nobilòmini* rubbed shoulders in harmony. One well-known such establishment was in Calle delle Rasse and another of equal fame in Calle dei Fabbri, though that no-one could compete with polenta of that in San Pantalon in terms of sheer size. The last of these locales, and we are speaking of no more than twenty years or so ago, were those of Toneti in San Cancian and of Aristide in Calle della Regina in San Cassiano. I still remember the former for its *baca'là mantecato* washed down with a very full-bodied *Merlò* (I know that it is spelt 'Merlot' but in my days our hosts wrote it like that). Aristide remains in the memory for its massive portions of polenta and particularly tasty and crunchy fish. As we were saying earlier, there are fortunately still a few surviving guardians of the culinary heritage, steadfastly holding out against such the fashionable delights of the likes of fast-food. They number no more than a dozen but comprise a diverse range of eating establishments in terms of price and elegance; from the extremely chic (though loyal to the tradition) to the popular and homely. They can also still be found in the estuary's islands, despite the constant tourist onslaught right from spring through to the first frosts. These are veritable oases of a seafaring cuisine well able to adapt to prudent and subtle innovation without the need for broccoli or bell-pepper creams. Not everyone knows where they are, not even those who write the ever more numerous good-eating guides. They would do well to compile complementary guides of the restaurants to avoid, making many enemies in the process, but gaining the eternal gratitude of the rest of us. It has to be said that there are some guides, such as the exemplary Accademia Italiana della Cucina, that provide detailed information on the gastronomic traditions of the Veneto, and at least two fine books on Venetian cuisine, such as that of the cultured patrician Ranieri Da Mosto and that of the late Bepi Maffioli, both successfully tried and tested by ourselves. There is also the now impossible to find *Gastronomia Veneziana* written by my father Elio Zorzi. Despite these exceptions there can be no doubt, however, that Venetian cuisine is largely disregarded by the public at large. This is perhaps only to be expected, but it is also an unknown quantity to those who should know more, by dint either of profession or culture. Even Luigi Carnacina, one of the most celebrated Italian connoisseurs of our times, in a widely-read paperback on regional cooking, introduced a drastic change to the typically Venetian dish of *bigolì in salsa*, where the salsa in question becomes the quite irrelevant tomato sauce. The fact is that changes in the conditions and life-styles of the population remaining in Venice have profoundly affected its traditional eating habits. Even if the *pescheria* fish market of Rialto is always extremely well stocked, the women who shop there now not only have to consider the prices of the food but also their cooking and preparation times. The ever-increasing numbers of working mothers no longer have the time to patiently mix the polenta in the pot, still less over a wood fire, nor has she the patience of Job to prepare the "baccalà" with a drop of oil to serve the *mantecato*. The tradition's dishes have thus lost their everyday nature and are no longer part of daily life. Our haste demands other, more easily prepared dishes, while fashions in food advance on the back of science, as well as the flourishing pseudo-science of fad diets. Together these factors relegate to prehistory the dishes that graced our family tables such as the classic *risi e verze* (rice and cabbage), the delectable *risi, se'leno e pomidoro* soup and many another soup really halfway between soup and the risotto all'onda that ennobled the potato, artichoke, salad and even turnips and onions. There was *bigo'li in salsa* on Fridays, in the wintertime

bisato in tecia; Venetian style liver and Venetian potatoes, *verze sofegae*, *sepe roste*, *ton rosto* and boiled *asià*; there was abundant *siévoli*, much appreciated by the poet D'Annunzio, and also *bòseghe*. The recipes for most of the dishes referred to in this introduction are reproduced in the main section of this book. During wartime want there was the bony but, all things considered, delectable *papa'line*. After the terrible winter shortages of 1944-45 which saw also the fleet of boats in Chioggia decimated to make improvised bridges over the rivers Adige and Po, even these humble substitutes for sardines became impossible to get hold of.

There are however some premonitory signs of a re-assessment of the culinary heritage even in the family home, though these are not yet visible in the women's magazines that still rigorously recommend dishes seemingly designed to play havoc with the coronary arteries. As is the case with fashion, for better or worse, we are often ten years behind what is happening in America, so we should perhaps draw some comfort from the average American's rediscovery of the pleasures of cuisine. That is to say, not only that of eating well but also the pleasures of cooking. Many American men and women are increasingly going off the idea of going out for the evening to ever more anonymous restaurants, with also the possible attendant dangers of venturing downtown. There is an increasing preference for staying at home and, instead of basking in the company of the television, spending the evening with a group of friends for a convivial evening on the backyard decking or around the fireplace. Americans are spending more time at the barbecue or in the kitchen, making salsas, baking cakes and hovering over stews. Big businessmen proudly present the fruit of their culinary labours and as part of the same trend, the drinking of wine with the meal is becoming ever more popular. This has to be regarded as a great improvement on the robust concoctions prevalent since the twenties with the ever-present Scotch and soft-drinks that go so well with no known dish on Earth. It is to be hoped that the re-launch of traditional gastronomic values carried out by many restaurant owners, despite more or less subliminal attempts to undermine them from other quarters, will also be followed by a rebirth of the love

Banchetto alla Giudecca (Banquet at the Giudecca) from the Longhi school; Ca' Rezzonico, Venice.

of cooking in the domestic environment. There are now many technological aids available that speed up and simplify many thankless and laborious tasks in the kitchen and solve a whole range of food preparation problems; some of these could scarcely have been dreamed of by the housewives of times gone by. Available free time has increased for most people and now many young couples choose to spend some of this time together trying out their hands at preparing meals. We can dare to hope that a rather grey age may see the rebirth of true cuisine. If this rebirth does in fact come about, we are confident of the contribution that this book could make. From among the various recipes presented in a clear and lively way, the reader cannot fail to be tempted, strongly tempted, by some of them. When he or she personally gets a taste of this heritage, it will most surely be a pleasurable surprise.

Not all of the recipes included come from the cuisine of the Serenissma Republic as there at least twenty traditions represented from Italy's north east, including those of the Veneto region and in particular of Vicenza and Verona, Treviso and Chioggia, as well as another I willingly have left out, i.e. the wholly alien but inevitable "spaghetti alle vongole" of Neapolitan origin. The book is about an essentially poor and wholesome cuisine that is also healthy, even in such rich desserts as *frito'le*, with its use of olive oil rather than animal fats, its love of deep sea fish and garden vegetables. The variety and tastiness of these recipes, almost all of which date from olden or even ancient times, make them full of delightful surprises. In conclusion, the book aims to make a real contribution to the survival of Venetian civilisation, rocked as it has been by so many trials since its loss of its thousand years of independence in 1797. This civilisation has not yet wholly disappeared and still contains much of merit. Our task is to keep what has remained alive.

THE ORIGINS OF VENETIAN CUISINE

Whatever may be the truth about the real origin of the first Venetians, one thing is certain, and that is that they were not able to rely on the fruits of the soil to nourish them. It seems that at least until the fifth century AD this land made up a large swathe of fertile soil on which stood, among others, the magnificent villas of the Altinate Campagna that so captivated the poet Marziale. For almost three centuries the area was devastated by every kind of calamity that turned it into what we have today, or rather what there was before the land reclamation work caused a part of Venice's lagoon and the whole of the lagoon from Jesolo to Marano and Grado to disappear. This geography consists of large stretches of salty water enriched by the daily tides and occupied on the margins by "barene" and reed beds with slender banks and narrow shores, that where once narrower than they are now, and the hundred islands of Venice and estuary. While the lagoons teemed with fish, the green shores were home to pine woods and most of the islands that now make up the city contained vegetable plots, salt-pans and fish pools. What could not however be grown was the staple of wheat, as well as much of what added flavour

and pleasure to the cereal. Foodstuffs had to be sought and bought in from elsewhere as the ancient Venetian Duchy did not extend as far as nearby Mestre, even when it was a Mediterranean power and European super economy. The celebrated cattle of the Bovense shore, no mere legend, could not alone possibly support the developing community. In the early tenth century a functionary from Pavia recorded to his astonishment that the Venetians did not sow, did not plough and did not harvest, but were able to buy wheat and wine at all their ports. Six hundred years later that most accurate and prolific chronicler of Venetian affairs and politics, Marino Sanudo il Giovane, described in the most minute detail the daily life of a city that was then a great metropolis, the third-largest in Europe and the most refined and opulent of them all. In the year 1494 he wrote «And here in this land no thing grew, and yet everything was here in abundance… because everything from every land and every part of the world that could be eaten was brought here». He went on to

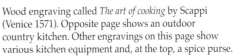

Wood engraving called *The art of cooking* by Scappi (Venice 1571). Opposite page shows an outdoor country kitchen. Other engravings on this page show various kitchen equipment and, at the top, a spice purse.

add that of all the fish and meat, wine and every kind of food that flooded the markets of Venice, nothing remained come the evening. The finest of these markets was at Rialto but there was another important one at Campo San Polo, a fish and meat market close to St. Mark's Square that was also the location of the *Magazzini al Formento*, the Republic's granary where today we find the Giardinetti Reali.
«It's because everyone has money», he explained, no doubt exaggerating, while it is true that the standard of living of the typical Venetian in Renaissance times was well above that of the dwellers of any other European city. It had long been the case that Venice not only imported wine and grain but also large quantities of other foodstuffs. The pricing authority of the time of the Doge Sebastiano Ziani spoke in 1173 of sturgeon and trout, rombe and orate, mullet and gilthead, scorpion-fish, sole, pike and tench. There were therefore plenty of fresh water fish as well as those from the Adriatic. The records of the same authority also show that beef from oxen and cows, pork and the dried meats of Lombardy were priced quite low, meaning that their consumption was substantial and widespread. In later times this consumption was to become positively excessive; fourteenth century accounting records studied by Gino Luzzatto showed so high an average intake of meet and wine, in statistics that included also the new-born, that mean life expectancy was no more than thirty years even in a privileged family like that of the Morosini of San Tomà. The main source of Venice's extraordinary wealth, accumulated over a period of at very least seven centuries, was the so-called spice trade. These included all kinds of spices and aromas from the Orient. Pepper first appears in a record of the year 853 of Bishop Orso of Olivolo, i.e. of Venice, followed by ginger, cinnamon, saffron, coriander, cumin, cubeb, mace, nutmeg and a host of other delights. They were purchased at the ports representing journey's end for the caravans, and especially those of Alexandria, Trebisonda, Beirut and Constantinople. These were all then exported with a large mark-up throughout the whole of Europe. The continent could not get enough of these products, stimulants being in those days thin on the ground with coffee as yet unknown, tea still not in use, and spirits a rarity. In addition to this it was difficult to conserve food, especially meat. Salt was the most commonly used preservative, itself to Venice's advantage as a major

producer. The result was a crying need to spice up the food to counter its high taste and odour in the absence of refrigeration. Greater and lesser feudal lords and the more or less bloated bourgeoisie of France, Germany, Flanders and England, willingly quaffed spiced wine punches, while many also believed in their medicinal properties. Such almost magical powers were thought to be possessed even by the likes of cane sugar, grown and refined since the fourteenth century in Cyprus by the Corner family of San Luca, Venice, in what could almost be described as an industrial process. Some of these goods stayed in Venice itself where they were widely used in cooking, while the state itself exercised very firm control over any fraud or tampering with the products, as indeed it did in all areas of the food industry. The spices came from afar but mutton was shipped in from just across the Adriatic, an area under Venice's control from the time of Pietro Orseolo II around the year 1000, subsequently lost and finally retaken in the fifteenth century. The best known delicacy was the smoked, salted and sun-dried lamb taken to the Dalmatian ports from Cattaro, Budua or even from Bosnia or Albania. Until not so long ago the *castradina* lamb Venice's traditional dish for the day of the Madonna della Salute. Until the fourteenth century the traditional policy of the Republic affected complete disinterest in conquering or exercising dominion over the mainland, even after the fourth Crusade when the Doge held the titles of «Duke of Venice, Dalmatia and Croatia, and lord of the fourth part and half of the whole of the Eastern Roman Empire». The boundaries of the Venetian dominions inland hardly extended beyond the limits of the salty water of the lagoon, excepting a few negligible holdings. Venice was however in possession of Crete, Eubea, the Cyclades and Sporades, Istria and Dalmatia, but neither mainland Mestre nor Oriago. Although the Venetian gentlemen were primarily merchants, they turn not turn their back on opportunities to invest in land. In November 1289, when the population showed a dangerous enthusiasm for Jacopo Tiepolo, son of the Doge Lorenzo Tiepolo and grandson of Jacopo, he decided to let the electoral college off the hook by withdrawing to his seat in Morocco after the death of Giovanni Dandolo, as there would have been a real risk a dynasty establishing itself in the Republic. The San Leonardo branch of the Querini family enjoyed feudal revenues from their Papozze in Polesine area

Filippo Zaniberti, *Banchetto del Doge Giovanni I Corner*
(Doge Giovanni I Corner's banquet); Ducal Palace, Venice.

then in the hands of the Marquis of Ferrara. Before becoming Doge, Marino Falier had acquired the great fiefdom of Valmareno. As celebrated in a play by Byron, he then went on to be executed for conspiring to seize power for himself. It was probably as this that situation that the Venetian patricians voted in favour of the rule prohibiting any Doge from possessing estates *extra Dominium*. From these estates

however, both in the middle ages and the high Renaissance periods, flowed those copious quantities of fruits of the land of which Sanudo had spoken. Those of the Corner family of San Cassiano for example, from which Caterina Queen of Cyprus was to come, contained truly vast tracts in the marches of Treviso and Padua. With these foods also came the recipes and culinary customs of the terra firma. These were to combine in the lagoons with those from lands under Venetian dominion beyond its shores as well as those from those areas still further afield where the tireless merchants of Venice had established continuous links both east and west. The galleys of Venice regularly moored in Sicily, at Aigues Mortes on the coast of Provence, and then onwards to the Atlantic ports of Bordeaux and up to Southampton, London, Antwerp and Bruges. There was also constant trade with the German world, whose importance was confirmed in the early sixteenth century by the construction of the grandiose Fondaco, or warehouse, at San Bortolomio, decorated by Giorgione and Titian. This commercial exchange also served to maintain the prosperity of Venetian business in Augusta and other imperial cities. Other much more distant lands were visited by noblemen adventurers born beneath the shadow of the tower of St. Marks Square. In 1245 in Kiev, Giovanni da Pian del Carpine met with the two Venetians Nicolò Pisani and Giacomo Venier on his way to the extremely distant court of the Great Khan of Mongolia; in Tabriz in 1264 the Venetian Pietro Vilioni left, among other things, many glass and crystal artefacts in his will, and while Nicolò, Matteo and Marco Polo are famous for travelling the immensity of China for so many years, they were also followed by many other Venetians including "the great merchant" Pietro di Luca Longo who made a fortune in Beijing. He was also to be famous for generously funding there the construction of a catholic cathedral. Other adventurers include the likes of Luchetto Duodo and Francesco Giovanni Loredan; the latter was known as the Vacca or cow and died in Delhi in India, itself also the objective of many Venetian trading expeditions.

The reason we have made much of the Venetians' legendary mercantile ability has been to emphasise the variety of ingredients that were to enrich the Venetian cuisine. These merchants had ensured an inflow of great wealth to Venice that was only finally to lose its energy in the first half of the seventeenth century. This cuisine fell into two main types: the records show that until recently there were the festive, heavily flavoured and spiced dishes of feasts on the one hand and homely, modest fayre based on a few simple local foods on the other. These latter were often just as much appreciated by the great and good in Venetian society. Records from the middle ages show the appearance of some of the foods that are still to be found in our local cuisine, such as the likes of the bread-based *salsa peverada* containing pepper and ox marrow. This was considered by the judicial

authorities of the "Giustizieri Vecchi" to be so important to the city's nourishment that in 1310 they made a special rule that the spice-sellers should not dare or presume to «make or have made *peverada* containing any other spices than good-quality pepper and good "unwetted" saffron». It was further decreed that that the grinders «must not pound *peverada*… that they knew to contain any ingredients other that those of good quality». As with many preparations of this kind it was ground in a stone pestle and mortar. A document dating from 1299 records the menu for a nuptial banquet that was not especially elegant but was very substantial. The beef and pork, chicken and game birds were all accompanied by the *peverada*.

Great quantities of chicken were sold at the Rialto market and in 1173 we see the first regulations governing the activities of the *gallineri* or chicken vendors. Game was abundantly available throughout the fourteenth century with falcons and gerfalcons even for exportation; in 1364, for example, sixty live and twelve dead gerfalcons arrived in a Venetian galleon at Alexandria in Egypt where they were exchanged for a batch of sugar. Other documents refer to wild duck, quail, wild doves, partridges, black partridges or francolins, marsh waders, thrushes, lapwings, squid, wild chicken fowl and even swans and cranes. Jellies were also much appreciated by the gentry, as were goose, domestic duck and doves well into the eighteenth century. You can feel the great chronicler of the sixteenth century Marin Sanudo positively salivating in his records of these. At the table of the Doge himself figured such delights as *lotregani* and *verselate*, varieties of mullet that were offered as dues or tributes. Alongside these could be found the oysters and salted eels that would grace the dining room for centuries. The *zentilomeni*, or gentlemen, also sat down to botargo dishes, especially mullet, and caviar whose price was determined by the authorities between the years of 1460 and 1464. As regards sweets and desserts, there are records of *zelatiam* jelly as far back as 1304 and in the fifteenth century we find increasing references to the a range of sweets that included biscuits, *bozolatos* or *busso'lai* doughnuts, candied pumpkin, marzipan, *pignocade*, *storti* (still to be found when I was a boy, as were the cialdoni eaten with whipped cream), quince jam, boxed *ze'li* biscuits, candied pasta, musky sugar, and *sca'lete* or grilled offal whose makers (the *sca'leteri*) even gave their name to some

Venetian cook, engraving from the Gherro collection
(volume IV, n° 2003); Correr Museum, Venice.

of Venice's streets. The fifteenth century also provides
us with many other records, including one of the bread
that made at least one consumer swoon with delight, saying
in 1427 that he had paid six *soldi* «*pro panibus optimis visu
ac candidissimis et deliziosissimus*» (the best bread you
could set eyes upon, brilliant white and quite delicious)
as well references to the prized vegetables, lettuce and
endives of the monks' vegetable gardens. These included
spinach, chervil, carrots, cabbages, leeks, garlic and radishes,
beets, Egyptian capers, red chickpeas, kidney beans, lentils,

peas, fresh or dried broad beans and the asparagus that was
"to be eaten before lunch on Holy Saturday". There was
also an abundance of fruit that included gooseberries, pears
(with those of San Nicolò reputed to be especially good),
fresh figs, water melons from Ferrara, dry marasca cherries,
fresh Arbe figs, fresh grapes, the *cimbybo* (sweet "zibibbo"
grapes), almonds, chestnuts and dates and prunes, while the
olives were served with oil and fennel. There is also mention
of a Holy Christmas "focaccia" for which one customer
in 1460 bought twenty-four eggs, at three eggs per soldo,
though it is not known how many people would have
eaten it with him. The state itself was ever vigilant in
the avoidance both of possible shortages and of hoarding
or monopolies, as well as any adulterating of products,
paying especial attention to the wine trade. There were
an abundance of provisions made to prevent sophistication.
As far back as 1173 the Doge Sebastiano Ziani prohibited
innkeepers from watering down or from mixing wines.
The state exercised a true wine monopoly in the fourteenth
century, importing malmsey from Peloponnesia and Crete,
red ribolla and *tribiano* from Istria and all kinds of other
wines from the Marches, Abruzzo, Puglia and Calabria,
as well as from the nearby marches of Treviso. It was
however permitted under certain circumstances to dilute
wines and 1339 it was even established what exactly was
the best degree of alcohol for the diluted wine; such wine
being known as "prima acqua", or first watering, wine.
The legislature turned its attention in the fifteenth century
to the food on the table, particularly addressing real and
presumed wastefulness by the rich. There was an ever-
present concern that the excesses of luxury could lead
to what the poet Andrea Calmo was to call the *"desfation
de le famigie"*, or the break-up of the families. Thus it was
that the Maggior Consiglio prohibited in 1473 the eating
of pheasant, francolin, peacock, Indian fowl, mountain
chicken, trout and other freshwater fish and only
allowed jelly and *frito'le* for dessert. It was with this order,
published by Bartolomeo Cecchetti, that these most
Venetian of Carnival sweets came to the fore. Needless
to any such rules to curb excess were as unceremoniously
disregarded as the exhortations of Manzoni. For the whole
of the sixteenth century the Magistrates of the high counsel,
highly unpopular with the patrician class, did everything
they could to put in place prohibitions and restrictions.

These even involved domestic staff who were theoretically under a duty in law to report any flouting of the regulations by their masters. The agents of the inspectorate, and their sorties, were not suffered gladly, as was demonstrated by the need for yet another provision aiming at punishing those "presumptuous persons" who welcomed them with a hail of bread and oranges. The refined manners of Venetians at the dining table can trace their origins to the influence of the Byzantine Court. The Doge Domenic Salvo married a Byzantine princess who introduced the fork to the lagoons in the period between 1071 and 1084, fully two and a half centuries before Brother Bonvesin da la Riva recommended his table companions, in

Franceso Zugno, *Il banchetto di Antonio e Cleopatra* (Anthony and Cleopatra's banquet); Ca' Rezzonico, Venezia. Bonifacio de' Pitati da Verona, *Il convito del ricco Epulone* (banquet of the wealthy Epulone); Accademia Gallery, Venice.

his *Cortesie da desco*, not lick their fingers and scoop food to their mouths. At least as time went by, this sophistication came to be paralleled by that of the meals themselves. Some of the fourteenth century Venetian recipes published by Zambrini in 1863, in the *Libro di cucina*, records this fact and enables us for the first time to see a link between the ancient cooking and that of our times, or those just past. We see that some of today's "discoveries" in fact date back six centuries. An example of this is the *Bramagere*, a dialect variation of blancmange or "eating white", i.e. chicken with almonds and sweet rice and cloves. Another example is the true *quiche* and *torta di herbe*, or herb pie, with beet, parsley, spinach, mint, lard and eggs. There was also the *torta de faxoli freshi*, or fresh bean pie, cooked with belly of pork and then ground with the pestle and mortar to make the "perfettissima" pie. Recipes included orange sauce and walnut bread, hard-boiled eggs stuffed with cheese and fine herbs *(erbe bone)*, a great variety of fried ravioli with raisins and pine-seeds and cheese and herbs fillings, using the likes of lean Tuscan cheeses. There were almond

more the feel of Arabia or the Maghreb desert, as well as green *capreto* sage and rosemary sauce for kid and lamb, while for the suckling pig was reserved the "perfettissimo" tartar sauce with egg added to the usual spices. Culinary canons demanded the use of aniseed, almond, ginger, nutmeg and sugar dissolved in vinegar in the cooking of boiled meats. Such recipes are far from the habits of our times; medieval Venetians loved the so-called "dolce-forte", sweet-strong taste, that survives today only in Tuscan boar with chocolate and a few other Italian recipes. Giuseppe Maffioli records for us how the printing boom

quinquinelli and the *licaproprii* "as big and round as apples" to be cooked in lard and dusted with sugar powder. We find elder-flower fritters that are still around today, and the apple fritters for Lent. Quadragesimal fritters were made with vegetables and pomegranate chicken, much as still seen nowadays in Vicenza's *paéta al malgaragno*, and there was also stracciatella, known in my mother's day by the fourteenth century name of *sansare'li* or *sassare'le*. As well as several varieties of *peverada*, sauces included one based on grilled garlic that has a feel of Provence or Catalonia about it, the "salsa saracinesca" made with cinnamon, cloves, cardamom, nutmeg, ginger, yet other spices and almonds, raisins and verjuice that has much

of the early sixteenth century saw more books printed in Venice in any given year than in all the other cities of Italy put together. This explosion did much to contribute to the birth of European haute cuisine. The new century brought with it a proliferation of cookery books. Claudio Benporat traced to the Vatican Library what was perhaps the prototype for many other works: the *Refettorio* of Eustachio Celebrino of Udine. This was published by Francesco di Alessandro Bindoni and Maffeo Pasini in Venice in 1526 and contained fifteen pages aimed at teaching the reader how to «lay the table for guests, carve all kinds of meat and present food in accordance with the tenets of the carvers' guild for the honouring

of foreign guests… with the addition of cooking secrets and how to conserve meat and fruit». Benporat considers the menu for a winter luncheon: after the guests have washed their hands in scented water they arrive at a table laid with bread, biscuits and *pignochati* (sweet bread with pine-seeds), as well as a knife and fork for each person, something still rare in continental Europe. They are then served a *coletione*, consisting of green ginger, small bitter lemons *(cetrangoli)*, nuts and candied fruit. These are followed by biscuits dipped in Malmsey; artichokes; fresh cheese scented with rose water and sweetened with sugar; chicken, capon or veal liver in damask sauce; platters of pheasant, partridge, roast pigeon, capon, chicken and roast veal with slices of orange and pickled lemon. Following these are sweet lemons sliced in rose water, pear tarts, jelly, boiled capon, veal and tongue with broth or *blanc manger* or ravioli with mustard and the peppery *peverada*.
At the end of the meal marzipan is served, the tablecloth and dishes are changed and various jams are provided with dark and white liqueur wines diluted with water. Here we have, then, a clear order to the servings: antipasti followed by roasts, followed in turn by the boiled meats, and dessert at the end of the meal. The use of lemons as a returning feature between courses is worthy of note, as well as the use of oranges to accompany the roasts. The rightly celebrated *canard à l'orange* of French haute cuisine is thus foreshadowed in this fourteenth century text, in which appear the words «an orange flavour… to be given to each roast dish»; though by this are intended oranges washed in wine and salt, sliced into quarters and soaked in the wine. Platina, that most erudite of men and founder of the Vatican's Apostolic Library during the reign of Sisto IV, in the year 1473 proudly had printed in Venice a compendium of recipes in his «*honesta voluptate et valetudine*».
These were inspired by the classics works, especially of Apicio, though even he gives us a recipe for *sassarèle*, «*cibarium quod vulgo zanzarellas vocatur*», consisting of egg, cheese and bread chopped into a saffron broth. Much more extensive and systematic treatment of the subject in the common language of the day was provided in the works of a number of authors. These notably included those of Cristoforo Messisbugo, first printed in Ferrara in 1549 and reprinted in Venice no less than seven times between 1552 and 1626; that of Domenico Romoli, known as Panonto,

first published in Venice in 1560 and that of Bartolomeo Scappi with seven printings from 1570 to 1642. None of these gentlemen was from Venice but we know that Messisbugo stayed in Venice and Scappi's work contained a dedication to the «Magnificent Maestro Matteo Barbiero, most celebrated Chef and Scalco (official carver) of the City of Venice». There is no doubt that the choice of location for the printing of these works was not only determined by the primacy of Venice's publishers in Europe, but also to the widespread use of such works by Venetian society in the sixteenth century. At that time the art of putting on a banquet had become a highly sophisticated affair and was a matter of considerable pride. Entertaining became an important ritual, not just for private parties but also for state occasions. The Doge's banquets were the living incarnation of the majesty and splendour of the Serenissima, the most serene republic, and met real political needs. These included the rotation of carefully planned guest invitations, so that all the officers of the government were assured at least one convivial informal encounter with the Doge every year. Such meetings with the head of state would be less dominated by the rules of procedure and protocol that governed normal practice. While the pomp and splendour surrounding the head of the government gave him all the appearance of a monarch, his power was in fact extremely limited, and as a rule he was always seated close to the Serenissima Signoria, the six ducal councillors, together with other influential figures in the republic.
We cannot really know exactly in detail how it was to dine in the Banqueting Hall of the Palazzo Ducale, to the strains of music of St. Mark's Chapel. We do know that much depended on the personal tastes of the Doge. Sanudo often praises the exquisite *pasti di pesse*, or fish dishes, of the magnificent Doge Andrea Gritti. In his youth this Doge had been a merchant in Constantinople, then a much-decorated general in the wars against the Cambrai coalition and later an extremely shrewd diplomat involved in the dismantling of the doomed league assembled by Pope Julius II. Gritti, whose majestic features survive in a portrait by Titian, was a politician of great energy and temperament and a figure of high culture but these qualities did not stand in the way

Paolo Veronese, detail from *Convito in casa di Levi*
(Banquet at the Levi household); Accademia Gallery, Venice.

of his also being a quite unrepentant glutton. It seems he was mad about beans, garlic and onions and would stop at nothing to gorge himself on eel kebabs on Christmas Eve. We can be assured that other Doges, like the generous Lorenzo Priuli, the prudent Alvise Mocenigo and above all the most splendid Marino Grimani, willingly partook of the recipes in vogue, with a view also to further endear themselves to the guests at the banquet who would, with their votes at the political meetings, be the arbiters of policy.

FROM THE RENAISSANCE TO MODERN TIMES

Giuseppe Maffioli noted that several of Messisbugo's recipes were destined to be handed down with slight modifications to ourselves, or at least to those of very recent times. The *mariconda* is an example that re-appears, albeit with many changes, in the celebrated and classic work of Artusi. Also surviving to our times are the *mostarda*, a typically

Renaissance dish in its marriage of jams, candied fruit and strong mustard and the *capirotta*, a sort of capon, veal or game soup and fricassee thickened with egg yolks and lemon juice. This latter is still enjoyed in central Italy with lamb, while the egg and lemon sauce is none other than the *avkolémona* that today's Greeks pour over all kinds of dishes. Panonto presents us with a pluck-based dish that is the ancestor of the *fongadina* of our grandparents' day. The cuisine offered by Scappi seems to be less heavy and spicy than that of the other writers and sings the praises of the *pesce gho*, or whitebait from the lagoon that still figures today in many delicious local risottos. It has to be said that the above three recipe books also contain many concoctions that would be unacceptable to the modern palate, not to mention the liver or arteries. Such instances include such delicacies as Scappi's fritters made with goat's milk, sugar, rose water, salt, saffron, white sugar, egg and lard, and Panonto's butter-fried bread. There are however other recipes that could be well worth rediscovering, such as the fried string beans, *pesce in casonada* (fish boiled in wine and vinegar with sage), Messisbugo's apple, raisin and pine nut fritters, Panonto's roast lamb and a curious recipe for the conserving of caviar. Something of the atmosphere of the setting for these recipes is conveyed in the many works depicting banquets by great Venetian painters of the Cinquecento. The first of these was Paolo Veronese, master of the splendid dining scene, with such works as the *Nozze di Cana* (Cana's wedding feast) and the *Convito in casa di Levi* (banquet at the Levi household) in the Accademia gallery in Venice. While Tintoretto was the greatest artist of his time, he showed little interest in capturing the convivial aspect of his dining scene paintings, more concerned with the spiritual aspect dramatically emerging through strong contrasts of light and shade. Bassano was more attentive to the details of the life of the kitchen. As regards the literati, no-one better embodies the spirit of the age than Pietro Aretino. He was a master of sensual writing, friend and patron of artists, correspondent to the powerful, and dining companion to the most beautiful courtesans. The famous portrait by his friend Titian shows the features of an impudent gourmand, nonchalantly dressed in sumptuous clothes and fully expressing the merriment and conviviality that characterised that century. Aretino also knew a thing or two about food, and it is

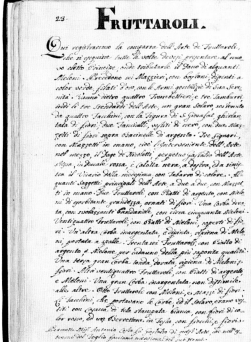

Giovanni Grevembroch, *L'offerta dei meloni al Doge*
(offering melons to the Doge).
Fruttaroli (fruit vendors); Correr Museum, Venice
(Gradenico-Dolfin codex).

not difficult to picture him at the dining table in his house
on the Grand Canal, just opposite the great market of Rialto,
with an arm around the milky white shoulders of the
fine courtesan and woman of spirit Angela Zaffetta whose
company he enjoyed so much. In his other hand we may
picture a diaccio glass of the vinello he praises in a letter,
toasting the health of Titian Vecellio and Jacopo Sansovino,
his most frequent of guests. Those particular evenings were
however dominated more by business matters than by sex
or good food, as the triumvirate of Artetino, Titian and
Sansovino represented something of the gathering of bosses.
Overall, the most gluttonous event of the century overall
must have consisted in the series of uniquely splendid
celebrations in which the Republic welcomed the king
of France and Poland, Henry III di Valois. He came to the
city to consolidate a long alliance, as well as to shore up the
coffers. Much has already been written of the encounters
so we need not dwell on them here. We cannot however pass

over the «most beautiful luncheon of confettioni, candied
fruits, with cutlery, tablecloths, dishes, and napkin holders
made of icing sugar» served on the occasion of the visit
to the Arsenale, nor that other "finest of luncheons "
offered him a few days later in the hall of Scrutinio of the
Ducal Palace in the presence of «diverse statues, icing sugar
figures of men, nymphs, lions, dwarves and griffins made
by the expert in such things Nicolò della Pigna».
The Republic set out to amaze and astonish its illustrious
guest, and it succeeded, especially when the king tried
to unfold his table napkin only to find it crumbled in
his grasp, it too made of icing sugar.
In contrast to all this splendour, a contrast that was to last
for the whole of Republic's existence, there persisted a great
simplicity of taste and customs, even among the privileged
patrician class. This is illustrated in the expenses ledger
of 1509 of the high-ranking nobleman Marco Falier,
published by Pompeo Molmenti. It speaks of "eggs and
herbs", *barbonzini*, the small mullet still much appreciated
by Venetian connoisseurs of good food, the *bresole de ponta
de schena* chops, figs and sorb apples, two lira's worth
of tripe, one soldo of fish, and two lire and seven soldos

23

Bartolomeo Litterini, *Nozze di Cana* (Cana's nuptial feast);
San Pietro Martire, Murano.

for "4 buckets of wine at 12 soldos a bucket". With the happy
conclusion of the wars that had afflicted the republic
in the early sixteenth century, a long period of peace was
to begin in the land of the Veneto that was now an
established part of the Serenissima republic of Venice,
and would be right through to 1797. With peace and final
dominion over the mainland, the interest of well-to-do
Venetians shifted more and more from the traditional
industries of armaments and sea trading to landed property.
For the whole of that century and into the early seventeenth
century, the two areas of interest lived side by side.
It was at this time however that what is today known as
"villa civilisation", began to develop, flourish and become
truly splendid. The greatest surviving monuments to that
time are the villas designed by Andrea Palladio and
commissioned by wealthy Venetians such as the Badoer,
Zeno, Emo, Barbaro, Foscari and Pisani families, as well
as the Veneto families of Capra, Serego, Pojana and others.
Running parallel to the outward spread of patrician Venice
into the terra firma and their villas, with a consequent
rediscovery of country life even by the provincial aristocracy
itself, there began the farming of new crops, the most
important of which was maize. This was a profitable cereal
to grow and was soon planted throughout the mainland
dominions which included even half of Lombardy up to the
river Adda. A popular song of the early twentieth century
reflected this in its line *«un bel dì, fra l'Oglio e il Brenta / venne
al mondo la polenta»* (one fine day, twixt the Oglio and Brenta
/ there came to the world the – good dish – polenta).
Polenta was to become a staple of the Veneto region, at once
the delight of the gourmand and the consolation of the poor
who then existed in large numbers in the countryside and
did so up until not many years ago. The reliance on polenta
was such that in the nineteenth century the dreaded pellagra
was endemic as a result of a lack the vitamin niacin.
The year 1881 saw no less than a hundred thousand cases
of the disease. Polenta also made its way to Venice itself, and
it came to stay. Eighteenth century cuisine welcomed it with
open arms and glorified the dish. The playwright Goldoni
placed it at a focal point in the tasty gastronomic seduction
scene in his *Donna di garbo*, when Rosaura says to Arlecchino:

«Empiremo una bella caldaia d'acqua e la porremo sopra
le fiamme. Quando l'acqua comincerà a mormorare io prenderò
di quell'ingrediente in polvere bellissima come l'oro chiamata farina
gialla e a poco a poco andrò fondendola nella caldaia nella quale tu
con una sapientissima verga andrai facendo dei circoli e delle linee.
Quando la materia sarà condensata la leveremo dal fuoco e tutti e due
di concerto con un cucchiaio per uno la faremo passare dalla caldaia
ad un piatto. Vi cacceremo poi sopra di mano in mano un'abbondante
porzione di fresco, giallo e delicato butirro, poi altrettanto grosso,
giallo e ben grattato formaggio, e poi? E poi Arlecchino e Rosaura,
uno da una parte, l'altra dall'altra, con una forcin in mano per
cadauno prenderemo due o tre bocconi in una volta di quella ben
condizionata polenta e ne faremo una mangiata da imperadore…»[1]

This is the stuff of the refined and illuminated eighteenth
century. The previous century, which saw Venice victorious
in its jurisdictional battle with Pope Paul V, it had lost Crete
and but briefly conquer Peloponnesia through Francesco
Morosini. The century also left no great impression on the
gastronomic arts aside from a book by Giulio Cesare Tirelli.
The Doge's chef's work was succinctly entitled *L'arte di ben*

cucinare, or The art of Good Cooking, and was published
in Mantua in 1662. According to the experts it was notable
for the range of its innovations, including such recipes
as *latte alla spagnola* precursor to today's *rosada allo zambalione*,
consisting of egg yolks, sugar, and white wine, his pumpkin
and artichoke bottoms and a general reduction in the use
of the hitherto ever-present spices and the tradition
of the "dolce-forte". The new century saw the Most Serene
Republic impoverished by the ruination of its trade with
the Orient and a drastically diminished role in international
affairs as against the great continental monarchies.
It became less and less a capital of high politics
and increasingly a capital of worldly pleasures; what
Talleyrand was to call *la douceur de vivre*.
France had indeed become the foremost continental power
and was by now dictating trends both in fashion and cuisine.
The reign of Louis XIV saw the rising talent of the great
French chefs such as Carême and Vatel, while during that

of Louis XV French cuisine made some excellent discoveries
such as mayonnaise and lamb chops à la Villeroy.
The influence of French cooking spread throughout Europe
so that we have, for example, the birth of Neapolitan
"monzù" cuisine, from *monsieur*, as they called the chefs
come down to the city from France. They also came
to Venice and imported all manner of dishes and ways
of serving them to the more fashion-conscious stratum
of society. Again it is Carlo Goldoni who gives us a flavour
of the scene in a dialogue from his *Spirito di contraddizione*:

DOROTEA: Venga un piatto alla volta. Conte, che ve ne pare?
CONTE: Certo un piatto alla volta. Questo è il vero mangiare.
FERRANTE: Anch'io così lo intendo. Pria la minestra, e poi…
DOROTEA: No, la minestra in fine. Conte, che ne dite voi?
CONTE: Dico che va benissimo. La Francia a noi maestra
ora accostuma all'ultimo la zuppa e la minestra.
FERRANTE: Ma non è ben dapprima lo stomaco scaldarci?
DOROTEA: No signore, alla moda dobbiamo uniformarci.
(Al servitore) Lascia il salame in tavola. Porta il resto in cucina.[2]

We can rest assured that every century has its own *nouvelle cuisine*. The large number references in the works of Goldoni, himself a connoisseur of the dining table and acute observer of the manners and ideas of his time, nevertheless convince us that despite the many dishes imported from French haute cuisine, most people steadfastly remained faithful to tasty, local and simpler food. To hear such dishes described by the characters in Goldoni's plays is enough to make the audience lick its collective lips.

When asked how she is treated by her master, Brighella responds, in *La cameriera brillante*:

> «Alla casalina, ma no gh'è , mal. La so manestra, per consueto de risi o de pasta fina… La so carne de manzo con un bon capon. Un rosto de vedelo e do oseleti… Un piatto de mezzo, che vol dir o un stufadin, o quatro polpete o cosse simili, el so formagio, i so frutti… Ma no gh'è torte, non gh'è pastizzi, no gh'è selvadego…»[3]

The setting is that of what may today be called a well-to-do home. If we take a look at dinner being prepared for successful artisans in *Una delle ultime sere di Carnevale*, we hear:

> DOMENICA: E avanti a principiar, sono andada in cusina, ho dà i me ordeni; ho aiutà a far suso i raffioi; ho fatto meter el stuffà in pignatta, e ho volesto metterghe mi la so conza; ho fatto che i torna a lavar el pollame; ho fatto el pien a la dindietta; ho volesto veder a impastar le polpette; ho dà fora el vin; ho messo fora la biancaria. No me manca altro che tirar fora le possae, le sottocoppe, e quelle quattro bottiglie de vin de Cipro.[4]

Ravioli (*raffioi*), stew (*stuffà*), poultry, tacchinella – stuffed turkey hen (*dindietta*), rissoles, good wine and, to end up with, the Cyprian wine that was so fashionable in the eighteenth and part of the nineteen centuries. The theme is that of substance and simplicity. Rather more whimsical is the feast of the *Morbinosi*:

> GIACOMETTO: Gran risi!
> ANDREETTA: E quela sopa?
> OTTAVIO: La carne era squesita.
> FELIPPO: Che castrà! Che fritura! Mi ghe andava de vita.
> GIACOMETTO: Quele quatro moleche non gierele perfete?
> ANDREETTA: I s'ha desmentegà de tagiarghe le ongiete.
> FELIPPO: Boni quei colombini.
> ANDREETTA: Boni per la stagion.
> GIACOMETTO: E quel salé co l'agio mò no gerelo bon?
> FELIPPO: La torta veramente gera assae delicata.
> GIACOMETTO: No cavàvela el cuor quela bela salata?
> FELIPPO: E sto desser? Dasseno, no se pol far de più…[5]

Pietro Longhi, *Venditrice di frittelle* (Fritters vendor); Ca' Rezzonico, Venice.

Risotto, soup (*sopa*), meat, lamb, fried food, *mo'leche*, small pigeons, garlic salami, salad and dessert. Not bad for a banquet for a hundred and twenty to serve, despite some grumbles from Signora Andreetta who is never without a corkscrew in her pocket and proceeds to uncork a bottle of cinnamon rosolio. By the time Goldoni describes the meals of eighteenth century Venice, the taste in food is very close to that of our times, differing significantly only in terms of quantity, as we eat much less. Others of the innumerable records of eighteenth century life confirm that we are faced with a simple, flavoursome cuisine where meat and fish figure equally while rice is dominant in first course dishes and the roasts are prevalently poultry. The century saw the rise of coffee drinking. The "bottega del caffè", or coffee house, emerged to become the meeting place for high society and the bourgeoisie. Meanwhile the common people

of Venice continued to drink wine, with that of the Vicenza area being rightly popular; still today some delicious wines come out the Colli Berici hills. Among these are the sparkling Durello and the delicate red Tocai, neither as well known as they deserve to be. The wine was consumed in the *magazeni* (stores) that also doubled as pawn shops, and the *bastioni*, lower ranking public houses, as well as in the *malvasie* or malmsey houses which, like the *magazeni* left their trace in the form of many street and place names in the Venetian landscape. Such establishments were also frequented by members of the nobility who fancied a glass of Greek or Cyprian wine. The *malvasia* in Calle del Rimedio was one such well-known gathering place. It was not unknown for patricians to take a young colleague here for a glass or two of malmsey into which they would dip slices of *busso'la*, the fragrant Venetian doughnut. The ritual may well have followed the round of handshaking at the *Broglio*, the square in front of the Ducal Palace, on the young man's debut in the Maggior Consiglio, the Republic's sovereign assembly.
During the course of that century increasing numbers of the ruling class abandoned active participation in the political life of a republic that had lasted longer than any other European state. This was largely due to the loss of the underlying conditions behind Venice's raison d'être. It became common for the members of the patrician order to take on an ecclesiastical role as "abbots", simply to avoid having to take on the compulsory *cursus honorum* of political office. All social classes took refuge in pleasure, as the continuous partying of the *garanghé'lo* helped divert their thoughts from what practically everyone considered to be an inevitable decline.
Some dulled their senses by indulgence in the most extravagant luxury; the Pisani family of Santo Stefano, for example, spent a fortune to prepare a welcome for King Gustav III of Sweden who was to frankly admit he would not have the means to return the compliment on such a grand scale in Stockholm. The Nani family organised a great dinner at the Giudecca for the archbishop elector of Cologne, Clement of Baveria, that has been recorded for posterity by an amusing painting. An endless string of parties runs as a thread through the unfolding century; aristocratic parties, bourgeois parties and popular parties, with everyone eager to organise dances in the squares or "Campielli" and take part in the *sagre*, local fetes. The most famous of these was that of Santa Marta that always ended with a great buffet of stuffed duck and *sfogi in saòr*. The Venice Carnival itself lasted for more than half of the year. Molmenti published a list of the wines and liqueurs served at the nuptials of the "Cavaliere" Giorgio Zorzi Contarini dal Zaffo and Caterina Civran in 1755. The wine list is enough to make your head spin; there were twenty-four different wines including Tocai, Burgundies, Champagne, Graves, Rhine wines, Malaga, old Cyprian wine and Cyprian muscatel.

---

[1] «Let us fill a good hot pot of water over the fire. When the water starts to bubble I'll take that beautiful golden powder called yellow flour and mix it little by little in the pot where you, with artful stick, will trace lines and circles. When it is thick you'll take it off the fire and together we'll take from the pot to a dish. We steadily add abundant portions of fresh, yellow and delicate butter and then some copious amounts of equally yellow well-grated cheese, and then? And then, Harlequin and Rosario, you for your part and my for mine, forks in hand, we'll take two three mouthfuls at a time of that fine polenta and stuff ourselves like emperors…»

[2] DOROTEA: Have one dish brought at time Count, don't you think?
COUNT: Oh yes, one dish at a time. That is true dining.
FERRANTE: I understand it to be so too. First the soup, and then…
DOROTEA: No, the soup comes at the end. Don't you think so Count?
COUNT: I think that's fine. France teaches us that it is now the thing to leave the soup to the end.
FERRANTE: But is not perhaps a good idea to first warm the stomach?
DOROTEA: No sir, we must not fly in the face of fashion.
(to the servant) Leave the salami on the table. Take the rest to the kitchen.

[3] «As a housekeeper, but well. His soup, usually rice or small pasta soup… His beef with a good capon. A veal roast with two small birds… A middle course, that is a stew, or four rissoles or suchlike, his cheese, his fruit… but no cakes, no pasticcio and no game…»

[4] DOMENICA: Before starting I went to the kitchen and gave the orders; I helped to make the ravioli sauce; I had the stew put in the pot and I decided to add the condiment to it myself; I made them wash the poultry again; I prepared the stuffing and the turkey hen; I saw over the making of the rissoles; I distributed the wine; I put the table linen out. Then I had to get the cutlery out, the saucers and those four bottles of Cyprian wine.

[5] GIACOMETTI: Great risotto!
ANDREETA: And that soup?
OTTAVIO: The meat was delicious.
FELIPPO: What lamb! What fried food! I love it!
GIACOMETTO: Weren't those mo'leche just perfect?
ANDREETA: They forgot to clip the ends of the feet off.
FELIPPO: The pigeons were good.
ANDREETA: Good for the time of year.
GIACOMETTO: The garlic salami was excellent don't you think?
FELIPPO: The cake, it must be said, was very delicate.
GIACOMETTO: Didn't you just love the salad?
FELIPPO: And this dessert. You really couldn't do any better…

There was even South African wine from the Cape of Good Hope, Jamaica rum, vermouth, four types of rosolio, beer from England and the highly expensive Picolit from Friuli and ratafee from Grenoble. With such lifestyles becoming something of a habit it is not perhaps surprising that when the Lodovico Manin was elected the last Doge in 1789, the treasury spent the enormous sum of 47.298 ducats in just eight days to maintain the electors, with a terrible waste of meat, fish, prized crustaceans, salads, vegetables, fruit, sweets, ice-cream, wine and rosolio. Money was also squandered on board the Venetian war vessels; the embarkation inventory of Lunardo Correr, the shipping magnate or "Patrona delle Navi" provided in 1793 for a quantity of plates and crockery and an impressive list of foodstuffs. These included four 200 lb jars of butter, 400 eggs, 32 barrels of red wine, 100 lb of rice, 150 lb of barley, 150 lb of *macaroni* from Naples, 100 lb of *fidelini* from Genoa, 50 lb of *semette*, a kind of pasta from Puglia and more than 300 lb of other types of pasta; 30 hams, 20 garlic salamis, 93 *ossocolli*, 387 lb of dried salted cod, 150 lb of salmon and 20 ½ lb of caviar; 16 forms of various kinds of cheese, 100 lb of sugar in loaves and 800 lb of miscellaneous sugars, 300 lb of coffee and 130 lb of chocolate; 2 lb of truffles, 8 lb of gherkins, 8 lb of capers, 8 lb of pickled bell peppers and almost 200 lb of dried fruit and 44 lb of candied fruit. The list of wines includes no less than 36 bottles of Picolit, even then both rare and costly. As if all this were not enough, at Rovigno the ship took on board a further three beef carcasses, 25 live lambs and a cart of hay for their feed, 64 lb of oil and a bushel of salt. The mania for self-indulgence was a long-standing vice of the Venetian naval captains. In Venice's heroic years the ships' rowers faired rather less well with biscuits, inevitably, dipped in oil and sea-water, though in truth it should be said that these were very well made in the ovens of the Arsenale, and bean soup with or without the addition of pieces of meat. Each rower in a sixteenth century galley was given a ration of 676 grams of biscuits a day. The sailors and even the galley slaves of one time ate much better before the crew came to be made up of common crime convicts or prisoners of war. The way of life and working day was very different in the eighteenth century from what it is today. Some time between 11 a.m. and midday, work stopped for *marenda*,

a light lunch usually of one course. A more substantial "lunch", known as the *disnar*, was served at five in the afternoon. Those in society had a late, even night-time, dinner while the rest had no evening meal. There were however very few Venetians who stayed in their homes after *disnar*. They made their way to the coffee houses, the *malvasie* malmsey pubs, and the *magazeni* and the *bastioni*, which swelled with people. Those who still felt peckish could go to the *furato'le* where they would be offered food but not drink as these were unlicensed premises. These habits continued for many a long year, even after the fall of the Serenissima, the republic occupied as it was by the French in May 1797 and handed over to the Austrians at the end of that unfortunate year. The *furato'le* were to continue well into the nineteenth century when they were mentioned by the learned Giuseppe Tassini who wrote of the «little shops similar to delicatessens selling fried fish and other victuals eaten by the poor». Those wishing to learn more of the *furato'le*, the *frito'lini* and the hostelries of the nineteenth century and of what was eaten and drunk there, need look no further than the fine *Osterie Veneziane* by my much-lamented father Elio Zorzi. In that volume we learn of the classless nature of the *frito'lini* and how the customers of the one in Calle della Regina picked up takeaways of a good helping of fried fish and polenta wrapped in paper. One of these customers was S.A.S. Prince Bernhard von Bülow former Chancellor of the German Empire, soon to attempt to prevent Italy entering the war against the Central Empires. The year was 1912. It is said that the nineteenth century, with the Austrians present for a total of seventy years (1798-1806, 1814-1848 and 1849-1866), brought with it the potato to the Veneto region. It is true that the vegetable had first been imported some ago but its possibilities had still not been fully exploited. The course of the century continued nevertheless to be dominated by the hegemony of polenta, sold even on the streets "piping hot with butter and cheese", as were the boiled *folpi* octopus and the *peri coti petora'li* baked pears saw on sale in our youth. Towards the latter part of the eighteenth century the poet and physician Lodovico Pastò celebrated the worthy staple in an amusing ditty:

Pietro Longhi, *La Polenta*;
Ca' Rezzonico, Venice.

«La me piase dura e tenera,
in fersora e su la grela,
in pastizzo, in la paèla,
con sponzioi, coi fonghetti,
co le tenche, coi bisati,
con le anele per i gati,
co de schile, coi marsioni,
coi so bravi scopertoni…»[6]

The period of Austrian occupation represented a distinctly low ebb in the city's history and many left the city for good during that rule. With depopulation some traditions and customs were lost, including culinary habits. Certainly it was not all doom and gloom however: Christmas times saw butchers and poulterers putting on great displays of meat and poultry in front of their shops, while the larger traditional *sagre*, or saints day festivals, such as those of the Redentore (Redeemer), Santa Marta and the Madonna della Salute, brought together people of high and low birth in great feasting. In the words of Petro Gasparo Moro-Lin in 1841 *«Capitale peccato dei Viniziani è la ghiottoneria, ma la è una ghiottoneria chiacchierona viva…»*, i.e. «A capital sin of the Venetians is gluttony, but it is a lively convivial gluttony…». This was certainly true on days like that of Santa Marta when the stalls where put out, in the words of the chronicler of the time Tommaso Locatelli: «bedecked with a profusion of flowers and herbs», where there were also «splendid shining kitchen dressers of pewter ware and appetising fumes wafted up from the ovens…». The party ended up at in the vegetable gardens of the Lido, where banqueting took place on the grass. The "tapinelli" or disinherited ones also abounded «hoping to pick up bits of bread and leftovers like dogs thrown bones, while others stuffed themselves in luxury until fit to bursting». The dishes recalled by Goldoni were still there. During Carnival time there were *ga'lani*, strips of sweet pasta fried in lard and then coated with sugar, and the traditional *frito'le*, or fritters. These were at their best, in the words of the poet Lamberti, when they were cooked *«in tanto agio da farve sofegar»* («cooked in so much garlic as to almost make you choke»). An engraving of the 1830s illustrates one these masters of street-fried fish hard at work in his noble calling, complete with a standard of the double-headed eagle and a large board bearing the proud legend "here works Zamaria". Fish continued to be abundant in the sea and in the lagoon. The basins of the Arsenale produced the best oysters

and *peoci* (mussels). After Venice was unified with Italy in 1866, the patriotic Prefect Count Luigi Torelli set about establishing the creation of a large mollusc farming area between the Giardini di Castello and Sant'Elena. In 1850, Luigi Plet, professor of holy music at St. Mark's basilica and fine composer of sacred works, published a dythramb to the "baccalà" or dried cod:

«lesso, in umido, rosto, o se se vol
in quattro modi co la salsa, e po
frito in tre altri; in pezzi, a mustacchio,
in turbante, in adobo, co l'inchiò,
in carta, in tripa, revoltà…»[7]

and so on. Naturally there was also the classic "baccalà mantecato" that has fortunately survived to the present day. The period of Austrian domination did not leave a significant mark on Venetian cooking. Maffioli lists among the dishes "inherited" from the imperial and royal tradition that of *gulasch*. This is not however really the case as *gulasch* was traditionally only served in the occasional, originally "German" beer house, and did not become part of domestic Venetian life. Venice already had something better, namely the highly flavoursome *cavroman*, a sort of mutton stew recalled by Teofilo Folengo in his macaronic poem *Baldus* (*«da carne guazzettum / quem pevero spargit Venetus striccando sacchettum»*) involving the use of spices other than just *pevero* or pepper. I can think of little to say on the subject of the empire's culinary legacy apart from the fact that it brought us the *Krafken* doughnuts that became common throughout the Veneto and Lombardy, and of course the potato, so beloved of the Teutonic peoples. On descending the steps of the Ducal Palace after the 9th Congress of Italian Scientists, Giovanni Prati was heard to pronounce on the subject, «Between ourselves, only the Germans really like potatoes, and may they go and eat them in blessed peace in their own countries and not sully our lands with them…». The potato was however happily adopted as ingredient

---

[6] I like it hard and soft, / cooked in the pan or on the grill / baked in the pan, / with morel mushrooms, with button mushrooms, / with pork, with small birds, / with tench, with eels, / with little fish for cats, / with shrimps, with bullheads / with fine kippers…

[7] Boiled, stewed, roast, or if you like / four different ways with sauce, and then / fried three other ways; in chunks, spiced, whole, with anchovies/ wrapped, in a stew, over-under…

for *gnocchi*, while the only other mention should perhaps go to what my generation called "Aus flour", the name by which the "00" standard flour was known.

The Great War put Venice in the front line. When our lines were broken at Caporetto, the Austro-Germans established a bridgehead at Piave, just a few kilometres distant. The aircraft attacked incessantly and dealt the surviving Venetian traditions the coup de grâce. Far too many Venetians were forced into exodus as refugees all over Italy, while the assiduous moral and material support provided by their patriarch La Fontaine and Mayor Grimani were not enough to conserve what was already a weakened and crumbling identity. The post-war years brought with them different habits, both in the structure of the working day and in the kind of food that was eaten. The ubiquitous pasta-eating habit became established, along with that of the Milanese fried cutlet. Some customs remained to be enjoyed by children of my generation, including the *persegada* of the festival of San Martino, with images of the saint figuring on quince jam tarts studded with silver sugar-icing balls and also in gingerbread. There were also the dry and crunchy "beans of the Dead", made with a sweet almond paste we ate every November 2nd. The *peri coti* (baked pears) mentioned earlier were carried around on the vendor's back in a magnificent copper boiler, now, I am told, very much a collectors' item. The *folpeti* were sold to the street seller's shouts of «*Caldi! Caldi de bogio!*» («Come and get it hot! Piping hot!»), while you could also still buy roast chestnuts and sweet potatoes. For us kids it was party time when the *caramei* or sweet vendor came to the beach at the Lido, then as now selling also selling his treats in the streets. I have been told they even turn up as table ornaments in fashionable jet-set dinners. The cry was the unmistakable «*Xe qua Bepi, putèi! Coi caramei*» («Beppi's here kids! With sweets!»). Street vendors also sold *caragòi* and *garùso'li*, tasty shellfish that the municipal health department, run for many years by a venerable health enthusiast, eventually succeeded in banning. A great many of Venice's trattorias were still places where all sorts of wonders could be discovered; historical, artistic and literary discoveries as well as those of a culinary nature. The young Marcel Proust for example, together with his friend the painter Kees van Dongen, stayed at the famous Taverna La Fenice of the equally famous Ottavio Zoppi. With the disappearance of the *magazeni* and *bastioni*,

the man in the street frequented the *bàcari* where they served the grosso "Trani" originally brought to Venice by the enterprising Pantaleo Fabiano from Puglia. Then came the other the world war, the one we called number two. This is a matter of modern history, made difficult to swallow by the wholesale exodus of the city's inhabitants, half of them leaving in the years since the war. This is not a book to dwell on regrets, its aim rather is to lift our spirits by revisiting our cuisine with precise and accurate recipes that are wholly faithful to the originals, with also a little local history and philology thrown in. The intention is to be truer to this culinary heritage than any previous works of its kind have been, as well as being more accurate in its re-evocation of the Venetian tongue, where *supa*, for soup, once again becomes *sopa* as it should be, and where *vedel* returns to its Venetian *vedèlo*… and so forth. I wish you the greatest of pleasure in the reading of this book and, above all, enjoy the food!

Giovanni Grevembroch, *Nobili alla Malvasia* (Noblemen at the malmsey house); Correr Museum, Venice (Gradenigo-Dolfin codex).

31

VENETIAN CUISINE

Pino Agostini

Antipasti

sarde'le in saòr

MARINATED SARDINES

The saòr *(meaning flavour) is a marinade whose principal ingredient is onion. The Venetian habit of marinating food with onions has a very long history, with records dating back to the fourteenth century. It was a typically seafaring custom as it helped to avoid the onset of scurvy in the course of extended voyages at sea. The traditions of our times have it that this dish, in which* sfogi, *or sole, may also be used, should be eaten aboard boats the night of the Redentore, the third Saturday of July. It is however served all year round as a very appetising antipasto.*

Ingredients
for 8 servings
1 kg (2 lbs) of sardines
½ kg (1 lb) of white onions
3 spoonfuls of white vinegar
white flour
extravirgin olive oil
salt

Preparation time
1 hour, plus the marinating time

The sardines are cleaned by the removal of head, fins and entrails. The fish is then washed and coated with flour.

——

Pour a good quantity of olive oil into a pan and heat. Fry the sardines until both sides are golden brown. As they are cooked take them out of the pan and place on food quality absorbent paper to make them less greasy. Add salt.

——

Chop the onion into slender fillets or rings according to taste. Heat a glass of olive oil in another pan and add the onions, browning them gently over a low flame. Pour in the vinegar and leave over the low flame until a soft, quite dense, sauce is produced in which the onion continues to keep its appearance.

———

Arrange a layer of fried sardines on the bottom of a heat-resistant glass or earthenware dish and cover with the sauce. Add another layer and cover again and so on until all the sardines and *saòr* have been used. At the end all the fish must be covered in the sauce.

———

Place a cover over the dish and leave to rest in a cool place for at least two days.

Recommended wine
Because of the presence of the vinegar it is difficult to advise a wine that will always be suitable; however a red Breganze or Bardolino is suggested

Variations
Instead of the common *sarde'le* or sardines, the classic *saòr* of the old days made use of the more up-market *sfogi* (sole) or, failing that, *passarini* (plaice). Other fish that can however be used as an alternative, include anchovies (*sardoni*) eels (*anguè'le*), whitebait, and small trout or mullet, in which case, however, we have fish *in salsa* rather than in saòr. An ancient wintertime addition of calories to the *saòr* custom, still revived today by some people, involves the use of wine-softened sultanas, together with pine-seeds and a pinch of cinnamon here all sprinkled here and there over the layers of sardines before the sauce is poured on. That was in fact the recipe for this dish in its oldest conception.

granseo'le a' la venessiana

SPIDER CRAB ALLA VENEZIANA

Spider crabs (Latin Maja squinado) *are large crabs that inhabit the sandy and detritus covered beds of the Mediterranean Sea where they often camouflage themselves by covering themselves with small bits of seaweed. The crab has a hard red spiny heart-shaped shell, or carapace, and can grow to as much as 20 cm in length. The species is common in the Adriatic Sea and has always been one of Venice's best-loved foods.*
Both the male and the female are cooked but the males, distinguishable by their larger claws and thin abdominal plate, have less but tastier meat. The females have more meat as well as eggs that are protected by a thick plate on the underside.
The best time of the year for this dish is in the autumn, between October and December, when their so-called "coral", the redder meat, is at its fullest. This flesh is the tastiest and densest part of the meat.

The largest granseo'le *(of 400-500 g) are considered a main course, though more commonly the medium-sized specimens are those served (250 to 300 g) due to the delicacy of the meat that makes it excellent as an antipasto.*

. . . .

I n g r e d i e n t s
f o r   4   s e r v i n g s
4 medium-sized spider crabs
2 lemons
a handful of chopped parsley (if desired)
extravirgin olive oil
salt
fresh ground peppercorns

P r e p a r a t i o n   t i m e
1 ½ hours

Clean the shells thoroughly with
a small brush. Tie the legs to the bodies
using kitchen string to avoid problems
at the next stage.

——

Drop them while they are still alive
into a pot of boiling water with half
a lemon, salt and a few peppercorns.
Let them cook for about twenty
minutes. When cooked they will turn
a bright scarlet. Leave them to cool
in their own water.

——

Take them out, drain them and cut
the kitchen string. Clean the shell
once again to remove the most stubborn
encrustation.

——

Remove the female's abdominal plate,
extract the eggs and place them
in a bowl. Then take out all the part
underneath the shell and detach
the legs one at a time close to the shell,
taking care not to break them.

——

Take out the "coral" and place it
in a separate container. Patiently also
remove all the meat and divide it up
into small pieces. Using your hands

separate the meat from the tough and
cartilaginous parts that should be thrown
away. Put the meat in the container
with the coral. Take a pointed stick
to complete the task of removing the
flesh from all the nooks and crannies.
At this stage you will also find the
creamy brown parts that go in the bowl
containing the crab eggs.

——

Use crab pincers or a nutcracker to break
the legs and remove the flesh from inside
the shell. Break this meat up into pieces
and place it with the rest.

——

Season the meat and coral with a pinch
of salt and an abundant quantity
of fresh-ground pepper; add the juice
of a lemon and sprinkle on a little
extravirgin olive oil.
Gently mix it all together and place
back in the shells, garnishing with
a chopped parsley if you wish.

——

Finally mix the eggs and creamy
parts in their bowl and serve these
separately to those guests who wish
to add it to the meat.

GRANSEO'LE A'LA VENESSIANA

Recommended wine
Sauvignon dei Colli Berici
or Soave classico

Variations
The version given above is the classic
Venetian preparation but some people prefer to add mayonnaise or a little
Worcester sauce. Another version
involves the use of melted garlic butter
instead of the oil. It is a question of taste,
but the classic recipe is the best in that
it maintains and enhances the natural
flavour of this prized crustacean.

cape sante a'la venessiana

**COQUILLES
SAINT-JACQUES
ALLA VENEZIANA
(SCALLOPS)**

The molluscs that the Venetians call cape sante *are known around the world by their French name* coquilles Saint-Jacques *("St. James' shellfish") due to their excellent use in French cuisine, as well as by the familiar name of scallops. In the Venetian and French their are "sainted" because they were fished in medieval times off the coast of Galicia in Spain where their shells were used as emblems for pilgrims reaching Santiago de Compostela to venerate the relics of James the apostle, reputedly buried there. In Spain they are thus called* conchas de peregrino, *or the pilgrims' shells. They are also known by other names in other parts of Italy including "pettini" or combs, (from the Latin* Pecten jacobaeus), *and "ventagli" or fans, from their shape. These shells have ribbing radiating outwards in a fan shape with concentric growth lines. The valves are unequal with one notably convex and the other flat. They live on sea beds were there is seaweed or a sandy bottom and move by way of the reactive force produced by flapping the valves. This movement creates a jet of water that pushes them off in the opposite direction as they zig-zag to move around or to escape from predators. The best time year to eat* cape sante *is between September and May when they reach their ideal size of 10 to 15 cm in diameter.*
Most of the cape sante *eaten in Venice are trawled in the open Adriatic though some are now also farmed. When buying them you should check that they are fresh, i.e. closed with a good "sea odour".*

*Ingredients
for 6 servings*
18 *cape sante*
1 clove of garlic
1 lemon
a bunch of parsley
1 glass of extravirgin olive oil
and a knob of butter
a small quantity of very finely grated
   bread crumbs
2 spoonfuls of dry white wine
salt (if necessary)
freshly ground pepper

Preparation time
20 minutes,
plus ½ hour's preparation

40

The first task is to buy and open
the raw shells and take out the soft parts.
This preserves their aroma that
would otherwise be lost if they were
opened hot like mussels (see pages
43-44 for mussels). Using your left hand
and a table napkin for a better grip,
take hold of each *capa* with the flat
valve facing upwards.

Insert a kitchen knife to penetrate
deeply between the two valves
and run along the hinge to separate
them and simultaneously cut
the muscle.

The flat valve is then removed and,
using a table napkin again, pass
a small flexible knife under the mollusc
of the other valve to remove it.

The coral is separated from the "nut"
(white muscle), while getting
rid of the greyish skin or mantel

that covers it, as well as the black part.
The nuts and coral need to be washed
several times in water to eliminate
all the grains of sand.
The very decorative convex shells
also need to washed well, scrubbed
on their outer side and then dried.
The cooked shellfish will later be
placed in these.

Roll the nuts and coral in
the breadcrumbs.

Heat the oil and butter with the clove
of garlic in a shallow pan.
Remove the garlic when they are hot
and gently fry the bread-crumbed
cape sante until they are golden brown
all over. Just before they are fully
cooked drop in the chopped parsley,
pour on the dry white wine
and a squirt or two of lemon juice.
Taste the sauce to see if you need
to add a little salt and season with
freshly ground pepper.

Take the *cape sante* out of the pan,
place them on the shells and
pour over each a little of the juice
and serve hot.

R e c o m m e n d e d   w i n e
Tocai dei Colli Euganei
or from the Colli Berici

V a r i a t i o n s
If you are sure of where your *cape sante*
are from you can also eat them raw
with lemon juice and pepper.
The most usual way of cooking is
however either *in forno* (in the oven)
or *in tecia* (on the top).
If cooked in the oven, preparation
is as above with the shellfish cooked
au gratin in the oven and in the
latter case it is cooked in the same
way as sautèed mussels or *peoci saltati*
(next page).

cape 'longhe a scotadeo

**RAZOR CLAM
A SCOTTADITO**

The razor clams are bivalve molluscs (Solenides) that are easily picked up in the early morning at low tide when they are briefly above the water line at the Venetian lidos. They are long like an old-fashioned cut-throat razor, measuring from 12 to 16 cm depending on the particular species. In Venice they are also known as **cape da deo** (finger clams) because of the curious method used for fishing for them; at dawn they usually point upwards out of the sand with the valves open and all the fisherman has to do is put his little finger in for the creature to close up and hold on to its "prey". This fatal error means all the man then has to do is quickly pull up his finger and the mollusc is caught . Usually the little finger is too large for the aperture, so the Venetians use an iron rod widening slightly at the end. The rod has to be used cautiously or the clam will be alerted to danger and immediately bury itself under the sand. Another stratagem employed is to surprise the shellfish by approaching it from the side by pushing a hand underneath the clam and cutting off its escape route. Perhaps the most surprising system of all is that of pouring a pinch of salt into the shellfish that then comes out of the sand up to half the shell's length, as if the low tide were passed. The harvest is usually abundant. Even more highly prized are the **cape 'longhe da bàil**, or shovel razor clams, that are dug out with a shovel so that no sand gets in between the valves. The **cape 'longhe** are sold at the fish stalls. They should only however be eaten when they are really fresh.

*Ingredients
for 4 servings*
800 g (2 lbs) of razor clams
extravirgin olive oil
lemon juice
pepper

Preparation time
10 minutes after the initial
preparation

Wash the clams very thoroughly
and for some time under running
water to ensure all the sand has
come out of the shell.

Prepare a dip bowl for each
guest, mixing together a sprinkling
of olive oil, lemon juice and
a pinch of pepper.

Place an iron plate on the heat
and pour the clams onto it when hot.

As soon as the heat has made
them open take the clams off

42

the hot-plate and serve them hot.

___

The edible part is removed with a fork and dipped into the bowl.

Recommended wine
Garganega dei Colli Berici

Variations
These molluscs are also very tasty with just a few drops of lemon squirted onto them at the moment they are removed by fork. Another way of washing them is to immerse them for a couple of hours in bucket of salted water and then rinse in running water.

---

p e o c i   s a l t à i

SAUTEED MUSSELS

Molluscs in general and shellfish in particular are a natural part of the local cuisine in a seafaring city such as Venice. A prominent place is held by the peoci, also known in Italy as mitili from the Latin Mytilus, which itself comes from the Greek for "shell". In English they are mussels and moules in France where they are sometimes called huîtres du pauvre or poor man's oysters. They are bivalve molluscs found in all seas ad oceans and are generally deep blue-black or black. They differ slightly in shape and colour depending on where they come from. They valves are equal in size, of a triangular-rectangular form, with patterns of growth lines and a highly developed goat's beard of fibres that come out of the valve.

At one time in Venice they ate mussels taken from the open sea beyond the lidos that form the lagoon's barriers, but they were always more commonly taken from within the lagoon itself, often close to the city or even in St. Mark's bay. Here close near the city they were taken from the poles to which they attached themselves. Mussel-culture began only recently in the second half of the nineteenth century in Venice's lagoon and soon met all local needs as well as those of the Veneto region as a whole. Of the three basins in the lagoon only two were used, the lagoon areas served by the harbours of Chioggia and Malamocco where the waters were "clean" and pollution free, unlike that towards Marghera into which the city's factory effluent and sewage flows. The lagoon mussels are excellent and pure, but even so no Venetian would risk eating them raw even when really fresh, as long experience has taught them that the risks of polluted shellfish are serious indeed. Peoci, yes please by all means, but always cooked and aromatised with the traditional Venetian flavourings of garlic, parsley and pepper.

. . . .

Ingredients
for 6 servings
1 ½ kg (3 lbs) of *peoci*, or mussels, (or 6 dozen but it does depend on their size and guests' appetites)
2 cloves of garlic
2 bunches of parsley, either chopped or not
100 ml (½ cup) of extravirgin olive oil
salt (if they do not taste salty enough)
freshly ground pepper
a few lemon wedges

Preparation time
A quarter of an hour, plus 1 hour's preparation

Detach the beard-like fibres from each mussel.

___

Wash the mussels carefully and repeatedly in a basin under running water, scraping each one with a hard bristle brush or other such

43

instrument until all the encrustation
has been removed.

——

In a pestle and mortar grind together
some parsley, the two cloves of garlic
with any green shoots removed,
and a little oil.

——

Lightly oil a wide-bottomed pan,
add the contents of the pestle and mortar
and gently add the mussels. Place
the pan over a strong heat and cover.

——

After 5 to 10 minutes, depending
on their size, the mussels will be ready.
They will have opened and produced
a sauce that is already salty.
Throw away any mussels closed
or empty mussels.

——

Take them out of the pan with a skimmer
and place them on a tureen for serving.
Pour their juice over them after filtering
it first. Sprinkle some freshly ground
pepper over the top, mix and garnish
the dish with parsley.

——

Serve the mussels hot with lemon
wedges. The guest takes the shellfish
out of its shell with a small fork after
trickling a few lemon drops over it.
If he or she wishes, the guest can
spoon up the remaining juice with
a used mussel valve, dipping pieces
of bread into it.

Recommended wine
Gambellara or Bianco di Custoza

Variations
The most common variant of the dish
is to arrange a layer of slices of toasted
bread on the plate before pouring
on the mussels and their sauce.
These are then eaten at the end when
they have absorbed plenty of the juice.
Others prefer to serve the lemon wedges
apart so that each guest can add the
lemon juice directly to the mussels
before mixing them. The recipe given
above is both the simplest and the
most common but another widespread
version is the oven-baked mussel dish.
In this case the *peoci* are opened
with a small knife, the top valve
is dispensed with and the mussels
are laid on a large oven dish.
Over these is sprinkled a paste made
from grinding together garlic,
oil and parsley with a little grated bread
and the whole preparation is placed
in a hot oven at 200 to 220 °C where
it is cooked for about a quarter
of an hour. The dish is then served
straight from the oven.

c a p a r o s s o ' l i

SEA TRUFFLES These bivalve molluscs (Venus verrucosa) *belong, like the* vongole *clams, to the Venerides family. The species eaten in Venice and environs come from clam farms in the lagoon basins of Chioggia and Malamocco. Their common name derives from the shell's similarity in colour and roughness to the well known and delicious underground mushroom. They are to be eaten fresh and, as they live on sandy beds, have to be thoroughly cleaned of all sand before cooking. This operation is performed by leaving them immersed for at least 12 hours in a basin of sea water or suitable salted water.*

CAPAROSSO'LI

Ingredients
for 6 servings
2 kg (4 lbs) of sea truffles
extravirgin olive oil
a clove of garlic
some chopped parsley
pepper (no salt)

Preparation time
45 minutes

Wash the shells repeatedly and very
thoroughly in running water and
scrub them with a brush to get rid
of all incrustation and seaweed.

Pour a little oil into a pan, place over
the heat and brown a clove of garlic
with the central green sprout removed.

Take the garlic out and add
the *caparòssol'li*.

The shells release a salty juice
as they cook.

Remove them from the pan using

a ladle with holes in it and lay the
shellfish in tureen. Sprinkle the chopped
parsley on top and pour on their juices
and mix. If there was not enough time
to thoroughly clean them, it is a good
idea to filter any sand remaining
out of the juice through a cloth before
pouring it on.

The shellfish are eaten with the end
of a fork that is used to take the mollusc
directly out the shell. It is best not
to eat any whose shells have not open
during cooking as this may mean
that they were not fresh.

Recommended wine
Vespaiolo di Breganze
or Pinot grigrio del Piave

Variations
If you are sure that they are completely
fresh, these molluscs can be eaten
raw like oysters, after all the necessary
washing and cleaning. In that case,
just open them and add a few drops
of lemon and a little pepper to taste.

garuso'li

SEA SNAILS

In the history of the civilisations of the Mediterranean, these gastropods (Murex brandaris *and* M. trunculus) *were rather more sought after and exploited for their economic importance than for any culinary significance. Even the connoisseurs have not shown any great interest. Their value lay in a particularly well-developed gland under the shell that secretes a white substance that turns first yellow-green and then reddish purple under the sun's rays. The Greeks called them* porphyra, *i.e. purple, but their value was discovered by the Phoenicians who used them to dye prized cloth (the* purple of the ancients *and Tyrian purple). This pigment is now produced synthetically by chemical means, but the term has remained to indicate the colour. Nowadays these* gauso'li *are of interest only to malacologists and chefs, especially in Venice. Here they are used to make excellent antipasti or appetisers. Since these are shellfish that are fished rather than farmed, it is very important to be quite sure they are very fresh. According to tradition, and there are those who still follow this,* garuso'li *should be eaten by removing them from their shells with a needle or toothpick.*

Ingredients
for 4 servings
1.2 kg (2 ½ lbs) of *garuso'li*
some lemon rind
chopped parsley and garlic
2 spoonfuls of vinegar
extravirgin olive oil
salt and pepper

Preparation time
1 hour if they are light in colour,
which means they are young,
or 1 hour and 15 minutes if they
are older and dark in colour

Wash the *garuso'li* thoroughly
and repeatedly in running water.

——

Pour them into a saucepan of cold
water that has the lemon rind,
vinegar and a pinch of salt in it.

——

Place the saucepan over the flame
and bring to the boil. Allow to
the *young ones* to cook for 45 minutes
and the *old* snails for one hour.

——

Drain and remove the sea snails
with a needle or toothpick and place
them in a tureen. While doing this be
sure you get rid of the tough opercolum,
the shell's hard plug protecting
the fleshy insides.

——

Dress with oil, chopped parsley
and garlic, salt and pepper.

——

Serve cold.

Recommended wine
Pinot bianco dei Colli Euganei
or Soave classico

Variations
In the hostelries of Pellestrina
and San Piero in Volta, a little further
out than Venice, and where the
snails are especially appreciated,
they are also made in a kind of stew
with slowly fried onions and
tomatoes in the manner of *bovo'leti*
(see the next recipe).

b o v o ' l e t i

SMALL LAND SNAILS

The bovo'leti (or bogoeti) are small land snails (Helicids) that can be gathered in abundant quantities on lettuce leaves from vegetable gardens or from country hedges, especially after rain or in the early morning when there is still dew on the leaves. They can also of course be bought in the fish market. Traditional Venetians' favourites are those collected from vine leaves. The local culinary skills of Venice, Treviso and thereabouts have succeeded in transforming this humble dish into a connoisseur's delight. Nowadays it is even offered as a speciality on the most refined menus, though it really belongs in the popular culinary tradition as they are sold on some Venetian street corners and in village fêtes. The vendor offers wrapped bov'leti scooped from a great earthenware pot.

They are normally eaten as a small snack between meals, but they easily betray this purpose as "just one more" easily leads to another and so on until the stomach is completely full!

· ·

I n g r e d i e n t s
bovo'leti, as many as you like,
   but at least 100 g (¼ lb) per person
garlic (to taste)
parsley (if you wish)
extravirgin olive oil
salt and pepper

P r e p a r a t i o n t i m e
After initial preparation
they take at least 2 hours

to prepare, plus the time
for them to take on the flavour
of the dressing

Wash the snails thoroughly and
repeatedly under running water.

———

Heat a large pan of water until
it is lukewarm and then add
the washed *bovo'leti*.
Bring to the boil and allow to cook
for ten minutes.

———

Drain the snails and leave
them to drip dry and cool for
an hour or so.

———

Flavour with a *pesto* of ground
chopped garlic and oil, seasoning
to taste with salt and pepper.
If you wish abundant chopped
parsley can also be added.

———

Let the *bovo'leti* take on the
flavourings for a few hours and
serve them cold. They should
be picked up with the fingers and
sucked out of their shells or
extracted with the use of a toothpick
or, as Venetian tradition has it,
with a *pomo'lin*, pin.

48

Bardolino chiaretto

The Venetian street vendors wash
the *bovo'leti* by leaving them for
at least two hours in a vat of cold
water and then under running
water. They do not put them into
lukewarm water but place them

in cold water that they bring
to the boil. A good deal of foam
forms on the surface when
the water is boiling, and this has
to be removed. They are then
left to boil for 5 minutes,
are drained and dried and dressed
as above. In Venice, the *caragoi*
(small sea snails) are prepared
in the same way.

---

po'lenta e sa'lame coto

POLENTA
AND COOKED
SALAMI

*B*oth polenta and salami have always been considered roba da poareti *(poor folk's food),
even if nowadays there is a smart trend to eat them as antipasti on many occasions. Until
not so long ago the pot of boiling water was always ready in the Veneto region's country
fireplaces for the cooking of polenta, just as the salami and soppressa sausage was always to be
found in the cellars. Even in times of war the rural population never went entirely without as the
vegetable plot could always be relied on to provide fresh vegetables, the fields gave them wheat and
maize for polenta, there was pork and salami from the pigs, milk from the cows and so on.*

*The maize, known here quite erroneously as Turkish corn, came from Spain and originally from
America, imported by the* conquistadores *and distributed all of Europe including to the Serenissima republic of Venice. By the end of the seventeenth century it was widely grown all over the
Veneto region. The whole of the plant was put to good use; the leaves and haulms or stems were
broken up and fed to the livestock, the cobs were used for making fires, the dry cob husks were used
to stuff mattresses and naturally the caryopses were turned into yellow or white flour. Polenta was
eaten more than bread because it cost less and because bread usually had to be bought from the
forneri, or bakers. Polenta went with everything: with fish (white polenta), cheese,* tocio *or stew
dips, mushrooms, figs and even radicchio and salad.*

Not many years ago, after the maize harvest in late autumn or early winter, se faséa su el porco
*i.e. the pig was slaughtered, and the work of making the various kinds of salamis began. These in-
cluded, soppresse, ossocolli, sausages, "cotechini" and others. The traditional household manner of
making the salami was, and still is, to mix one part of fat pork and five parts of lean, chop them together to the desired consistency and add a very finely ground "pesto" of garlic (that could be omit-
ted if so desired) and plenty of salt and peppercorns. These ingredients were mixed together again,
encased in the thoroughly cleaned intestines of the pig and finally tied off with a piece of string at
the top and bottom and around the middle. The salami sausages were then hung in the well-aired
cellars and left to mature.*

*Meat has always been salted, encased and also smoked in the northern countries, where it has
been one of the best ways of preserving it. Those of you who have been fortunate enough to taste
home-made salami in various parts of the Veneto region will have noted that although they have
much in common, each has its own personality. This is because each area, or we could even say
each household, has selected over time small but nevertheless significant variations peculiar to its
own particular environment, e.g. the addition of various aromatic herbs.*

Thus in the Valpolicella area of the province of Verona, for example, the homemade mixture for the soppressa sausage has a good helping of the traditional recioto amarone wine and aromas. This wine producing tradition can even be seen in the area's name as "Valpolicella" itself translates as "the valley of the many wine cellars". The above mixture is worked by hand for a long time and the sausages are then left to mature in the dark in a cool dry and airy place. This is possible in that area as the valley is almost entirely free from the winter mists and fogs that afflict the plain below.

. . . .

Ingredients
for 5 servings

FOR THE POLENTA
1 kg (4 cups or 2 lbs) of yellow larger
  grain polenta (like the marano
  of Vicenza or Verona) or the more
  classical fine grain flour
3 litres (3 quarts) of water
15 g (1 tablespoon) of salt

FOR THE SALAMI
10 thick slices of homemade salami
50 g (2 oz.) of lard
2 spoonfuls of white vinegar

Preparation time
½ hour to 1 hour

Bring the salted water for the
polenta to the boil in the seamless
bowl-shaped copper pan known
here as the paiolo.

———

Shake a little of the yellow flour
at a time into the water to avoid
it lumps forming.
Keep stirring in the same direction
with the traditional wooden stick.
Stir frequently also while
it is cooking.

———

The polenta is ready when
the even mixture comes easily
away from the sides of the paiolo.
It will cook in just half an hour
though some people like to
go on cooking it for up to hour
to improve its taste.

———

Pour the polenta onto the chopping
board and leave it to become firmer
as it becomes lukewarm.

———

Cut into about 2 cm slices using a knife
or the traditional wire.

———

Chop the lard and slowly melt in
a wide-bottomed pan over a low heat.

———

Place the slices of salami into the
pan when the lard is ready, without
really cooking them but just heating
up both sides.

———

Place two slices of warm polenta
on each place together with two slices
of the cooked salami.

———

Pour two spoonfuls of vinegar
onto the remaining lard
and heat just slightly for one
minute. Pour a little over each
place and serve.

Recommended wine
Valpolicella classico
or Merlot del Piave

Variations
Polenta is also excellent left to cool,
cut into slices and browned on the grill.
It is toasted to taste and according
to what is served with it.
As for the salami, it is of course also
good raw, perhaps lain over piping
hot polenta. Soppressa salami
is particularly good and goes well
with a robust red.

fiori de suca o de suchete friti

FRIED PUMPKIN OR CORGETTE FLOWERS

This dish has the freshness and delicacy of spring, when the flowers of the pumpkin or tender young courgettes first appear in the vegetable garden. Pumpkin flowers are picked before they open. The point is cut as well as the stem and the fibrous parts are removed. In the case of courgette flowers, these are picked when open. They are cut at the base and the pistil is removed. Both should be washed and left to dry on a linen cloth.

. . . .

Ingredients
for 6 servings
12 pumpkin or courgette flowers
100 g (¼ lb) of best flour
1 egg
a glass of milk
olive oil or frying oil (as you prefer)
salt and pepper

Preparation time
20 minutes

Beat the egg and mix in the flour after diluting it in cold milk. Do not add the salt now if you want a crisp result.

———

In the meantime get a pan ready with a good depth of boiling oil.

———

Gently coat one flower at a time with the mixture, let the excess drip off and place in the pan.

———

Turn the flowers over when they are frying so that they are evenly browned. Take them out of the pan using a skimmer and place them on some absorbent kitchen paper to stop them being too greasy. Sprinkle on salt and pepper seasoning to taste while they are still hot. Serve hot.

Recommended wine
Durello or Bianco di Custoza

Variations
The quantities given above are intended for when the dish is prepared as an appetiser. If they are made as an accompaniment to the main course the quantities can be increased at will. The mixture can also be made using only the white of the egg, beaten with a little white wine and best flour. Instead of seasoning with salt and pepper, the cooked flowers can be sprinkled with sugar for delicious desserts. If they are prepared in this way remember to add a pinch of salt to the frying mixture. The same method can be used for frying bunches of false acacia flowers (*Robinia pseudoacacia*). The flowers are widespread in the lagoon and in the Veneto region where they grow along irrigation and drainage ditches or at the edges of tilled fields. As the flowers are naturally sweet they are more suited for use as a dessert, adding a little grated lemon peel. Corymbs, or clusters, of white elder flowers (*Sambucus nigra*) can be given the same treatment. They both make delicate and surprising dishes. If you don't believe me, just try them out.

First courses

bìgo'li in salsa

SPAGHETTI AND SARDINES OR ANCHOVIES

An oft-repeated and generally believed myth has it that spaghetti was introduced to Venice and thence to the rest of Europe from China by Marco Polo. It is said that the great Venetian explorer and merchant, on his voyages to China in the thirteenth and fourteenth centuries, send a servant to get provisions from a village on one such journey. The servant reputedly saw the women making strange food in the form of long strings that were then cooked in boiling water with dressing added later. He had the women tell him the ingredients and give him the recipe, reported these back to Marco Polo who spread the word in Venice. Recent historians of the culinary tradition have however shown that it is not possible to say that spaghetti comes from one country rather than another, as they are «among those spontaneously arising types of food that every population comes to without the need for inspiration from others» (Alberini). In Venice and the Veneto region this "spontaneously arising food" is known as bìgo'li. These are prepared in the home using a small hand-press through which is passed a dough made from flour, egg, very little water and salt. A holed copper disk extrudes long large fleshy strands of spaghetti. The classic bìgo'li of the Veneto are brown because they are made with whole-wheat, though nowadays white flour is used, later darkened by the addition of the sauce. At one time this was a dish for holy "Eves" such as Christmas Eve, Ash Wednesday, Good Friday and many other Fridays throughout the year, i.e. those days for which Roman Catholicism imposed abstinence, fasting or abstention from meat, as well as requiring "pure oil" rather than animal fats. It has always been a major part of the cuisine of the Veneto region and as such eaten on all occasions.

. . . .

53

Ingredients
for 4 servings
FOR THE PASTA
300 g (¾ lb) of wholemeal flour
   or white flour (if preferred)
3 whole eggs
3 pinches of salt
water as required

FOR THE SAUCE
4 salted anchovies
a medium-sized onion
a glass of extravirgin olive oil
freshly ground pepper

Preparation time
1 hour

Spread the flour out over
a baking-board in the form of a crater
and pour the whole eggs into it,
along with the salt.

—

Use a fork to slowly bring together
the flour, egg and a little water until
the dough is firm.
Knead the dough well and long,
turning and pressing with the palms
until you have an even and very
elastic mixture.

—

Let the pasta rest for twenty minutes
or so wrapped in kitchen cloth lightly
coated with flour.
Then cut the dough into two halves,
which will reveal the characteristic
air bubbles, and pass it through
the press to finally get the *bìgo'li*.
This resulting strands should
be collected in a tureen containing
bran to stop them sticking to each other.
Lay them out on an kitchen cloth
and leave to rest for the time you
are preparing the sauce and bringing
the water to the boil.

—

Prepare and clean the anchovies
by removing the heads, bones

and if necessary the scales.
Wash them thoroughly under running
water to get rid of excess salt
and cut them up into small pieces.
Cut the onion into thin slices.

—

Heat the olive oil quite strongly
in an open pan and pour in the chopped
onion and anchovies together.
Slow down the cooking with a couple
spoonfuls of water or white wine before
the onions go brown, lower the flame
and cover the pan.
Cook slowly, stirring occasionally,
until the sauce is quite smooth.

—

Place a covered pan full of plenty
of lightly salted water over another ring.
The rule is one litre of water per hundred
grams of pasta, so in this case we would
need about 4 litres of water.
Not too much salt should be added
as the sauce is already very salty.
Otherwise the rule would be 10 grams
of salt per litre of water.

—

Bring the water to the boil and lower
in the *bìgo'li* an unravel immediately
with a carving fork so they do not
stick to each other.

—

Adjust the flame so that the water
starts to boil again as quickly as possible,
while not boiling over.
The pan should be left uncovered.

—

Keep a close eye on the cooking pasta,
stirring with the fork from time
to time. There is no fixed rule about
how long the *bìgo'li* need to cook
as the desired consistency for serving
is a matter of taste, as well as varying
according to the grain size and
ingredients used. Ideally the pasta
should be *al dente*, in our case being
after 5 to 8 minutes, when the *bìgo'li*
are still hard in the centre rather
than a gooey mass.

—

BÌGO'LI IN SALSA

and serve hot to the guests.
They should not be served with grated
parmesan cheese.

Recommended   wine
Garaganega dei Colli Berici
or Tocai italico dei Colli Euganei

Variations
The *bìgo'li* can be brown or white.
Variations on the salsa are necessarily
limited. Nowadays there is a
preference for using ready-made
anchovy fillets in oil as opposed to salted
anchovies. Some people add some
chopped parsley, capers or onions
as the case may be. The most interesting
variation, however, that *all'ebraica*
using a tiny amount of ground garlic
in place of the onion. There are those
indeed who affirm it was in fact
the Jews in the Venice Ghetto that were
the inventors of *bìgo'li in salsa*.

Drain quickly but not excessively
so that there remains a little water
still in the bundle. Pour into a tureen
and serve. Dress with the sauce

---

bìgo'li   co'   l'anara

**BIGOLI WITH
DUCK SAUCE
ALLA VICENTINA**

Both the lagoon and the inland areas of the plain right up to the foothills, abounding as they do *in ditches and springs, are ideal breeding grounds for water birds like wild duck as well as the domestic duck that was bred from them. There is thus hardly a smallholder in the Veneto without ducks in the yard. They practically raise themselves and need little in the way of special care. It is interesting to note that some historians are of the view that duck, goose and turkey were introduced into Venetian cuisine by the Jews in the Ghetto. They soon became ubiquitous among the "Christians" too, a word that is used in Venice and around in a non-religious sense for people in general. Even talking of the house cat you can still hear the expression* el par un cristian *i.e. he seems like a Christian, i.e. a human being. The dish is found all over the Veneto and Venice to where it spread from the hills above Vicenza, particularly in Thiene where it is known as* bigo'li co' l'arna.

· ·

Ingredients
for   4   servings
400 g (1 lb) of wholemeal *bìgo'li*
1 young duck, not too fat
2 carrot and a onion
a stick of celery
a bunch of sage

50 g (3 ½ tablespoons) of butter
50 g (3 ½ tablespoons) of grated
    parmesan cheese
salt and pepper

Preparation   time
1 ½ hours

Pluck the duck, if this has not already been done for you, and singe. Cut the head and feet off and throw them away, although these also were used at one time. Empty the bird and keep the giblets to one side, i.e. the heart, liver and the gizzard or *dure'lo*. Make sure you get rid of the gall bladder from the liver (known here as the *vessigheta del fiel*) as it is very bitter. Wash the duck and giblets.

Take a large pan of slightly salted cold water and bring to the boil with the duck, celery, carrot and onion. When water comes to the boil, cook for at least a further hour.

In the meantime roughly chop the giblets. Gently fry the butter and sage in a small frying pan and pour in the giblets. Ladle in some of the boiling duck broth. Add some salt and pepper and cook over a low heat for about 30 minutes.

When the duck is cooked take it off the heat and out of the pan. Filter the broth through a fine strainer and bring it back to the boil. Pour in the *bìgo'li* and cook as in the previous recipe.

Drain the *bìgo'li*, pour into a hot spaghetti dish and add the giblet sauce. Sprinkle on some good quality parmesan.

Boiled duck may be served as a main course with a suitable sauce for boiled meats (see the section on *salse*).

R e c o m m e n d e d   w i n e
Cabernet or Merlot del Montello and Colli Asolani

V a r i a t i o n s
If you wish to lighten the dish you can boil the duck after first removing the skin, which is very fat.

---

s p a g h e t i   a' l e   v o n g o' l e

SPAGHETTI ALLE VONGOLE (WITH CLAMS)

S paghetti is not really a typical Venetian food, except in the form of wholemeal bìgo'li *(see above). The fact however remains that anyone venturing into a restaurant in Venice or its surrounding area will inevitably find the aboves dish on the menu. It in fact originates from Neapolitan cooking, though it is also true that the basins on the eastern side of the lagoon, as well as the open sea, abound in these clams that are harvested daily for sale at the fish markets. These are veneride molluscs like the* caparosso'li, *or sea truffles (pages 44-46), though a different species. Spaghetti are dried pasta strings that are usually industrially produced and the Venetians tend to lump them together with other similarly produced pasta, referring to them as* paste conze, *i.e. pasta for sauces, rather than distinguishing by name all the various forms of penne, pennette, maniche and so an and so forth.*

. . . .

I n g r e d i e n t s
f o r   4   s e r v i n g s
320 g (¾ lb) of spaghetti
600 g (1 ¼ lb) of fresh clams
400 g (1 can or 14 oz.) of tinned
   peeled tomatoes
or 4 large ripe tomatoes

100 ml (½ cup) of extravirgin olive oil
2 cloves of garlic chopped parsley
salt and freshly ground pepper

Preparation time
40 minutes

Wash the clams thoroughly, place in
a low pan with a drop of water and a little
oil and leave to boil until they open.

Take them out of the pan with a skimmer
and place them in a container to cool
down a little. Keep the liquid they were
cooking in and let it settle in its pan.

Heat the saucepan with plenty of salted
water for the spaghetti and cook as for
bìgo'li (see above pages 54-56).

Pour the rest of the oil into another
pan and heat up. Put the chopped garlic
cloves into the oil, together with the
tinned peeled tomatoes (or the filtered
fresh tomatoes), a pinch of salt and
the cooking juice rom the clams
(after filtering it through a fine strainer).
Make sure no grains of sand get through.
Reduce for half and hour or so, stirring
occasionally with a wooden spoon.

In the meantime take the clams out
of their shells and put them in the juice
only when it is well reduced.

They are already cooked and only need
to be heated up again. Add the chopped
parsley and freshly ground pepper.

The spaghetti should be placed in
the boiling water a few minutes before
the sauce is ready so that they are
al dente just when the sauce is cooked.
As the pasta is factory made its cooking
time is generally indicated on the pack.

Drain the spaghetti and pour onto
each guest's dish. Add the sauce
to the top and mix together gently.
Serve without adding grated cheese.

Recommended wine
Pinot grigio from Breganze
or Lison-Pramaggiore

Variations
While the clams and sauce are cooking,
the addition of olive oil is not essential.
This can be added raw at the end straight
onto the spaghetti on the plate to make
it a lighter dish. A small hot chilli pepper
may be used instead of the ground pepper,
this being cooked together with the sauce
and removed before dressing the
spaghetti. As a final note for lazy people
or those unable to get hold of fresh clams;
a successful dish can also be prepared
using clams preserved in brine, following
the manufacturer's instructions.

papare'le coi bisi

**TAGLIATELLE
AND PEAS**

A classic springtime dish from the Veneto mainland that is at its most delicious when the
first sweet and tender peas are ready for picking. Their delicate flavour goes well with the
homemade pasta that does not overpower their subtle taste. Generations of housewives
have taken much pride in the making of the tagliatelle as a way of showing their skills and honouring their guests. A proverb from Verona says on the matter, parché la paparela sia bona,
bisogna che mena el cul la parona *(for the taglietelle to be good, the lady of the house has to work
her socks off – or words to that effect).*

Ingredients
for 4 servings

FOR THE PASTA
300 g (¾ lb) of white wheat flour
3 whole eggs
a pinch of salt
water (sufficient for making the dough)

FOR THE SAUCE
100 g (4 oz.) of shelled small peas
50 g (3 ½ tablespoons) of butter
50 g (2 oz.) of lean bacon
a small onion
a small ladle of hot broth
a tablespoonful of chopped parsley
grated parmesan cheese (to taste)

Preparation time
1 hour

Make the flour, egg and salt into
a dough, knead on a baking board
as explained in the recipe for *bìgo'li*
and divide it up into two halves.
Roll each half out flat with a rolling-pin,
starting from the centre and working
out until the pasta is sufficiently thin,
even and not torn.
Let it dry for a few minutes, not too
much, and then roll and cut up with
a sharp knife into 5 to 8 mm strips
(the *papare'le*). Spread them out
on a kitchen cloth so that they do not
touch and stick to each other and once
again leave them to rest while you
prepare the sauce.

Chop the bacon and the onion
and gently fry them in half of the butter.

Add the peas and ladle in the broth
when the onion begins to brown
and the bacon is half melted.
Cover and cook for 10 to 15 minutes,
depending on the size of the peas,
and season with salt and pepper to taste.
Add and mix in the chopped parsley
when the sauce is cooked.

In the meantime place a large saucepan
of slightly salted water over a strong
heat and bring to the boil.
Pour the *papare'le* in and cook until
al dente. Keep a close watch over
them as they cook as homemade
pasta is soon ready.

Drain the pasta without shaking away
all of the water. Place in an earthenware
pot, add the remaining butter and
pour the sauce on top, together with
a handful of grated parmesan cheese.
Mix carefully and serve.

Recommended wine
Soave classico or Bianco di Custoza

Variations
A more complicated version involves
the addition of several ladlefuls of broth
in the pan with the peas and cooking
the *papare'le* together with them.
When so cooked they absorb all
the cooking water and do not have
to be drained when ready.
This method requires a good deal
of experience and skill or you may
end up with something that more
resembles soup.
A similar dish using the same
cooking method is *papare'le e figadini*
(tagliatelle with chicken livers).
In this dish chicken livers gently
fried in butter are at the essential
feature of the recipe.

g n o c h i   d e   p a t a t e

POTATO GNOCCHI

Gnocchi *are really a dish from Verona rather than Venice, but the city was for centuries a part of the Serenissima Republic. What the Venetians used to call* macaroni, *and were in fact* gnocchi, *were made with white flour. The gnocchi consisting of boiled potato were the glory of the city of Verona where it is said that they began with the sixteenth century carnival. What is known for certain is that their use was widespread by the time of Austrian domination at the beginning of the nineteenth century. Verona was then one of the fortresses of the Austrian Quadrilateral. It was nevertheless felt, with something of an air of superiority, to be* roba da foresti, *i.e. stuff for foreigners or for the mountain folk. It may then be that it was the Austrians themselves who provided the example that led to the use of the potato in the gnocchi.*

There is a very old tradition that is still alive and well in Verona where gnocchi are given away from enormous pots to anyone who happens by in the square in front of the basilica of San Zeno on the last Friday of carnival. This custom is followed by a parade of carnival floats through the streets of the city centre, led by the papà del gnoco, *or father of the gnocchi festival and symbol of abundance. His retinue continue to distribute the delicacy along the way to the assembled crowds. That day in Verona, known there as* vènardi gnocolàr, *there is hardly a family that does not celebrate the occasion without piping hot gnocchi on tables laid for a feast.*

The gnocchi of Venice, that hardly anyone still actually makes, date from the times before the introduction of the potato into Italian cooking, and thus to a more ancient tradition. There are still traces of this tradition in, for example, the malloreddus *of Sardinia made from flour and water, or the "strangolapreti" of the Trento region, as well as all those recipes involving the use of breadcrumbs that resemble the* Knödeln *of the Tyrol. Boccaccio talks of these in his description of Bengodi, the land of idleness and luxury, in the fourteenth century, as does Merlin Cocai (Teofilo Folengo) in his* Baldus *of the sixteenth century, both calling them "maccheroni" (from* ammaccati, *or dented pasta) for a pasta that was like a bean-shaped polenta. The gnocchi today of Verona are now "sanzenati", i.e. have been officially accepted into the Venetian tradition.*

. . . .

I n g r e d i e n t s
f o r   4   s e r v i n g s
FOR THE GNOCCHI
2 kg (4 lbs) of large floury potatoes
500 g (1 lb) of very fine, sifted, white flour
2 eggs and salt

FOR THE SAUCE
1 kg (2 lbs) of peeled tomatoes
100 ml (½ cup) of extravirgin olive oil
a large onion
a few bunches of parsley or basil
a clove of garlic
salt and pepper
grated parmesan cheese

P r e p a r a t i o n   t i m e
1 ½ hours

Wash the potatoes with their peel on and place them in a large, well covered casserole dish of cold water, bring to the boil and cook.

———

Meanwhile prepare a board by lightly sprinkling it with flour, (in Verona a marble surface is de rigueur). Drain the potatoes, peel them and mash them. Gather the mashed potato onto the board and work in the flour and salt to taste. Knead the mixture thoroughly until you have an even soft and lump-free dough.

———

Divide the dough into small pieces and with floured palms roll into little sticks about 2 cm in diameter.

61

GNOCHI DE PATATE

Cut the pieces off at about 3 cm lengths and lightly press each with the prongs of a fork or the concave part of a grater to give the pieces the typical dimpled shell shape that also favours good distribution of the sauce.

———

Place the *gnocchi* on a kitchen cloth that has been lightly sprinkled with flour. Keeping them separate from each other to prevent them sticking.

The tomato sauce is made as follows: heat the olive oil in a casserole and pour in the finely chopped onion; when the onion starts to brown, pour on the peeled tomatoes, the finely chopped garlic clove which has had its green shoot removed and season with salt and pepper; when the sauce is thick enough, add the chopped parsley or basil, mix and remove from the heat; add a little more salt if required.

———

Bring a large pot of salted water to the boil and pour in the *gnocchi*. They sink at first but as soon as the water comes back to the boil they start to return to the surface. As they come up take them out with a skimmer, let them drip and place on individual serving plates. Pour two tablespoons

of tomato sauce over each serving. Serve the *gnocchi* hot with plenty of grated parmesan cheese.

Recommended wine
Bardolino chiaretto
or Tocai rosso dei Colli Berici

Variations
In addition to the different ways of making gnocchi indicated in the introduction, the variations for the potato version largely regard the sauces added to them. The sauce described above, which is also ideal for various types of pasta, is that most commonly used in the Verona area where they also however sometimes adopt fried butter and parmesan or melted butter, sugar and cinnamon (in the proportions of two parts sugar and one of cinnamon) and, once again, parmesan cheese. An excellent alternative sauce is ragout, or the sauce made from horsemeat soaked in wine as in the *pastissada de cavàl* (pages 100-102). As for the dough itself, there has in recent years been an increasingly widespread use of tomato sauce, very finely chopped cooked spinach or cooked pumpkin to respectively "dye" the dough red, green and yellow. These are all just variations on the theme.

pasta e fasioi

PASTA AND BEANS

I t is not strictly correct to call this a Venetian dish as it belongs to the whole of the Veneto region, where there is no home, trattoria or restaurant that does not sing its praises. They were certainly however the merchants of Venice in the sixteenth century who brought the beans to their homeland from Spain, where in turn they had been imported from the Americas. The cultivation of the crop took on apace in the whole region where it obtained the considerable success that has endured to this day.
The characteristic thing about this dish is that it brings together beans and pork rinds. Traditionally it was at its very best in the early autumn when the pigs were slaughtered and the skin and the bones were fresh. In addition to this, the beans themselves were harvested just before where the smallholders had planted them in the fields between one maize plant and another.

The beans climbed almost to the tops and the pods ripened at just the same time as the corn cobs. Nowadays we are almost unaware of these seasonal rhythms and much of the ritual has disappeared as we can buy whatever we want all year round. The recipes nevertheless in some way continue to enshrine that intimate relationship with the land and nature that enriches the significance of the culinary tradition. The classic **pasta e fasioi** *uses the Lamon bean. That is the name of a village to the north of Feltre, in the area of Belluno, whose claim to fame is that it has thin-skinned floury beans that are perfect for this recipe. Flavour is usually added to the dish with the inclusion of pork rind, though some areas also use fresh bones, a ham bone or lean unsmoked bacon.*
The preferred pasta is that known as the **tirache** *of Treviso, the name being a local one for trouser braces and hence a type of thick tagliatelle, made with wheat grain and water with no egg. Every area uses its own favourite pasta however, and this may be in the form of lasagnette, bìgo'li, subiotini (ditolini) or others besides. The result is never however in doubt, and always excellent.*

. . . .

I n g r e d i e n t s
f o r   4   s e r v i n g s
200 g (½ lb) of the *tirache* from Treviso
   or other type of pasta
300 g (¾ lb) of fresh beans from Lamon
100 g (¼ lb) of pork rinds or a ham bone
a large onion
a carrot
a stick of celery
a clove of garlic
a bunch of parsley
100 ml (½ cup) of extravirgin olive oil
salt and freshly ground pepper
grated parmesan cheese

P r e p a r a t i o n   t i m e
3 hours

Chop the vegetables up well,
not including the parsley, and brown
in a large pan in hot oil.

———

Add the beans, 2 ½ litres of cold water
and the pork rinds or ham bone.

Bring to the boil and leave to simmer
for about 2 ½ hours. So that the beans
stay more tender add the salt and
a little pepper half way through
the cooking time.

———

Remove the pork rinds or the ham bone.
In the case of the pork rind, cut into
strips and keep on a side dish for those
who wish to add it to the soup and in
the case of the ham bone, take any meaty
bits off and place it back in the soup.

———

Sieve half of the cooked beans
and pour them back into the soup.
If necessary add salt.

———

Keep the soup on the boil, pour
in the pasta and allow to cook.
At the end of cooking add the chopped
parsley and mix it in.

———

Place the *pasta e fasioi* in earthenware
bowls and leave to rest for ten minutes
or so until a thin film forms on the surface.
Serve with grated parmesan cheese
(if desired), freshly ground pepper and
excellent quality olive oil. Before tasting
there should at least be a cross shape
of olive oil trickled over the surface
as well as freshly ground pepper to taste.

R e c o m m e n d e d   w i n e s
Tocai rosso dei Colli Berici

Variations

If you have to use dried rather than
fresh beans, they must be left to soak
overnight in warm water with a pinch
of bicarbonate; then throw the water away
and proceed as with the recipe above.
If the soup is too thick it can be thinned
with boiling meat extract broth, while
if it is too thin a spoonful of potato
or corn flour can be added. The end result
should in any case be a fairly thick soup.
The ingredients that come from the pig can
naturally be varied. If fat or froth comes
to the surface it must be skimmed off
as *pasta e fasioi* has to remain, despite what
you might think, an essentially "light"
dish. The choice of chopped vegetables
can also be varied to taste. In Venice,
and especially in Polesine, *risi e fasioi*
goes down very well, i.e. rice and beans.

m i n e s t r ò n

**VEGETABLE
MINESTRONE**

M inestròn *means a big soup and is the most common first course on the tables of Venetians and those in the Veneto, who were converted from the habit of dry first courses
with the nationalisation of regional cooking. What better welcome home could there be
after a day toiling in the fields or factory that a hot bowl of vegetable soup? Especially in the autumn and winter evenings when the body feels the need for something to warm it up. The ingredients come readily to hand with the homely vegetable plot providing all the season's requirements.
Each* minestròn *is a unique and unrepeatable masterpiece; it depends on the skill of the cook to
vary the choice of vegetables from season to season, as well as the inspiration of the moment. There
is therefore no area without its own culinary variations or that does not produce a minestrone that
it cannot claim to call wholly its own. There is no iron rule that says there must necessarily be pasta included, it is a question of taste. There are those who use toasted bread cubes, others who use*
maltagliati, *i.e. leftover bits of pasta from pastry-making, and still others who use rice or similar-
shaped short pasta grains, and so on. The dish is also traditional in other Italian regions such as
Liguria, where they add* pesto alla genovese *at the end, or in Lombardy, where rice is almost always added. Minestrone is also a favourite in Tuscany and according to Artusi it is that region
that is the true home of minestrone. It is however in the Veneto region that its use is so common
that it earns the right to be considered a regional dish. Invariable ingredients include Lamon beans
(see previous recipe) while as for the rest, anything goes.*

· ·

*Ingredients
for 8 servings*
400 g (1 lb) of fresh Lamon beans
200 g (½ lb) of courgettes
4 potatoes
4 fresh peeled and chopped tomatoes
2 carrots
2 sticks of celery
a onion
some chopped parsley
a glass of extravirgin olive oil
salt and pepper
grated parmesan cheese

Preparation time
2 hours

Lightly brown the onion in the olive oil in
a large pan. Add the 2 ½ litres (2 ½ quarts)
of cold unsalted water, the beans
and the other vegetables, all chopped.
Do not add the parsley yet.

——

After 1 ½ hours remove some of the
vegetables, pass them through a sieve
and return to the soup. Add salt as

necessary and season with a little pepper.

─────

When the minestrone has finished cooking leave it to rest for a few minutes. Serve with freshly ground pepper, extravirgin olive oil and grated parmesan cheese.

Recommended wines
Soave classico

Variations
The gourmets in Venice maintain that you should not add parmesan cheese when there are beans in the soup, but the gourmands will have none of it. It is naturally a matter of taste. If you wish, shortly before removing from the heat, you can add a modicum of pasta grains so that the minestrone does not become too thick. In practice, however, this does preclude the possibility of enjoying the soup the next day. One of its virtues is that its taste gets more intense when allowed to cool down and it is heated up again some time later. The flavours blend together to make it even more delicious. As well as varying the actual choice of vegetables included, variations include gently frying the onion in lard or chopped melted unsmoked bacon rather than in olive oil. Some people add an extra clove of garlic.

s o p' a   d e   p e s s e

FISH SOUP

All the towns and villages on the gulf of Venice can boast a fish soup. These soups, like the minestrone above, are all different from each other. They vary according to the products available in the various markets on any given day as well as according to the species available in each locality. In the morning the household cook makes his or her way to the Pescaria, the fish market on Venice's Grand Canal where fishermen have been selling their catch under the shadow of San Pietro since the ninth century AD. The ingredients may also be varied with the whim of the moment. Of all the various ways of preparing this dish, which may also be considered a main course, it has been decided to give the recipe for the current fish soup of Chioggia. This is because it is the most widespread version and because Chioggia sits at the mouth of the lagoon's southern basin where there has remained a direct line of descent through the culinary traditions of Venice in matters of fish, crustaceans and molluscs. The dish can of course be cooked in other ways as it is, for example, in the villages of Caorle, Grado, Trieste, Comacchio and the Polesine lands. Incidentally this latter area makes up the southern part of the Veneto region between the lower reaches of the river Adige and the Po delta where they prepare the "land-lubbers" fish soup, often using species that are not the favourites of the population of the city. All of these soups take that of Chioggia as their reference point from which, to a greater or lesser extent, they are all variations. Another reason for choosing Chioggia is because every August it holds a sagra del paese, or town fair, which sees the place full of fishing nets, sails and illuminated local Adriatic fishing vessels such as the braghe, bragozzi and bragozzetti. Stalls spring up in the streets offering fried fish and polenta, folpeti (small octopus) and much more besides. It is also the ideal moment to try out the fish soup.

· ·

SOPA DE PESSE

I n g r e d i e n t s
f o r   6   s e r v i n g s
2 kg (4 lbs) of assorted fish (scorpion-fish,
    eels, sea-toad, bass, small octopus,
    squid, cuttle-fish, scallops etc.)
600 g (1 ¼ lbs) of mussels, to one side
100 ml (½ cup) of extravirgin olive oil
3 ripe tomatoes
2 carrots
2 sticks of celery
2 cloves of garlic
2 bay leaves
a onion
a few slices of toasted or lightly
    grilled bread
half a glass of fine quality vinegar
2 litres (2 quarts) of water
salt and pepper

P r e p a r a t i o n   t i m e
About 1 ½ hour

Clean and wash the fish, throwing away
the shells, gills, and innards. Cut off
the heads and fins and remove the bones,
but keep all these for the preparation
of the fish broth. Cut the fish into pieces.

———

Chop the carrots and celery and pour
them into a pan containing 1 ½ litres
of water, 2 bay leaves and a little
salt and pepper. Add in the heads
and bones etc. and bring to the boil.

———

Put another large pan on a high heat
until a 100 ml of olive oil starts smoking.
Add the onion and the two cloves of garlic
that have been very finely chopped.
When the onion is soft but not brown
add half a glass of water, the pieces
of molluscs and crustaceans.
Ten minutes later add the other fish
pieces and allow to lightly brown.

———

Add the half glass of vinegar, followed
by the peeled and chopped tomatoes
when this has evaporated.

———

In the meantime sieve the fish broth and
pour into the fish pan. Add some more
pepper and bring to the boil. Let the soup
boil simmer for half an hour.

———

Five minutes before removing from
the heat, add the cleaned mussels
that were kept to one side.
(The way to clean mussels is explained
in the recipe on page 43).

———

In the meantime toast the bread and
place a couple of slices on the bottom
of each guest's bowl. Add any salt that
may be required to the soup when it
is cooked and pour it hot into the bowl
on top of the toasted bread. The result
must be a soup with the fish submerged
in the broth. It is not intended to be
served with grated parmesan cheese.

R e c o m m e n d e d   w i n e s
Pinot bianco superiore di Breganze
or Gambellare superiore

V a r i a t i o n s
The vinegar, bay leaves and tomato
are all in the original Chioggia fish soup
though the latter ingredient came late
on than the others and some suggest
it does not really belong. All the fish
soup you will find nowadays in the area
of Venice is however reddish in
colour and sometimes this is further
emphasises by the addition of a spoonful
of concentrated tomato paste.
The bay leaves add a flavour that is not
everyone's favourite so many households
choose to leave it out. Finally, a glass
of dry white wine is an excellentvariation
instead of the vinegar.

t r i p e   i n   b r o d o

TRIPE SOUP

Tripe is part of the giblets and as such was exclusively fit for the poareti, *i.e. the abject poor. In the case of tripe this thinking changed long ago and nowadays it is thought of as a delicacy for the connoisseur. Walking round the calli of Venice, or tree-lined avenues in the Veneto, it is not unusual to find "Tripe today" or "Hot tripe" chalked invitingly on the menu boards of many a trattoria. This is one tradition that is very much still alive and kicking. The area that has most developed the tradition of the dish, whether as a soup or a stew (see pages 110 to 111) is that of the marches of Treviso. This is a rural environment but many Venetian nobles built their summer villas there and took on local serving staff. Tripe is from the stomach of cattle and calves. The cow has a stomach system divided into four parts that provide us with four different types of tripe. The first is the rumen, making up 80% of the stomach; the second the honeycombed reticulum; the third is the moasum or manyplies (known as* sentope'le *in Venice), made up, as its name suggests, of numerous layers and fourth is the abomasum or true stomach (*prete, *or "priest" in Venetian). Each type of tripe is now sold ready-washed and pre-cooked by the* bechèri *or butchers. If this were not the case it would be essential to careful and thoroughly wash the tripe, then scald it and finally cook for a long time in slightly salted water with an abundance of aromas to taste (typically celery, carrot, onion, rosemary and others). The reason is that tripe itself is not blessed with a notable flavour of its own. The most tender tripe comes from the young calf but the tastiest is that of the steer or the fatted calf. Naturally the fresh variety is to be preferred to the frozen product. At one time people also used pork tripe (*tripe de porse'lo), *but you practically never see that nowadays.*

. . . .

I n g r e d i e n t s
f o r   6   s e r v i n g s
1.2 kg (2 ½ lbs) of tripe from the steer
   (*sentope'le* and *prete)*
50 g (2 oz.) of lard chopped into cubes
3 sage leaves
3 sprigs of rosemary
2 bay leaves
1 ½ large onions
a stick of celery
a bunch of parsley
the juice of a lemon
1 ½ litres (6 cups) of beef stock
half a glass of extravirgin olive oil
a few slices of toasted bread
peppercorns
salt and pepper
grated parmesan cheese

P r e p a r a t i o n   t i m e
3 to 6 hours

If the tripe is not ready-cooked
wash thoroughly and leave in
a bowl of water overnight with half
an onion, a stick of celery, some
parsley, lemon juice, peppercorns,
a sprig of rosemary, two sage
and two bay leaves.

———

The next morning throw away
the water and cut up into strips.

———

Prepare some stuffing from the lard,
the needles from a branch of rosemary
and two sage leaves.

———

Heat a little olive oil in a large
pan until it is hot, add the stuffing
mix and let it brown slightly.
Add the tripe, a little salt and a bay
leaf and pour in some water.
Raise the heat and let it boil for
a couple of hours if the tripe
is ready-cooked and for as much
as 3 to 5 hours if it is fresh.

If necessary pour in some more boiling water from time to time. At the end the tripe must be tender with almost all the water gone.

———

Finally add the boiling beef broth, season with salt and pepper if required and serve hot in earthenware bowls in which have placed the toasted bread slices. Add a generous amount of grated parmesan and freshly ground pepper.

Recommended wines
Tocai bianco dei Colli Berici

Variations
Tradition has it that the tripe should be served in broth in earthenware bowls as they hold the heat in. Tripe tastes better in fact when it is still hot and is also more easily digested. There is a clearer soup version of the dish known as *convent's tripe* where the aromas are placed in the broth in a muslin bag and then removed and thrown out. Some parts of the Veneto region prepare the stock with a pig's trotter but that does not go down well in Venice as it tends to thicken the soup and make it gelatinous.

sopa coada

BAKED PIGEON SOUP

This soup is called coada, (Italian "covata"), or "smouldered dish" because it is cooked for a long time in the oven. To understand the history of the recipe we need to consider that kitchen stoves were large wood-burning appliances and also that the household had the greatest of respect for their dovecotes where they raised their pigeons.

The dish takes a long time to prepare and is quite complicated to make so to offer it to guests was in itself an expression of the honour afforded them and the significance of the occasion. All the cookery writers agree that the dish dates from the first years after the unification of Italy, with the Veneto becoming part of the nation in 1866. This is also because it draws heavily on a similar dish of more ancient tradition from Sardinia, known as the "suppa quatta". This latter was a little simpler but prepared in the same way. It may well be that some Sardinian grenadier from the Piedmontese army was perhaps stationed in Treviso and taught the local people his favourite household recipe out of homesickness for his Mediterranean island. If that is so the dish soon caught on in the Veneto region and Venice.

The sopa coada can also be a main course and is at its best when young, tender pigeons are used rather than tough old birds. Its flavour improves overnight if it is eaten the day after it is cooked as the various ingredients blend their flavours together.

· ·

Ingredients
for 6 servings
3 young pigeons
500 g (1 ¼ lbs) of sliced stale homemade
   bread sautéed in butter
2 litres (2 quarts) of meat stock
2 carrots
2 sticks of celery

a large onion
half a glass of extravirgin olive oil
150 g (5 ¼ oz.) of butter
100 g (¼ lb) of grated parmesan cheese
a glass of dry white wine
salt
pepper

Preparation time
3 hours

Pluck, empty and clean the pigeons
(throwing the head and feet away
but keeping the livers), scorch the skin
and cut into halves or quarters.

———

Chop the celery, carrots and onion
and gently fry in the hot oil and butter.
Add the pigeons and lightly brown.
Pour in the glass of white wine and
when it has evaporated add the broth,
salt and pepper and cover the pan.
Cook for half an hour.
Add the cleaned pigeon livers 5 minutes
before taking off the heat.

———

Take the pigeons out of the pan
and remove the bones taking care not
to break the pigeons up too much.
Also remove the livers and cut
them in half.

———

Meanwhile pour the remaining
boiling broth into the pigeon juice
and simmer for 10 minutes or so.

Lay a slice of bread sautéed in butter
in an earthenware pot or oven pan.
Sprinkle with a good quantity
of parmesan cheese and place two
half pigeons and a few pieces of liver

on the top. Make another layer like
the first and so on ending up with
a layer of bread, with another sprinkling
of parmesan cheese. Finally pour
on the broth and pigeon juice mixture
until the whole dish is submerged
and place in a moderate oven
at 80-100 °C for 2 ½ hours.
Add a little boiling broth from time
to time to keep the mixture soft.

———

When the *sopa coada* is cooked,
the result is a thick bread and pigeon
pie to serve with a cup of broth to be
sipped separely while enjoying the meal.
No added is pepper is required.

Recommended wines
Pino nero del Piave
or Cabernet riserva dei Colli Berici

Variations
You can use stale bread without frying
in butter if you wish to lighten the dish.
A spoonful of tomato paste dissolved
in water can also be added if you wish.
In some areas, such as Oderzo,
they use small young chickens instead
of pigeons. To ensure the soup does
not dry up too much, press the top
layer of bread with a wooden spoon;
juice must always come out, if none
does then add more broth.

papare'le coi figadini

**PAPPARDELLE
IN BROTH WITH
CHICKEN LIVERS**

The civilisation that brought us the Ville Venete reached as far as Lombardy and it is in fact from the farthest reaches of the Serenissima Republic of Venice that this dish came to its capital city. Someone once said of it that it was "fit for a king's table", so delicious was it, and so it found its way to the Doge's table. Originally it came from Verona where it is still made today on special occasions when the household has honoured guests, when it is followed by several other courses.

A popular saying in Verona goes San Zen che ride, paperele calde, or "when we eat pappardelle in broth even the city's patron saint smiles", illustrating how the townsfolk have always revered the dish. Tradition dictates the use of an excellent chicken and turkey broth but the stock from boiled mixed meat dishes works equally well (see pages 95 to 96).

*Ingredients
for 6 servings*
400 g (1 lb) of homemade pappardelle
  (see pages 58 to 59)
300 g (¾ lb) of chicken livers
50 g (3 ½ tablespoons) of butter
1 ½ -2 litres (2 quarts) of good chicken
  and turkey stock
salt
grated parmesan cheese (to taste)

Preparation time
40 minutes (not counting making
the pappardelle and the broth)

Clean the chicken livers and cut into small pieces. Gently fry in butter with a pinch of salt.

Bring a pan of broth to the boil and add the cooked chicken livers and *papare'le*.

As soon as the pasta is cooked (don't leave it to rest), serve at the table with plenty of grated parmesan.

Recommended wines
Bardolino superiore

Variations
A very common variant is not to add the cooked chicken livers to the broth but to place them on top of the pasta soup on the guest's plate.
The above recipe is in any case very straightforward and familiar.

panada venessiana

**VENETIAN
BREAD SOUP**

The rule not to waste anything was well ingrained in that generation whose destiny it was to have to fight in two world wars. Nothing in the kitchen that could possibly be recycled was thrown out and waste was literally cut to the bone, and that bone had itself had the marrow removed first.

When stale bread began to pile up it was fed to the animals in the yard or also used in many ways in cooking for the household. It was grated for cutlets or pearà (see page 98), toasted or sautéed in *butter to go with broth or vegetable soups or even used in caffellatte in the morning. It was also used to prepare this dish, the* panada, *an easily digested soup that was ideal for young children still without teeth and for old folks who had lost theirs. These were days when dentures were unknown or prohibitively expensive.*

The soup was also known as panbogio, *i.e. hot bread. Its two overriding merits were that it was hot and it was tasty. The most surprising feature of the soup is how easy it is too make, even though there are now just a few elderly people around who like to recall the old days by preparing it. It is now therefore part of a dying tradition and it may well be that* panada *will be something only found in books. It was also a fasting times dish, eaten during such periods as Lent.*

. . . .

I n g r e d i e n t s
f o r   4   s e r v i n g s
400 g (1 lb) of stale bread
1-1 ½ litres (6 cups) of water
2 cloves of garlic
2 bay leaves
100 ml (½ cup) of full flavour extravirgin
   olive oil
grated parmesan cheese

P r e p a r a t i o n   t i m e
About 45 minutes

Break the bread up into pieces and place them in a terracotta casserole dish.

▬

Heat the water up to lukewarm and pour into the dish, adding the peeled garlic cloves, the two bay leaves and a pinch of salt.

▬

Leave to rest for 10 minutes or so then put the pan over a low heat and allow to simmer for about 40 minutes, stirring from time to time. When ready the soup must be thick, creamy and lump-free.

▬

Remove from the heat and add plenty of grated parmesan. When the soup has been poured into the guest's dishes, pour a little olive oil over the top of each.

Serve with grated parmesan and strong-flavoured olive oil for those who wish to add more of these.

R e c o m m e n d e d   w i n e s
Bianco di Custoza

V a r i a t i o n s
The above recipe is *panada* in its simplest form. To enrich the flavours, meat or vegetable extract can be added instead of salt. Some people grate the bread instead of breaking it, and bind it together with raw egg. Others use meat stock instead of plain water. Sometimes a little powdered cinnamon is added. The addition of aromas in general can vary according to taste, as well as depending on the traditions of the various localities. Naturally more water (or stock) can poured in if the soup gets to be too thick when cooking. Tradition says that the ideal amount of liquid is ½ litre per 150 grams of bread, but there is no reason why this cannot be altered to taste.

risi e bisi

RISOTTO WITH PEAS

This ancient dish originating in the time of the Serenissima Republic of Venice was customarily offered to the Doge on April 25, the Feast of St. Mark, patron saint of the city. Celebrated and loved in all the Venetian territories, this dish is common not only around the Veneto, where the sunny plains and hills make growing peas a tradition (many towns around the Veneto celebrate spring pea harvesting festivals), but even today, local variations can still be found in the coastal areas of Dalmatia, Greece, Turkey and Lebanon.

Ingredients
for 4 servings
800 g (2 lbs) of sweet and tender peas,
   with edible pod, enough to yield
   250 to 300 g (¾ lb) of shelled peas
250 g (1 cup) Vialone nano rice
60 g (4 tablespoons) butter
50 g (2 oz.) unsmoked bacon
a small onion
a bunch of parsley
salt and pepper
grated parmesan cheese

Preparation time
1 ½ hours

Shell the peas, separating the peas from the pods. Keep both separately and wash thoroughly.

Put the pods into 2 litres of lightly salted water and boil them for about an hour. Strain the broth and pods through a food mill (or sieve) in order to obtain a slightly dense greenish liquid that will be used as the cooking liquid for the rice. Keep the liquid hot over low heat.

Mince the onion and the bacon and fry them together with half of the butter in a heavy pot where the risotto will be cooked. Sauté until the onion is softened and the bacon has released its fat. Pour in the peas with two ladlefuls of hot broth. Cover and cook five minutes (if the peas are larger and not very tender, cook for 15 minutes).

Add the rice and mix with a wooden spoon until well blended. Add some more of the boiling broth and continuing mixing until the rice is almost tender and the risotto takes on a somewhat gelatinous consistency. Add the minced parsley a few moments before removing from the heat.

Turn off the heat, add salt and pepper to taste and add the other half of the butter and grated parmesan cheese. Blend well, cover and let the risotto stand for a few minutes.

Serve with an additional dusting of parmesan cheese to taste.

Recommended wine
Durello superiore dei Lessini

Variations
For a more simple preparation, many cooks replace the pea pod broth with bouillon and water, thereby shortening the cooking time to just half an hour. Others may prefer to add fennel seeds or a clove of garlic for added tang. One secret to a delicious risotto is to use shelled peas in equal proportions to the rice (or 3 to 1 if the peas are in the pod).

RISI E BISI

risi e spàresi

**ASPARAGUS
RISOTTO**

This risotto is a speciality of Bassano del Grappa, since the very best quality asparagus comes from that area. However, delicious asparagus is also grown in Chioggia, the Polesine, and the region around Verona on the banks of the Adige River, as well as in many other places. This quintessential springtime dish is prized in Venice and the entire lagoon area.

*Ingredients
for 4 servings*
300 g (¾ lb) asparagus tips
300 g (¾ lb) Vialone nano rice
100 g (7 tablespoons) butter
a onion, minced
a bunch of parsley, minced
a litre hot broth
half a glass of dry white wine
extravirgin olive oil
freshly ground pepper
salt and pepper
grated parmesan cheese

Preparation time
40 minutes

Pour a small amount of olive oil into a pot with just overhalf of the butter. Heat it up, add the onion, and sauté it for a few minutes until it softens.

—

Add the asparagus tips and sauté for a few minutes. Season with a little salt and pepper.

Pour in the rice and let it mingle with the other ingredients, mixing with a wooden spoon. Add the wine and let it evaporate. Add a ladleful of broth and mix. Add more broth by the ladleful as it is absorbed and mix well.

—

When the rice is cooked but still firm, add salt to taste and the rest of the butter (to give the risotto a glossy appearance), a generous handful of grated cheese and the minced parsley.

Mix well and cook for another minute or so. The risotto should be soft, creamy and dense, so that when it is poured out onto a plate and tipped, it moves slowly toward the edge.

—

Serve at the table with grated parmesan cheese.

Recommended wine
Vespaiolo Superiore di Breganze

Variations
Since it takes about a kilo of asparagus to obtain 300 grams of asparagus tips, the asparagus stalks are usually trimmed of the tough skin, boiled, and then strained in a food mill to give a slightly dense broth for the risotto.

This is the tradition method of preparation, however the risotto tends to be an amalgamation and the asparagus tips become practically invisible. Many cooks prefer to sauté the tips separately in a frying pan and add them to the risotto when it is already halfway through cooking. To give the risotto an attractive pink tinge, add a spoonful of tomato sauce.

risi e patate

RISOTTO WITH POTATOES

This simple and comforting first course is a popular Venetian dish during the winter months, because it is warm, soft and flavourful. It is not a very flashy dish, but no less satisfying.

*Ingredients
for 4 servings*
300 g (¾ lb) Vialone nano rice
200 g (½ lb) potatoes
50 g (2 oz.) unsmoked bacon
60 g (4 tablespoons) butter
a onion
a sprig of rosemary
a litre (4 cups) of broth
salt and pepper
grated parmesan cheese

Preparation time
40 minutes

Wash and peel the potatoes and dice them.

Chop the onion with the bacon and rosemary leaves.

Sauté this mixture in 30 grams of the butter then add the potatoes, salt and pepper and cook together for a few minutes.

Pour in the rice and let it mingle with the other ingredients, mixing with a wooden spoon. Add a ladleful of broth and mix slowly. Keep adding more broth as it is absorbed by rice, stirring well.

When the rice is almost cooked, taste for salt and add the rest of the butter and a handful of grated cheese. Mix the risotto well, leave it on the heat for another minute and serve it piping hot.

Recommended wine
Valdadige rosé

Variations
Once, this dish was frequently prepared during Lent. Then, the meat broth was replaced with vegetable broth and olive oil was used in place of the bacon. Outside Lent, many cooks use lard instead of bacon. Sage may also be used in place of the rosemary to give the risotto a more delicate flavour.

79

r i s o t o   c o i   b r u s c a n d o ' l i

**RISOTTO WITH
"HOP SPROUTS"**

Here is yet another peasant dish of the Veneto cuisine, one that has recently become popular in the more sophisticated restaurants. "Hop sprouts" are the tender top part of young shoots of wild hops that grow profusely in the spring along hedgerows, beside country ditches, and in abandoned fields. They have a characteristic slightly bitter and sour flavour. They should ideally be fresh, but if only dried hop sprouts are available, it is a good idea to plump them before cooking by putting their stalks in ice water and covering the tops with a plastic bag. Hop sprouts generally begin to appear on fruit and vegetable stands in April.

*I n g r e d i e n t s
f o r   4   s e r v i n g s*
300 g (¾ lb) hop sprouts
300 g (¾ lb) rice
60 g (4 tablespoons) butter
a onion
half a bunch of parsley, minced
half a glass of extravirgin olive oil
a litre (4 cups) of meat broth or bouillon
salt and pepper
grated parmesan cheese (to taste)

P r e p a r a t i o n   t i m e
40 minutes

Wash the hop sprouts and cut
them into pieces.

Mince the onion finely and sauté it in
a pot with the olive oil and half the butter.
Pour in the hop sprouts and salt to taste.

Keep the broth hot and ready to use.

After 10 minutes, add the rice and toast it
over a high heat, mixing for a few minutes
so that it absorbs flavour. Pour a ladleful
of broth into the rice, stirring constantly.
Keep adding small amounts of broth as it
is absorbed until the rice is fully cooked.

Remove the pot from the heat and
add the rest of the butter, grated cheese,
parsley, and a pinch of pepper and
stir until is well blended.

The result should be a moist and
creamy risotto that when poured onto
the plate and tipped, it moves slowly
toward the edge.

R e c o m m e n d e d   w i n e
Bianco di Custoza or Tocai del Piave

V a r i a t i o n s
In addition to hops sprouts, other
delicious variations include using tender
sprouts of burs, spiny asparagus,
or pokeweed, all wild plants that grow
spontaneously in abandoned fields.

r i s o t o   d e   s u c a   z a ' l a

**RISOTTO WITH
YELLOW PUMPKIN**

To make this risotto, use a piece of marine pumpkin or pumpkin from Chioggia, which in Venice is called suca baruca, meaning warty pumpkin because of its bumpy skin (see pages 181-182). It is a winter speciality, since these vegetables ripen in late autumn.

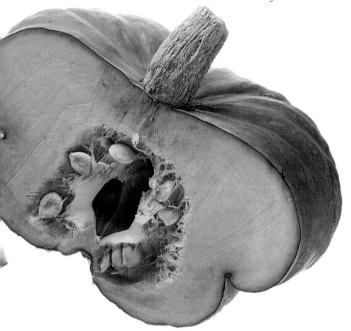

Mince the onion and sauté it in
the olive oil with 30 grams of butter.
Add the pumpkin, with a pinch of salt
and pepper and simmer, stirring from
time to time, until it cooks down to
a puree. It is best not to add any
additional broth or water in this step.

Pour in the rice and let it absorb
the flavours, stirring constantly with
a wooden spoon. Then add ladlefuls
of broth slowly as the rice absorbs it,
stirring all the while.

When the rise is almost cooked,
add the rest of the butter, minced parsley,
and a handful of grated parmesan.
Stir well, taste for salt and pepper
and continue cooking for a few minutes:
the risotto should be creamy and dense.

Serve piping hot with an additional
dusting of parmesan cheese.

Recommended wine
Pinot bianco superiore dei Colli Euganei

Variation
Other flavours such as garlic or cinnamon
are optional additions. When pumpkin
predominates over the rice, Venetians
call this dish *sucarisi*. To make this
speciality, just reduce the amount
of rice used. *Risi e suca* usually identifies
a drier, denser risotto.

Ingredients
for 4 servings
300 g (¾ lb) marine pumpkin
    or pumpkin from Chioggia
300 g (¾ lb) rice
50 g (3 ½ tablespoons) butter
a onion
a bunch of parsley
a glass of extravirgin olive oil
a litre (4 cups) of vegetable broth
salt and pepper
grated parmesan cheese

Preparation time
40 minutes

Clean the piece of pumpkin, trimming
away the peel and seeds, then dice
it or grate it coarsely.

risoto al radicio rosso

**RISOTTO WITH
RED RADICCHIO**

T his distinctively flavoured risotto became part of the Venetian culinary tradition relatively
recently, on the wave of the growing success of red radicchio from Treviso (see page 170).
However, pink radicchio from Chioggia or red radicchio from Verona, or a combination of
either type, can also be used to make this risotto. A pinch of sugar is often added to soften the characteristic strong and bitter flavour of the radicchio.

Ingredients
for 4 servings
300 g (¾ lb) rice
300 g (¾ lb) red radicchio from Treviso
50 g (3 ½ tablespoons) butter
a onion
a clove of garlic
a pinch of sugar
a litre (4 cups) of hot broth
a glass of extravigin olive oil
half a glass of red wine
salt and pepper
grated parmesan cheese

Preparation time
40 minutes

Clean and trim the radicchio,
then cut it into small dice.

Mince the onion and sauté it with
the garlic in the oil and a bit of the butter.
Add the piece of radicchio, salt,
and pepper and let it cook a while.
Add the red wine (which also lends
an attractive hue to the risotto)
and let it evaporate. Remove the garlic
clove and add a good pinch of sugar.

Blend in the rice and let it absorb

the flavours while stirring constantly.
Add the broth gradually as the rice
absorbs it, stirring constantly.

———

When the cooking is almost complete,
add salt and pepper to taste, stir
in the rest of the butter and a handful
of grated cheese, blending vigorously.

———

Serve the risotto piping hot and
creamy, with an additional sprinkling
of parmesan cheese at the table.

Recommended wine
Pinot grigio del Piave

Variations
Adding the red wine is optional.
White wine may be used or wine can
be eliminated altogether. This is also true
of the garlic, which as a rule is not used
in risotto. This recipe is too new for us
to know all the noteworthy variations.
However, the most interesting involve
using other types of red radicchio
which will slightly alter the appearance
and flavour of the risotto. Do away
with the pinch of sugar if other types
of radicchio are used as the red radicchio
from Treviso is the most bitter.

risi e verze

RICE AND CABBAGE

I n the dialect spoken in Venice, the word verza is pronounced with a soft "s" sound instead of the hard "zed". Verde in Italian means green and verze was named for the vibrant colour of the cabbage (see page 180). This first course risotto was once a typical autumn dish served in trattorie across the lagoon. It is very easy to prepare and always comes out flavourful and delicious.

. . . .

Ingredients
for 4 servings
half a Savoy cabbage
   (preferably sweet Padua cabbage)
200 g (½ lb) Vialone nano rice
40 g (3 tablespoons) butter

a small onion
a litre (4 cups) of meat broth
or meat extract
2 spoonfuls of extravirgin olive oil
salt and pepper
grated parmesan cheese

and oil is heated, add the chopped onion.

Remove the tough outer leaves from the cabbage, wash it and cut it into thin strips (or coarser strips if preferred). When the onion turns golden, pour in the cabbage with a ladleful of broth and a bit of salt. Cover the pot, raise the heat and cook for at least another 25 minutes.

Add the rest of the broth and the rice. Watch the cooking carefully and stir often.

When the rice is cooked but still firm, turn off the heat. Add a little salt and a handful of parmesan cheese. Stir well and let the rice sit for a few minutes. Serve.

R e c o m m e n d e d   w i n e
Gambellara classico superiore

V a r i a t i o n s
Excellent risottos can be obtained by following the same recipe, but replacing the cabbage with spinach, leeks, celery, fresh fennel, tomatoes or fresh mushrooms. For mushroom risotto, a couple of cloves of garlic might also be added.

P r e p a r a t i o n   t i m e
45 minutes

Put the butter and oil in a pan over low heat. In the meantime, chop the onion and when the butter

r i s o t o   d e   m a r

SEAFOOD
RISOTTO

This Venetian risotto is also called **risotto de pesse** *or a'la pescadora, not because fishermen are wont to make it but rather because it is made with a combination of different types of fish, shellfish, and molluscs. For the very best risotto, use a flavourful fish broth and present the dish garnished with cooked seafood and a few sprigs of parsley. There are many recipes for this dish, but we have selected the most simple to prepare.*

I n g r e d i e n t s
f o r   4   s e r v i n g s
300 g (¾ lb) Vialone nano rice
1 ½ kg (3 lbs) of mussels, clams and cockles
1 kg (2 lbs) of different types of fish
   (blacktail, scorpion fish, mullet)

a bay leaf
a onion
a carrot
a stalk of celery
a clove of garlic
a bunch of parsley

a glass of extravirgin olive oil
30 g (2 tablespoons) butter
a few black peppercorns
a glass of white wine
salt and pepper

Preparation time
1 hour

Clean and wash the mussels, clams
and cockles, then sauté them in frying
pan. Remove the meat from the shells,
setting aside a few mussels in the
shells for decoration at serving time.
Filter the broth obtained through
cheesecloth and keep it aside.

Clean the fish, removing the scales,
gills and insides. Poach the fish in water
with the bay leaf, a pinch of salt and a few
peppercorns. Remove the fish from the
poaching water and set it aside to eat as
the second course. Set aside the hot broth.

Sauté the onion and the clove of garlic
in the oil; when the garlic begins

to turn golden, remove it and discard.

Add the shelled clams and mussels
and white wine. When the wine has
evaporated, add the filtered shellfish
broth. Add salt and pepper to taste.
Pour in the rice and let it absorb
the flavours, mixing constantly.
Add the fish broth in ladlefuls as the
rice absorbs it, stirring constantly.

When the rice is almost cooked,
add the minced parsley and butter.
Blend the mixture vigorously and
leave it on the heat for a few minutes,
then turn off the heat.

Recommended wine
Gargenega dei Colli Berici
or Vespaiolo di Breganze

Variations
Small squid, small octopuses, and other
types of seafood may also be used in this
recipe. The broth can also be prepared
with scraps of any lean white fish.

r i s o t o   n e r o

**SQUID INK
RISOTTO**

*R*isotto with squid ink is not one of the great traditional Venetian dishes, but has gradually
made its way into classic Venetian menus. The person tasting this dish for the first time
may be initially put off by its unusually intense black colour, but is slowly won over by the
delightful flavour. Venetians heighten the surprise effect by serving this dish on brilliant white
porcelain plates. The strong contrasting colours deepens the visual contrast and thus, increases the
curiosity to taste it. One of the secrets to excellent squid ink risotto is a flavourful fish broth, prepared with lean fish scraps and some shellfish shells, boiled in water with herbs and then filtered.
Venetian housewives know this trick and usually prepare the broth with bits and pieces of the fish
that is to be served as the second course.

*Ingredients
for 4 servings*
600 g (1 ½ lbs) of medium sized squid
300 g (¾ lb) rice

30 g (2 tablespoons) butter
a small onion
a clove of garlic
a litre (4 cups) hot fish broth

RISOTO NERO

a glass of extravirgin olive oil
a glass of white wine
salt and pepper

Preparation time
40 minutes

Clean the squid, removing the skin
carefully and removing the bone
by pulling it out of the opening between
the tentacles and the body sac, or cutting
into the sac. Then separate the body
sac from tentacles with the innards
attached; remove the ink pouches
being very careful not to rupture them,
and set them aside in a cup.
Remove the eyes and the beak at the
centre of the tentacles with a paring knife.
Wash well and cut into thin strips.

Mince the onion and sauté gently
with a clove of garlic in a heavy pot
where the oil is heating.

When the garlic begins to turn golden,
remove it and discard it.
Add the squid strips. Add salt and
pepper and sauté the squid for a few
minutes, stirring well, and then add
the wine and let it evaporate.

Dilute the ink with a bit of water

and pour it into the pot. Simmer
the mixture for about twenty minutes,
stirring frequently.

Pour in the rice, stirring constantly,
and let it absorb the flavours, stirring up
from the bottom of the pot. Add a ladleful
of fish broth and gradually add more
as the rice absorbs it, stirring all the time.

When the rice is cooked to the right
degree of doneness, add the butter and
minced parsley, blending thoroughly.
Turn off the heat, and let the risotto
stand for a few minutes before serving.

Recommended wine
Vespaiolo superiore di Breganze
or Soave Classico

Variations
Remember that small squid are not
any more tender or less chewy
than the larger squid. Some
people like to add a little grated
parmesan to this risotto,
as in other types of risotto,
to enhance and soften
the flavour. That is fine
during cooking, but
grated cheese is never
added at the
table.

risi e scampi

**RISOTTO
WITH PRAWNS**

Prawns *(in Latin,* Nephros norvegicus) *are highly prized crustaceans with a light pink colour and claws, which are fished in the Adriatic as well as throughout the Mediterranean and in other seas.*

They are also exquisite as antipasti or as appetisers, but Venetian tradition has opted to feature them in a risotto whose delicate flavour and gentle pink colour has made it a sophisticated culinary favourite.

. . . .

Ingredients
for 4 servings
500 g (1 lb) of whole prawns
300 g (¾ lb) rice
30 g (2 tablespoons) butter
a small onion
a bay leaf
a clove of garlic
a glass of extravirgin olive oil
half a glass of dry white wine
salt and pepper

Preparation time
40 minutes

Wash the prawns well and boil them
for about 15 minutes in 1.2 litres of water
with a bay leaf and a pinch of salt.
Remove the prawns, filter the broth
and set it aside and keep hot.

———

Remove the shells from the prawns,
detaching the tails from the heads.
Discard the heads. Cut the cartilage along
the tails lengthwise along the back and
the belly, opening it out with the fingers.
Gently remove the flesh, being careful
to keep it in one piece. Another way
to do this is to remove the first belly ring
of the shell and press the end portion with
the fingers to make the flesh protrude.
Keep the meat from the shelled tails aside.

———

Heat up the olive oil in a heavy pot and
sauté the minced onion and the clove
of garlic. When the garlic is golden,
remove it and pour in the rice. Let it sauté
for a few minutes, then add the wine
and let it evaporate. Add a ladleful
of prawn broth and gradually add more
as the rice absorbs it, stirring all the time.

———

Halfway through cooking, after about
10 minutes, add the flesh from the tails
of the prawns and keep stirring.

———

When the rice is firm yet tender, turn
off the heat, add the butter and blend well.
The risotto should be creamy and dense.

———

Serve in brilliant white china,
foregoing the grated cheese.

Recommended wine
Bianco di Custoza

Variations
This same recipe can be used to make
risotto with shrimp, crab, lobster or any
other shellfish. To enhance the pink colour,
a spoonful of tomato sauce may be added
during cooking. Other herbs may be
added, such as a few sprigs of minced
parsley and a handful of grated cheese
may be tossed in at the end of cooking.

risoto de bisato

EEL RISOTTO

Bisato *means eel in the Venetian dialect and it is used widely in traditional dishes (see page 135-137 for recipe). Eel risotto is one of these specialities and was once served as a favourite first course on Christmas Eve. More generally, we might consider this risotto a paradigm of all risottos prepared in the inland areas with fresh water fish. The eel may be replaced with lake trout, carp or tench and risotto made with the latter is a speciality around the eastern banks of Lake Garda.*

. . . .

Ingredients
for 4 servings
400 g (1 lb) of eel
    (a large slice of fresh eel)
300 g (¾ lb) rice
30 g (2 tablespoons) butter
a onion, minced
a clove of garlic
a bay leaf
a sprig of parsley, minced
juice of half a lemon
1.2 litres (5 cups) of hot broth
    (made with bouillon)
half a glass of extravirgin olive oil
salt and freshly ground pepper

Preparation time
40 minutes

Clean the eel and cut it into slices.

———

Heat the oil and the butter
in a heavy pot. Add the onion,
the garlic and the bay leaf.

———

When the onion is soft, add the slices
of eel and a bit of salt. Sauté the
eel gently. Sprinkle on the lemon juice
and add a half a ladleful of broth.
Cook the mixture for about twenty
minutes.

———

Remove from the eel slices from
the broth. Remove the skin
and bones (removing the bones

should be quite easy at this point).
Remove and discard the garlic
and bay leaf from the broth.

———

Pour the rice into the pot and stir
it with a wooden spoon. Add the eel
pieces. Continue adding the hot broth
gradually as the rice absorbs it,
stirring all the while.

———

When the rice is cooked and has creamy
consistency, add the finely minced
parsley and grind in some black pepper.
Stir vigorously and serve piping hot,
without grated cheese.

Recommended wine
Soave classico superiore

Variations
The risotto is prepared in exactly
the same way when using trout or tench.
Clean the fish, cook it gently and then
remove the skin and bones and add
it to the rice in the heavy pot.
However, since trout is not as fatty
as eel, it is delicious with a bit of dry
white wine instead of the lemon juice.
On the other hand, tench, with
its distinctive earthy taste, improves
with the addition of a spoonful
of vinegar. Some connoisseurs
of *risoto de bisato* like to add fresh
peas to the dish, which are added
along with the eel slices.

risoto de rane

**RISOTTO
WITH FROG**

Frogs find an ideal habitat to grow and reproduce in the rice paddies, or at least they did before the introduction of chemical weed killers. They also thrive in the water-meadows and in
the ditches along the grassy plains or in the slow flowing waters of the Sile, the river that
cuts through Treviso and flows out into the lagoon.
What could be more genuine than reviving the felicitous combination of frogs and rice?

This dish is popular in the Veneto, Treviso, the alluvial plains and around lower Verona as well as across the plains of Padua. In Lombardy, it is also called "San Siro's rice" in honour of the bishop of Pavia, who legend has it, was both inventor and performer of miracles. This preparation (along with frog soup) has been credited with having miraculous healing properties for all sorts of maladies.

. . . .

Ingredients
for 4 servings
700 g (1 ½ lbs) of whole frogs
300 g (¾ lb) Vialone nano rice
30 g (2 tablespoons) butter
a onion, minced
a sprig of parsley, minced
1.2 litres (5 cups) of hot broth (made with
   the following herbs: a few celery leaves,
   a clove of crushed garlic, 2 bay leaves,
   a small onion studded with 2 whole
   cloves, a piece of lemon rind,
   2 bouillon cubes)
a glass of extravirgin olive oil
half a glass dry white wine
salt and pepper

Preparation time
1 hour

Put 1 ½ litres of water in a large pot
with all the herbs indicated for the broth
and the cleaned and washed frogs.
Bring to a boil and simmer the frogs
for half an hour.

Remove the frogs, detach the legs and
discard the bodies. Remove the meat
from the legs, discarding the bones.
Only the meat is necessary for the risotto.
Filter the broth through cheesecloth
and keep it hot.

Heat the olive oil in a heavy pot and
add the onion. Cook until soft. Add the
rice and stir with a wooden spoon to
mingle the flavours. After a few minutes,
add the wine and let it evaporate.

Add a ladleful of hot broth and keep
adding it slowing, stirring constantly,
as it is absorbed by the rice.

When the rice is almost cooked, add
the frog meat and taste for salt. When
the rice is cooked to the right degree,
add butter, the parsley and a sprinkling
of fresh ground black pepper.

Stir well and serve the risotto piping
hot with a bit of parmesan on the side.

Recommended wine
Tocai bianco dei Colli Berici

Variations
Considering the delicate flavour of the
frog legs, the risotto may also be made by
stewing the frog legs in a highly seasoned
sauce then pouring it over plain boiled
rice, like a pasta dish. Instead of using
parsley, this dish can also be flavoured
with a mince of mixed seasonal herbs,
such as basil, marjoram and tarragon.

risi e 'luganeghe

**RISOTTO WITH
SAUSAGES**

This risotto was originally prepared in the Marca Trevigiana, where many aristocratic Venetian families kept their summer homes. Thus, if someone in Venice or the surrounding area asks a restaurateur for riso e 'luganeghe, he might be a bit surprised by what is brought to the table.

The same name also belongs to a dish made with rice and sausages, plus a host of other ingredients, such as cabbage, cauliflower, potatoes and spinach. The common denominator that gives the strong flavour is the 'luganeghe, fresh Treviso pork sausages.

Ingredients
for 4 servings
150 g (5 ½ oz.) fresh pork sausage
300 g (¾ lb) rice
30 g (2 tablespoons) butter
a onion, diced
a stalk of celery, diced
sprig of parsley
1.2 litres (5 cups) of hot bouillon broth
half a glass dry white wine
a pinch of salt
plenty of grated parmesan cheese

Preparation time
40 minutes

Choose the freshest sausages, flavoured with any herbs desired. Remove the casing and cut them into pieces.

───

Fry the onion and celery in a little butter until soft. Add the pieces of sausage and cook them for a few minutes, mixing from time to time with a wooden spoon.

───

Add the rice and stir constantly, letting the rice mingle with the flavours until it becomes shiny. Sprinkle in the white wine and

when it has evaporated, add the
hot broth gradually by the ladleful
as the rice absorbs it.

———

When the rice is almost cooked,
add salt if necessary, stir in some
minced parsley and a generous
handful of grated cheese.

———

Serve the risotto when it is soft and
creamy, along with grated parmesan
cheese on the side.

Recommended wine
Cabernet di Lison-Pramaggiore
or del Montello e Colli Asolani

Variations
Traditional rules for preparing this risotto
lay down that one sausage is used for
every 100 grams of rice (sausages usually
weigh about 50 to 60 grams), but in order
to make a lighter less rich dish, the amount
of sausage can be decreased or the fat
can be removed by cooking it separately,
before using it in the risotto. Cooks
in the past did the opposite, cooking
the rice first and adding the sausages
whole and using them to make a pretty
garnish for the dish before serving.
If vegetables mentioned in the
introduction (cauliflower, cabbage, etc.)
are added, they should be almost fully
cooked before adding the rice.

risi col late

RICE COOKED IN MILK

To conclude our lengthy exploration into risottos – we've left out numerous recipes which
have fallen definitively into disuse – we felt we should add this simple but surprising dish,
which all Venetians of a certain age hold close to their hearts, when mothers of yore would
prepare this comforting dish in the evening for young children.
The flavour is pleasant even using the pasteurised milk found in the supermarkets, but to have
an idea of how delicious it used to be, just imagine using milk fresh from the farm and with all
the cream left in.

*Ingredients
for 4 servings*
300 g (¾ lb) rice
1 ½ litres (6 cups) of fresh milk
a pinch of salt

Preparation time
½ hour

Heat half the milk in a large pot.
As soon as it begins to boil,
add the rice and stir from time to time.

———

After 8 to 10 minutes, add the rest
of the hot milk and a pinch of salt.

When the rice is firm but tender,
taste for salt and… that's it.
The rice is ready. The risotto should
be very creamy and moist.

Variations
If desired, when the rice is just
about done, add a handful of grated
parmesan cheese. Another variation
which is rarely used these days,
is to make a sweet rice by adding
a spoonful of sugar in place
of the salt and perhaps a handful
of pine nuts or some raisins,
plumped first in warm water.

Meat and game

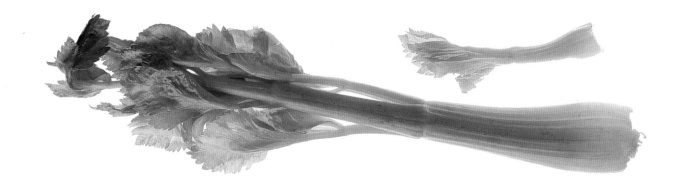

carne lessa

BOILED MEAT PLATTER

T his dish is found widely in most regions in Italy (the Piedmont has a celebrated version, called *büi*) but in Venice, this was a dish eaten almost daily by well-heeled Venetians from the 1600s until our days, because poor folk couldn't afford the price of meat. Meat began bubbling away in large pots in the early morning hours in household kitchens and mid-morning, the lady of the house would sip the delicious and fortifying broth, a pleasant habit still much in use today.

After cooking, the meat was kept warm and served with several different sauces on the side, so that each diner could choose the sauce he or she wanted. There are countless recipes for these sauces, but the most popular ones in the Veneto are given after this recipe.

. . . .

Ingredients
for 10 servings
1 kg (2 lbs) of beef
　(rump roast or other cut, as desired)
500 g (1 lb) calf head
500 g (1 lb) corned beef tongue
a piece of beef bone, with marrow
a free range hen, cleaned and plucked

a large pork sausage, about 500 g (1 lb)
3 carrots
3 stalks of celery
2 large onions, studded with cloves
2 bunches of mixed herbs
　(parsley, bay leaf and a clove of garlic)
black peppercorns
salt

95

About 3 hours at a very slow boil

Put a pot on the stove large enough
to cook beef and the hen.
Pour in 6 litres of water and 30 grams
of sea salt (the general rule of thumb
is to use 3 litres of water and 15 grams
of salt for each kilo of meat).
Add the beef bone, an onion, two carrots,
two stalks of celery, and one bunch
of herbs. Put the pot on high heat.

———

When the water boils, emerge
the beef and cover the pot almost
all the way. After a little while, a foam
will begin forming on the surface
(produced by the coagulating meat
proteins) which should be skimmed
off with a slotted spoon.
Lower the heat to a minimum and
after about an hour, add the hen.
Continue skimming off the foam
until the broth is clear.
Now add the peppercorns and
simmer the meats for another couple
of hours, partly covered. The beef
and the hen will be done when easily
pierced with a fork.

———

Cook the pork sausage and
the corned beef tongue in separate
pots, as indicated in the recipes

given on pages 114 and 107-110.

———

In another pot, cook the veal head.
Separate cooking will ensure that
the broth doesn't become cloudy.
Put it in cold, slightly salted water
with an onion, a carrot, a stalk of celery
and the herbs and bring to a boil.
Simmer the meat gently for a couple
of hours.

———

When all the meats are cooked,
remove them from their broth
and place them in a large metal pan,
basting with the hen and beef broth
to keep them warm. The other broth
made during cooking the other meats
can be discarded.

———

The host should serve the meat,
cutting it at the table according
to each guest's tastes.

Recommended wine
Merlot dei Colli Berici

Variations
To obtain a superior boiled meat
platter, the meat should be plunged
into boiling water, so the immediate
contact with heat instantaneously
coagulates the proteins and seals
in the internal juices that give flavour
to the meat. If you want to achieve
the most flavourful broth, do the
opposite. Begin cooking the meat in cold
water and bring to a boil very gently.
The selection meats can be varied
according to taste. Turkey, capon,
or breast of veal may be used.
The broth (served with small pasta
shapes, tagliatelle, or tortelloni,
or whatever is desired) will make
a splendid first course. In the Veneto,
many cooks serve the broth with very
narrow egg pasta (homemade angel hair)
with the addition of a spoonful of
sautéed chicken livers served at the table.

CARNE LESSA

SAUCES

In the Veneto region, sauces are never spooned on top of the meat, but served alongside so as to not diminish the flavour of the meat and to allow each diner to choose the best combination. The ingredients given are for 10 servings.

Pearà • PEPPER SAUCE

Legend has it that this sauce was invented in the sixth century by a cook in the court of the Longobard king Alboino, to tempt Queen Rosamund out of the fast she had begun in protest against her husband's oppression. The name comes from péar, which in the Veneto dialect stands for pepper, the ingredient that gives it its distinctive flavour.

Ingredients: *500 g (2 cups) breadcrumbs; 250 g (½ lb) beef marrow; 50 g (3 ½ tablespoons) butter; 1 ½ litres (6 cups) hot beef and hen broth; a generous handful of grated parmesan cheese; salt and plenty of fresh grated pepper.*

Chop the marrow and melt it with the butter in a heavy pot over low heat. Add the breadcrumbs and blend with a wooden spoon. Let the breadcrumbs absorb the marrow. Add the hot broth and simmer gently for 2 to 3 hours, mixing from time to time. Half an hour before serving, remove from heat and add salt if necessary. Toss in the grated parmesan and fresh ground pepper. Mix well.
Pearà sauce should be served piping hot.

Salsa de cren • HORSERADISH SAUCE

Less famous and more modern than the previous recipe, horseradish sauce gained popularity in Veneto in the 1800s, during Austrian domination.

Ingredients: *2 horseradish roots, about 200 to 250 g (½ lb) total; 100 ml (½ cup) white vinegar; 70 g (2 ½ oz.) white bread, without the crust, moistened with milk and squeezed of the excess; a pinch of salt; a pinch of sugar.*

Scrape, wash and grate the horseradish into a sauce boat. Add the other ingredients and mix well. Add a spoonful of sweet cream if desired.

Salsa verde • GREEN SAUCE

The Venetian version of this sauce has Jewish origins.

Ingredients: *200 g (½ lb) small leaf parsley; 2 hard-boiled eggs; 6 anchovies, rinsed to remove the salt; 3 handfuls of pine nuts; 40 g (1 ½ oz.) capers; 2 cloves of garlic devoid of the green sprouts; the soft part of 2 bread rolls, moistened with broth; a glass of extravirgin olive oil; the juice of a lemon; salt and pepper.*

Mince all the solid ingredients finely. Mix together well with the lemon juice and oil, and add enough bread to make it dense. Taste for sale and pepper.

Salsa coi càpari • CAPER SAUCE

We are giving a fairly simple version of this sauce.

Ingredients: *100 g (3 ½ oz.) capers; 70 g (2 ½ oz.) anchovies, rinsed to remove the salt; 2 cloves of garlic devoid of the green sprouts; 2 glasses of extravirgin olive oil; the juice of a lemon.*

Mince the capers, anchovies and garlic finely. Put them in a sauce boat and blend in the oil and lemon juice.

carne in tecia

STEWED BEEF

Brasàr *comes from the Venetian word* brasa, brase *("brazier") although the method of cooking that it identifies is performed in a pot and not on the brazier at all. Admittedly, both methods do call for searing the meat and require fairly lengthy cooking times. In Venice and around the Veneto, this recipe is also called* el lesso che no se lessa *or* el manzo che se cusina da so'lo *(meaning, "boiled meat that isn't boiled" or "beef that cooks by itself"), as cooking occurs slowly inside a tightly closed heavy pot (either in earthenware casserole or in stainless steel Dutch oven), needing very little attention. The most appropriate cuts of meat are the muscular parts (the round, for example) because they are tough when purchased but the lengthy cooking time softens them thanks to the lactic acid accumulation in the fibres. Shoulder is also a good choice, as is the rump.*

*Ingredients
for 4 servings*
800 g (2 lbs) beef rump
200 g (7 oz.) ripe tomatoes
200 ml (1 cup) of beef broth
a few strips of lard or bacon
a onion
a carrot
a stalk of celery
a leek
30 g (2 tablespoons) butter
a glass of red wine
half a glass of olive oil
a small amount of flour
salt and pepper

Preparation time
At least 3 ½ hours

Force strips of lard or bacon
into the beef along the grain, inserting
them a regular intervals.
To do this, use a special kitchen
tool called a larder. Otherwise, chop
the bacon or lard and add it to
the vegetables to be sautéed (further
in the recipe). The larding will make
the meat softer and more flavourful.
Dust the meat with flour.

———

Melt the butter with the oil
in a heavy pot and over high heat,
sauté the floured beef for about
15 minutes until a golden crust forms
that holds all the juices inside even
during cooking.

In the meantime, chop up the
vegetables and add them to the meat,
adding a glass of wine as well.
When this has evaporated, add the
peeled, drained and chopped tomatoes,
the broth and a little pepper.
Cover the pot tightly and cook very
slowly for at least three hours.

———

Check the sauce from time to time,
but not too often, so that it doesn't
get too dry. Add a little hot broth.

———

When the meat is cooked to tenderness,
add some salt to the sauce, cut the
meat into slices, arrange the slices
on a plate and garnish with the sauce.

Recommended wine
Raboso del Piave
or Valpolicella superiore

Variations
There are easy and there are complicated
variations. The easy variations entail
reducing the number of ingredients
by eliminating the chopped vegetables;
the more complicated variations
add ingredients that enhance the
flavour, for example *porcini* or *chiodini*
mushrooms (which then becomes
stewed meat with mushrooms)
or wine (Raboso is generally used
in the Veneto). If the gravy is still too
watery once the meat is cooked,
add a pinch of thickener (cornstarch
or flour) to give it more body.

---

pastissada de cavàl

**MARINATED
AND BRAISED
HORSEMEAT**

The custom of marinating meat and cooking it slowly in its juices is long established all over the regions of the northern Adriatic from Dalmatia to the Marches. However, one legend records the origin of this dish as being from Veneto, specifically from the city of Verona. The story goes that during the 5th century B.C., there was brutal clash between Theodoric's Visigoths and the Erules led by Odoacre. After the battle, several horses were left dead on the battlefield.

The local population then came up with a method for preserving the meat, which eventually gave rise to the pastissada de caval. *While a fairly unlikely tale, the legend still lends this ancient dish a colourful history and probably holds some degree of truth, at least in explaining the reason why many cultures use marinades to preserve meats.*

But, today, this dish has evolved and new ingredients have been introduced along the way: spices were introduced by Venetians only a short time before the year 1000; marinating meat has remained a popular custom with the Dalmatian populations; and as for the custom of eating horsemeat, horses once roamed free in the remote centuries of the Middle Ages in the maritime forests lining the Adriatic. At that time, Verona was the seat of tournaments and equestrian jousts and from the last century also became the seat of the most important European equestrian trade fairs.

. . . .

Ingredients
for 4 servings
1 kg (2 lbs) shoulder or round
   cut of young and tender horsemeat
a few strips of lard or bacon
1 litre (4 cups) Recioto Amarone
30 g (2 tablespoons) butter
2 small onions
2 carrots
2 stalks of celery
a clove of garlic
a bay leaf
4 cloves
a pinch of cinnamon
a pinch of paprika
a small amount of flour
half a glass of extravirgin olive oil
peppercorns and freshly ground
black pepper
salt

Preparation time
3 hours, plus marinating time

Force strips of lard into the horsemeat along the grain, inserting them a regular intervals.
To do this, use a special kitchen tool called a larder (see previous recipe for tips). Chop the carrot, onion, celery and garlic and pour the mirepoix into a glass or ceramic dish. Add the cloves, cinnamon, salt and some peppercorns.
Put the larded meat on top and cover with the wine. Let the meat stand in the marinade for 3 days.

———

After marinating, remove the meat, let it drip and then roll it in the flour to coat. Brown it in the olive oil over high heat. Remove the vegetables and add them to the heavy pot with the meat. When these have softened, add the wine, cover the pot and cook slowly for at least three hours.

———

When cooking is complete, remove the meat and pass the sauce through a strainer. Put it back on the heat, taste for salt and pepper and then add a little butter, a pinch of paprika and a pinch of flour.
Blend well and let the sauce thicken while stirring constantly.

———

Cut the meat into thick slices, arrange the slices on a plate and cover with sauce. Serve the dish with a soft yellow polenta.

101

Recommended wine
Valpolicella superiore
or Recioto Amarone

Variations
This method of preparation was also
once used to cook *pastissada de musso*
(marinated and braised mule).
A part from this variation, some people
cut the meat into cubes after marinating,
which makes a sort of stew, or use a
combination of meat and sauces blended
together to make a single dense gravy.

castradina s'ciavona

DALMATIAN MUTTON

This traditional dish is often prepared during the Venetian festival of the Madonna della Salute (21 November) the church designed and erected by Longhena on the Grand Canal to celebrate and pay homage for the ending of the plague of 1630 to 1631. Castradina is the meat from castrated mutton which is then salted, smoked and dried and which the Venetians once imported from Dalamatia (S'ciavona). Nowadays, it is difficult to find this imported meat even at the famous Rialto market, but a few loyal Venetians uphold the tradition by using local mutton.

*Ingredients
for 4 servings*
800 g (2 lbs) leg of dried salted mutton
a small onion
a carrot
a stalk of celery
peppercorns

Preparation time
4 hours of boiling time,
plus half a day to stand

Wash the mutton leg, cut into medium
sized pieces and put it into a Dutch oven
with plenty of cold water. Add the
vegetables and the peppercorns and bring
it to a boil. Simmer for a few hours.

Cool the meat in the cooking water
overnight, then skim off the fatty foam
coagulated on the surface.

Add a couple more ladlefuls of water
and put it back on the heat to simmer
for at least another two hours.

Remove the cooked mutton
and serve it with *verze sofegae*
(see recipe on page 180-181).

Recommended wine
Merlot dei Colli Berici
or Rosso Superiore dei Colli Euganei

Variations
Salted mutton from Dalmatia
or Albania would need a cooking
time of at least 6-7 hours.
It must be washed several times
in tepid water to eliminate
all traces of the unpleasantly
strong flavour and the water
from the first boiling is discarded.

ose'leti scampai

**SKEWERED MEAT
SHISH KEBABS**

The name of this dish is a play on words: it means that the little birds (ose'letti *in dialect*) *that were promised… would have none of it and flew away! In fact, the dish was a creative substitute for small game probably invented because the man of the house left early in the morning on a hunting trip and came back empty-handed or because game was not in season or because the lady of the house preferred not to work too hard on the meal that day.*
In short, this recipe proves that failing the genuine article, an alternative can often be just as good, making a virtue of necessity.

*Ingredients
for 4 servings*
200 g (7 oz.) veal
200 g (7 oz.) pork
200 g (7 oz.) unsmoked bacon
   cut into ½ cm strips
100 g (3 ½ oz.) chicken livers
100 g (3 ½ oz.) veal or pork liver
100 ml (½ cup) broth
100 ml (½ cup) extravirgin olive oil
30 g (2 tablespoons) butter
a glass of dry white wine
plenty of sage leaves
salt and pepper

Preparation time
1 hour

Cut the veal, pork, bacon, and veal
or pork liver into bite sized pieces.

Sauté the chicken livers in the butter
with a pinch of salt and a couple
of sage leaves.

Thread the ingredients onto
the skewers in the following order:
a piece of veal, a sage leaf,
a piece of bacon,
a chicken liver,
a sage leaf,
a piece of pork,
a sage leaf,
a piece of liver,
a piece of bacon,

another sage leaf.
Continue in this order until
all the pieces are used up.

In a large heavy pot, heat up
the extra virgin olive oil and add
the shish kebabs, browning them
on all sides over high heat.
Add salt and pepper and pour in
a glass of wine. Let it evaporate
and then add the broth a little
at a time. Continue cooking until
it leaves a good amount of gravy.

Arrange the skewers on individual
plates atop a bed of hot and
creamy polenta, covered with
the flavourful gravy.

Recommended wine
Cabernet del Montello e Colli Asolani

Variations
The order of the pieces of meat on
the skewers can be changed as can
the types of meat used. If desired,
the chicken livers can be replaced
with other types of organ meats
(brain sautéed in a pan) or left out
altogether. In some areas, *ose'leti scampai*
are prepared by wrapping a piece
of bacon around a piece of veal with
a few sage leaves, holding the roll
steady with a couple of toothpicks,
cooking as indicated above.

c a r p a c c i o

CARPACCIO

Toward the end of the 1940s, on a bright winter day in the late afternoon, Richard Cantwell, colonel of the infantry regiment of the United States army stationed in Italy, «threw open the door of Harry's Bar in Venice, and entered. He'd managed it again and felt right at home». *He took a seat at his usual table and waited.* «Then, she came into the room, a splendid young and slender beauty with her hair all blown from the wind. She had a pale skin with a slightly olive tone, and a profile that would have sparked emotion in anybody's heart. Her hair was brown, full and lustrous, falling around her shoulders.»

— Hello, lovely lady — said the Colonel.

— Oh, hello, how are you? — she responded. — I was afraid you would have gone by now. I am so sorry I'm late. (…)

— Waiter! — called the Colonel. He turned to her and asked — Would you care for a dry martini, too? — Yes, please — she replied.

— Two very dry martinis. Montgomerys, please. Fifteen to one. — ordered the Colonel. The waiter, who had served in the desert, smiled and vanished. The Colonel turned to Renata.

— You are sweet — he said. — You are also very beautiful and I love you.

— You always say that and I don't know what it means, but I still love to hear it. (…) «The Martinis were ice cold and they were true Montgomerys. After taking the first sip, they already began to feel a pleasant warmth throughout their bodies. (…) She turned her head and lifted her chin, with no sign of vanity nor flirtatiousness, and the Colonel felt his heart turn somersaults, as if an animal sleeping in his cave had awakened with exhilarating surprise to see another sleeping animal by his side.» *The delicious love story between the enchanting Renata, a nineteen-year old Venetian countess, and a fifty-year old American colonel soon to die, «beyond the river and amidst the trees» – as the title of the novel by Ernest Hemingway that retold it – played out in one of the most famous places in Venice: Harry's Bar. Here, not only were love stories consummated, but the crème de la crème of culture and world power congregated to be treated to exquisite service and utter peace. Hemingway (Cantwell), Adriana Ivancich (Renata), Churchill, Stravinsky, Orson Welles, and many other passed through these doors and have confirmed its magic. Veneto cuisine was revived in the 1930s in its kitchen, thanks to the ingenious intuition of its founder, Giuseppe Cipriani, who became a forerunner in a few basic criteria of simplicity and genuineness that would later become a shared heritage of the new culinary tradition. Today the prestige of the mythical restaurant, and the no-less celebrated Locanda Cipriani in Torcello, has been kept to its original standards by Giuseppe's son Arrigo, who claims to be the only person in the world to have been named after a bar. Among Giuseppe's culinary inventions, the most famous and legendary has to be Carpaccio. No less famous are the delicious cocktails he invented using the fresh and sparking dry Veneto white wine (Prosecco) with fresh fruit purées: the Bellini, Tiziano and Mimosa plus the very dry martini (the latter, as mentioned earlier, was a favourite of Hemingway-Cantwell). But let's let Cipriani speak for himself:* «How did you come up with Carpaccio?»

«Doctors had ordered the Countess Amalia Nani Mocenigo to follow a very strict diet. She was not to eat any cooked meat and so, to make her happy, I thought I could slice filet steak very very thinly. Meat by itself is a bit tasteless, but I knew a recipe for a very simple sauce that was wonderful with both meat and fish. I sprinkled a bit on the meat and called it Carpaccio in honour of the great painter whose exhibition was the talk of Venice that year [1963] and also because the colour of the plate reminded me of some reds he used in his paintings.» *Since then, this classic Venetian dish has won over all the most elite kitchens in restaurants across Europe and America.*

. . . .

Ingredients
for 4 servings
300 g (¾ lb) raw beef filet
a cup of mayonnaise
5 spoonfuls of sweet cream
4 spoonfuls of fresh tomato puree
2 spoonfuls of Worcestershire sauce
a spoonfuls of mustard

Preparation time
15 minutes

Cut the raw filet into very thin slices.
Arrange the slices, spreading them out
prettily on the plates.

———

Prepare the sauce by blending together
the mayonnaise, the mustard, the tomato
puree, the Worcestershire, and the cream.

———

Arrange the sauce decoratively
on the slices of meat, either in stripes
or spreading it evenly with the back
of a spoon. Serve.

Recommended wine
Vespaiolo di Breganze
or Bianco di Custoza

Variations
This recipe is more or less an original
creation of Giuseppe Cipriani.
However, he frequently used tomato
ketchup in place of the tomato puree
in the sauce and at times added a splash
of whisky or cognac. The simplicity
and the delicacy of this dish have also
sealed its popularity. Quite a number
of variations were made to the recipe,
none of which with much success.
These days, some cooks like to substitute
beef round or air-dried beef from
Valtellina *(bresaola)* and others replace
the original sauce with any number
of spur-of-the-moment creations.
Other ingredients can be used to garnish
the meat, such as *porcini* mushrooms,
truffles, slivers of parmesan,
rocket lettuce, and
so forth.

lengua salmistrada

CORNED BEEF TONGUE

Modern bechèri *(butchers) sell corned beef tongue ready for cooking, but in the old days, farmers in the hinterlands of Venice had to prepare it themselves, using a very special method. The name comes from salmistro a word that in the local dialect means saltpeter. This salt is the major ingredient in preparing the tongue, which was also a good preservative allowing the meat to be stored for a long time in days when there were no refrigerators.*
Farmers would procure a beef tongue, wrap it in coarse kitchen salt and then sprinkle on saltpeter (about 30 grams per kilo of meat). They put the tongue in a large earthenware dish with plenty of herbs and spices (juniper berries, black peppercorns, rosemary, sage leaves, and cloves of garlic). The dish was covered with a plate and a weight was placed on top to compress the tongue.
Put the dish into a cool place and let it marinate for 20 to 30 days, turning the tongue over from time to time. In the meantime, its juices will melt the salts and create a spicy herbal marinade. After the marinating time is over, the tongue was rinsed and cooked.

CARPACCIO

Ingredients
for 6 servings
a corned beef tongue,
   about 800 g (2 lbs)
a onion
a carrot
a celery stick

Preparation time
3 hours

Wash the tongue carefully and repeatedly
in running water. Put it into a pot
with boiling water and simmer for about
an hour.

───

Put another pot on the stove with water
and the vegetables and bring to a boil.

───

Remove the tongue from the first pot
and transfer it to the second pot without
stopping the boiling.

───

As soon as cooking is completed,
remove the tongue, put it
on a cutting board and remove
the tough skin surrounding the meat.
It should be fairly easy to do while
the tongue is hot (although be careful
to avoid burns).

───

Cut the tongue into thin slices
and serve it warm or cold on a serving
platter, with a side dish of spinach
or mashed potatoes or with one
of the sauces for boiled meats
(see recipes pages 98-99).

Recommended wine
Rosso superiore dei Colli Euganei

Variations
Excellent on its own as well as with
boiled meat platters (but cooked
separately), corned beef tongue lends
itself to creative preparations. It can
be thinly sliced, arranged on a serving
platter and covered with gelatine to
be served cold. Or it may be cut into
cubes and tossed with drained pickled
vegetables in a salad, dressed with a bit
of good quality extra virgin olive oil.

tripe a'la trevisana

STEWED TRIPE

T his dish originates from the Marca Trevigiana area and later spread to Venice and all over
the Veneto, where it has been given a variety of names: in tecia (in the pan) or a'la veneta or al parmesàn. It is frequently found on menus in informal country restaurants as a
one-dish meal. Veal tripe is generally used to make the dish because it is more tender, but less
flavourful, than beef tripe (see page 71-72 for recipe). If the tripe is not already cleaned and
blanched, it must be boiled for an hour in plenty of water with some herbs, then well-drained
and cut into thin strips.

. . . .

Ingredients
for 4 servings
1 kg (2 lbs) of veal tripe, already blanched
80 g (2 ½ oz.) lard or bacon,
60 g (4 tablespoons) butter

70 ml (4 ½ tablespoons) beef broth
a large onion, a sprig of rosemary
a generous amount
of grated parmesan cheese
salt and pepper

Preparation time
At least 2 hours

Chop the onion, lard or bacon, and
the rosemary leaves. Sauté the mixture
gently in the butter an earthenware pot.

———

Pour in the tripe and let the flavours
mingle, stirring with a wooden spoon.
Add salt, pepper, and add a half
a litre of beef broth.

Cover the pot and cook over a low
heat for about two hours, stirring
from time to time and adding the rest
of the broth halfway through cooking.

———

Once the tripe is tender, add a good
handful of parmesan cheese and stir.

———

Before serving, dust another handful of
parmesan on top of the dish and serve with
slices of rustic bread, toasted in the oven
or with a side dish of piping hot polenta.

Recommended wine
Cabernet del Piave

Variations
The version given here is the most
simple and can also be transformed
into tripe in broth, removing a little
of the tripe and transferring it to
a bowl of good hot beef broth.
Recipe variations mostly regard
the flavourings, which can be enriched
with a bunch of herbs (rosemary,
sage, parsley, bay leaf) that should
be removed once the tripe is cooked,
or a clove of garlic, chopped celery
and so forth. Stewed tripe can
be prepared with a tomato sauce
or with the addition of peeled
and chopped tomatoes, popular
some areas of the Veneto.
The recipe used around the Vicenza
area is particularly good, where
cooks add a handful of raisins
plumped in Bassano grappa to the
tripe just before serving.

figà a'la venessiana

**VENETIAN
STYLE LIVER**

Not everyone is fond of the slightly bitter aftertaste left by liver. This is why Venetians covered up the bitterness with the stronger flavour of onions and in doing so, have created a dish that has become popular all over Europe.

The custom of attenuating the flavour of liver with a sweetening ingredient dates back to very ancient times in areas around the Mediterranean. The name of the dish comes from the Latin, iecur ficatum, *where the first word means "liver" and the second word means "with figs". Veal liver is used in this version of* figà a'la venessiana, *as it is more delicate and less dark than beef or pork liver. If the liver is purchased whole, it is best to remove the membrane surrounding it by lifting it up with the tip of a small knife and pulling it away with the fingers. For slices of liver, just remove any bits of membrane that are left clinging to the meat.*

· ·

*Ingredients
for 4 servings*
500 g (1 lb) veal liver
2 large onions
30 g (2 tablespoons) butter

half a glass of extravirgin olive oil
salt and pepper

Preparation time
½ hour

FIGÀ A'LA VENESSIANA

Cut the liver into fairly short, narrow strips.

—

Slice the onion into thin rings.

—

Heat up the oil and butter in a frying pan. Add the onion rings and let them soften gently, making sure they don't brown, in an uncovered frying pan on low heat. Stir every so often.

—

After about 15 minutes, remove the pan from heat and cool the onions for a few minutes. Add the strips of liver (letting pan cool slightly will keep the liver tender) and put it back on the stove. Raise the heat. After two or 3 minutes, turn the slices over with a pancake turner (being careful not to puncture them)

and cook them for a few more minutes. Turn off the heat and taste for salt.

—

Serve the liver and onions a warmed serving platter, accompanied by slices of grilled polenta, or alternatively, freshly cooked soft polenta.

Recommended wine
Bardolino superiore

Variations
Frequently, a little dry white wine or beef broth is added to the frying pan along with the liver strips. Some cooks dust the cooked liver with a sprinkling of freshly minced parsley. Some people use milk or sweet cream in place of the broth.

---

porsè'lo al late

PORK COOKED IN MILK

Pork has always been highly regarded in Venice and in the surrounding area of the Serenissima. Every farmer had a pig, which was considered a valuable yet low-cost commodity considering that it ate just about anything. When butchered, nothing went to waste, not even the whiskers or the blood (which was cooked to make a pudding). Of the innumerable methods for preparing pork (roasted, sautéed, grilled, etc.), the most original has to be the one described in this recipe. The result is a tasty, delicate and unusual dish, perfect even in our modern times when weight-watching has become so important. For a truly delicious main course, use bone-in or boneless loin or saddle of pork.

. . . .

Ingredients
for 4 servings
800 g (2 lbs) of pork
1.2 litres (5 cups) of milk (as much as necessary to cover the meat)
1 litre (4 cups) of dry white wine
70 g (4 ½ tablespoons) butter
a sprig of rosemary
a few sage leaves
salt and pepper

Preparation time
2 hours, plus marinating time

Put the piece of pork with the white wine in an earthenware casserole dish (or in a glass pot) for a couple of days. After marinating, remove and drain the meat well.

—

Melt the butter in a heavy pot and brown the pork on all sides.

—

Add the rosemary, the sage, and the salt and pepper. Cover the meat with milk and simmer for a couple of hours over low heat, partly covered. Turn the meat over from time to time. When the pork is completely cooked, the milk should be reduced to a dense sauce.

———

Slice the meat, garnish it with the sauce and serve.

Recommended wine
Merlot del Montello or Colli Asolani

Variations
In the area around Padua, they allow the meat to marinate in the white wine and vinegar with herbs (garlic, onion, and herbs) and it is roasted in the oven, basting with milk as needed from time to time. Make sure the bottom of the pan is always coated with liquid and turn the roast over during cooking. In other areas of the Veneto, the preliminary steps, namely the marinating, are eliminated altogether and the roast is cooked as indicated above. The result will still be excellent.

muséto

PORK SAUSAGE (COTECHINO)

In Venice and in the nearby towns, the word muséto *does not exactly mean cotechino, the traditional pork sausage made with pork rinds, but a similar fresh sausage prepared with meats from the "muso" or head and face of the pig. To make muséto, farmers removed the tongue from the head of the pig and then blanched it to remove the skin and bones. The meat was ground up twice, first coarsely and a second time more finely. They would add 30% pork meat and rinds, salt, and spices, blend the mixture thoroughly and then would stuff the sausage into a beef casing. After a brief drying time in a cool place (two days is often enough), the sausages are ready to eat. They should be eaten fairly soon after being made.*

As a rule, codeghini are made up of fifty percent pork meat and fat and fifty percent rinds. Both are ground up finely, with 3% salt and 1% spices, and stuffed into beef casings. The distinction between muséto and cotechino is generally not strict because some cooks have always put pork rinds into the muséto and part of the pig's head into the codeghìn.

Besides, nowadays, the food industry has eliminated any differences by giving the name cotechino to any sausage made with a medium-fine mixture of rinds and tendons and the hard and soft parts of the pig's head and neck.

. . . .

Ingredients
for 4 servings
800 g (2 lbs) of pork sausage
 (cotechino)

Preparation time
2 ½ hours

Pierce the sausage all over with the tines of a fork or with a large needle, to keep the sausage from bursting during cooking due to excessive pressure formed by steam building up inside.

Put the sausage into a large pot with plenty of cold water and put it on high heat. When it begins to boil, lower the heat and cook slowly for at least two hours.

Serve the *muséto* hot, cut into slices, and serve it with mashed potatoes or a cold bean and onion salad.

Recommended wine
Cabernet del Piave

Variations
Add a glass of dry white wine
to the cooking liquid to eliminate

the flavour and odour of the fat, if desired.
Another way to prevent the sausage
from exploding is to untie the ends and
wrap the sausage firmly in cheesecloth:
most the juices of the meat will remain
inside during cooking.

'luganeghe co'la po'lenta

TREVISO SAUSAGE WITH POLENTA

'Luganega *is a Veneto dialect word whose roots lie in a far away land: in Lucania or Basilicata, where it is said that Venentian merchants brought this delicious recipe back from their travels, sailing far and wide across the Mediterranean. It is more likely that 'luganeghe were invented as a spur-of-the-moment dish, perhaps dating back to the ancient Roman times. What is certain, however, is that early in the Middle Ages the* Lucanicae tarvisinae *were already very popular.*
In the Marca Trevigiana and in the Veneto, every area has its own tradition for flavouring the fresh sausage mixture. However, despite the rise of standardised industrial food preparation, lugaghe are always the same and yet still different from each other, varying depending on the place and time. The meat mixture is made with pork and bacon without the rind and pork shoulder. After grinding, it is salted, spices are added and it is stuffed into a long pork casings, sectioned with a piece of kitchen string to make small uniform sausages.

. . . .

Ingredients
for 4 servings
4 to 8 (depending on hunger) *'luganeghe*
   pork sausages from Treviso
80 g (3 oz.) minced lard
2 spoonfuls of dry white wine
piping hot polenta
   (see page 50 for recipe)

Preparation time
20 minutes, plus the time to make
the polenta

Pierce the sausage all over with
the tines of a fork or with a large needle,
so that the sausages release some
delicious juice while cooking.

——

Melt the minced lard in a heavy
pot on low heat and add the sausages,
browning on all sides.

——

Add two spoonfuls of wine and cook
on low heat for about ten minutes, turning
the sausages over from time to time.

——

To serve, make a nest of steaming
hot polenta on each plate and arrange
a couple of *'luganeghe* on top. Garnish
with a bit of sauce and serve immediately.

Recommended wine
Refosco di Lison-Pramaggiore

Variations
'Luganeghe can either be cooked whole
or cut in half lengthwise.
They can be used in a number of
different preparations. They are delicious
crumbled into a meat sauce for serving
on pasta or gnocchi, cooked whole
with cabbage or beans, or diced into
omelettes or meatballs.

penin de porco (o de vedè'lo)

PIG'S TROTTER (OR VEAL FOOT)

Nowadays, this dish is largely found only in inland areas of the Veneto and is a classic expression of simple peasant cooking, where all the parts of the pig have always been put to good use. Either pig's trotters or veal feet can be prepared using the recipe below. The method of cooking is the same, however the broth resulting from cooking pig's feet is discarded, while veal broth is delicious (our ancestors used it as a tonic for many ailments). Pig's trotters and veal feet are purchased at the butcher, cut in half lengthwise, cleaned and trimmed of hairs and nails.

Ingredients for 4 servings
2 pig's trotters or veal feet
  cut in half engthwise
a large onion
a large carrot
a stalk of celery
salt

Preparation time
3 hours

Put the four feet halves into a large pot with the vegetables and plenty of cold water. Salt the water and put it on high heat.

When the water begins to boil, lower the heat and simmer the meat for at least two and half hours.

Remove the meat from the broth and serve half a foot to each person, accompanied by a selection of sauces for boiled meats or cooked vegetables. The hands are the best utensils for eating pig's trotters.

Recommended wine
Cabernet dei Colli Berici

Variations
Some people put 2 or 3 spoons of vinegar into the cooking water and then serve the pig's trotters with horseradish sauce (see page 99 for recipe). The feet can also be precooked for half the time and then transferred to a heavy pot where cabbage is cooking and to complete cooking. Pig's trotters cooked this way are called *penin co'le verze*.

po'lastro in tecia

STEWED CHICKEN

Tending to chickens and other poultry in domestic farmyards has traditionally been a job for the women of the village. The work is not complicated but is continuous, as having roosters, hens and chicks ensure a constantly replenished stock of meat. On the day set for the "cruel job", the housewife runs after the young chicken, generally pursued by a gaggle of excited children, grabs it, and holding it firmly under her arm, wrings its neck. She waits a few moments until it gives up the fight, then blanches the bird in hot running water and plucks the feathers. Chickens require no tenderising time. She then cuts off its head halfway down the neck and then makes another cut down the front to remove the trachea, lungs, and throat. She makes another cut at the tail to remove the entrails, careful not to rupture the bile sac, and removes and sets aside the liver for another use. Finally, she chops off the feet, singes them with a flame to remove the hair, and cuts them into eighths.

116

Po'lastro in tecia is the traditional and most common method for preparing chicken in Venice. Once, the feet (minus the hard external skin) and the head (after removing the beak with a pair of scissors) were cooked and eaten, but this is only possible with free-range chickens.

*Ingredients
for 4 servings*
1 young chicken, about 1 kg (2 lbs)
50 g (2 oz.) unsmoked bacon
50 g (2 oz.) tomato sauce
300 g (¾ lb) ripe tomatoes
50 g (3 ½ tablespoons) butter
a drizzle of extravirgin olive oil
a large onion, a carrot
a stalk of celery, a clove of garlic
a sprig of rosemary
a glass of dry white wine
salt and pepper

Preparation time
45 minutes

Chop the bacon and fry it in a heavy pot with the butter and a bit of olive oil until it softens.

In the meantime, make a mirepoix with the onion, carrot, celery and rosemary leaves, and toss it into the pot with the bacon.

Cook the mixture until the vegetables are tender, then add the chicken, cut into parts, and brown over high heat, stirring with a wooden spoon. Add salt and pepper.

Add the white wine and let it evaporate for a few minutes. Add the garlic clove and the tomato sauce (or the ripe tomatoes, peeled and diced). Simmer the chicken for about half an hour, stirring from time to time.

When the chicken is tender, there will be plenty of sauce left in the pan.

Recommended wine
Cabernet Sauvignon di Lison Pramaggiore

Variations
In the Veneto, many people like to add other spices, such as a little ground cinnamon or a couple of cloves, proof of Venice's past domination in the oriental spice trade in Europe. Other variations include adding other highly flavoured ingredients, such as mushrooms or bell peppers.

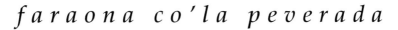

f a r a o n a   c o ' l a   p e v e r a d a

**GUINEA FOWL
IN PEPPER
SAUCE**

O*f all the poultry scratching freely in farmyards of the Veneto area, guinea fowl have been held in particularly high esteem. They have beautiful plumage and a certain cockiness to their posture as well as delectable meat that resembles pheasant. On the whole, this is a food for special occasions. Guinea fowl should be eaten between six and eight months of age because after a year, the meat tends to toughen and loses its delicate flavour. Guinea fowl may be prepared in a variety of ways (stewed, roasted, on skewers, or with other methods), but the original Venetian method is roasted with salsa* peverada, *whose name derives from* pevere *(pepper), the main ingredient.*

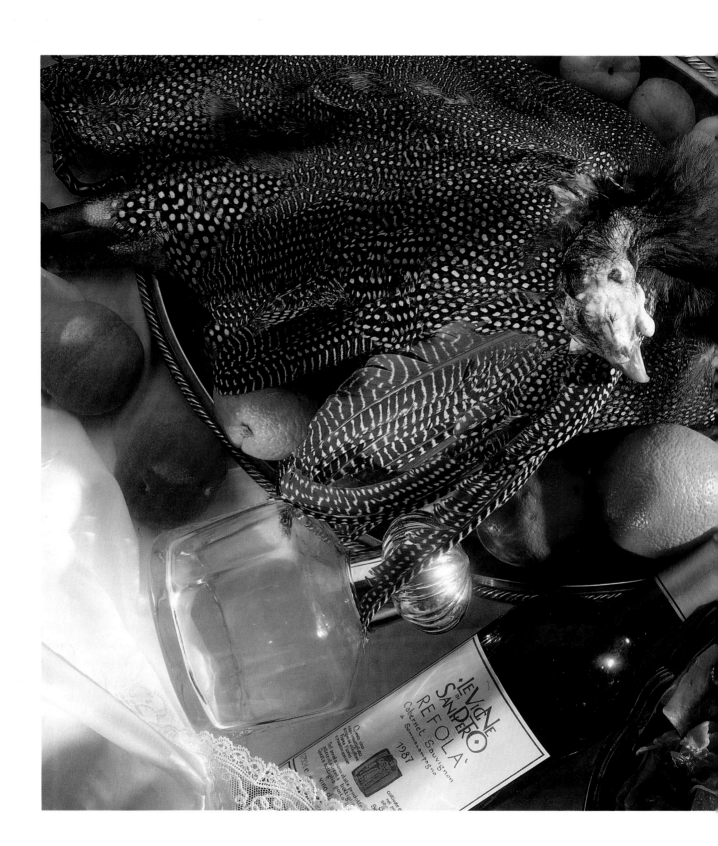

FARAONA CO'LA PEVERADA

Ingredients
for 4 serving
1 guinea fowl, 1 kg (2 lbs)
50 g (2 oz.) sliced unsmoked bacon
50 g (2 oz.) butter
a clove of garlic
some sage leaves
a sprig of rosemary
a glass of dry white wine
half a glass of extravirgin olive oil
salt and pepper

FOR THE SALSA PEVERADA
the guinea fowl livers
2 slices of Veneto salami,
    about 100 g (¼ lb)
2 cloves of garlic
a bunch of parsley
a lemon
2 spoonfuls of strong vinegar
a glass of extravirgin olive oil
salt and freshly ground pepper

Preparation time
1 hour and 15 minutes

Clean and trim the guinea fowl
as indicated for chicken (see page
116 for recipe) but leave it whole.
Set aside the livers. Discard the head,
feet and the wing tips.
Sprinkle the bird with some salt
and bard it with strips of bacon all
around and inside the cavity and
truss it with kitchen string.

——

Melt the butter with the oil in a heavy
pot. Add one of the cloves of garlic,
crushed, and the rosemary.
Add the guinea fowl and brown on
all sides. Pour in the wine and let
it evaporate, then put the pan in a hot
oven (200 °C) for 30 to 40 minutes,
basting the guinea fowl from time
to time with the pan juices.

——

In the meantime, prepare the sauce
as follows:

- mince the livers up finely with the
  salami, one clove of garlic, the parsley
  and the grated rind of the lemon
  (only the yellow part);
- squeeze the lemon juice and set it aside;
- heat the olive oil in a pan and add
  a clove of garlic. When it begins
  to turn golden, remove it and discard;
- add the finely minced salami and
  liver mixture, salt and pepper and fry
  at low heat;
- after about ten minutes, pour in the
  lemon juice and vinegar, let the liquid
  evaporate for a moment or two and then
  turn off the heat. The sauce is ready.

——

Remove the guinea fowl from the
oven, cut it into pieces and arrange
it on a serving platter.
Arrange the *salsa peverada* on top
and serve with piping hot polenta.

Recommended wine
Cabernet superiore del Montello
e Colli Ascolani

Variations
The Padua version of the *peverada*
sauce includes 2 to 3 anchovy filets
(or salted sardines, rinsed) and a small
pickled pepper. This sauce is also
excellent served with roast chicken
and game meats in general (hare, wild
duck, etc). The livers should be from
the same animal and weight about
150 grams. If there is not enough
of the same liver, chicken livers can
make up the difference.

anara co'l pien

STUFFED DUCK

R oast duck is one of the traditional dishes served on the most famous night in Venice, the night of Redentore (the third Sunday in July), which ends with a spectacular fireworks display lighting up the sky over the Giudecca island. There was a time when any farmer worth his salt in inland Venice and the islands kept a few ducks scratching around the farmyard. Ducks are lovely to look at for their proud demeanour, especially when followed by their ducklings. The male duck was so very snobbish that its name, màsoro, comes from the way many young and hearty men strut about their neighbourhoods, courting (or morosàr, in dialect) young marriageable women.

Today, local ducks have nearly all been replaced by products of industrial raising methods, which, however, strive to duplicate the traditional ways. Peking (white) and moulted ducks are also raised, both of which are valued for their delicious flavour and firm flesh and are for the most part stewed with the salsa peverada (see previous page for recipe), roasted or stuffed.

. . . .

Ingredients
for 4 servings
1 duck weighing, about 1.2 kg (2 ½ lbs)
2 slices of Veneto salami,
   about 100 g (¼ lb)
100 g (¼ lb) ground pork
100 g (¼ lb) unsmoked bacon, sliced
1 egg
a clove of garlic
a sprig of rosemary
a few sage leaves
a bunch of parsley
a pinch of nutmeg
one dry bread roll, grated
50 g (2 oz.) grated parmesan cheese
50 g (3 ½ tablespoons) butter
a glass of dry white wine
half a glass of milk
half a glass of extravirgin olive oil
salt and pepper

Preparation time
About 2 hours

Clean and trim the duck as indicated
for chicken (see page 116 for recipe).
Set aside the livers.

——

Mince the livers up finely with the salami,
the clove of garlic, rosemary, sage and

parsley. Add the ground pork, bread
crumbs, milk, grated cheese, egg,
nutmeg, and salt and pepper. Blend
the mixture well with a couple of knobs
of butter, forming the dense meatloaf
into a long roll.

——

Insert the meatloaf into the duck
cavity and sew the openings closed.
Lay some bacon along the outside
of the duck with a few slices of bacon
and a few more sage leaves and truss
it with kitchen string.

——

Melt a little butter in a roasting pan
with the olive oil and brown the duck,
turning it frequently to brown
on all sides. Add the white wine and
put the pan into a hot oven (200 °C).

——

Cook in the oven for about an hour
and a half, basting from time to time
with the pan juices.

——

When duck is fully cooked, cut
the string used for trussing and closing
the cavity. Cut the duck into pieces
and arrange the pieces in the centre
of a serving platter. Garnish with
the pan juices and the sliced stuffing.
Serve hot.

Variations
The herbs in the gravy and the stuffing
can be varied or supplemented to taste.
Instead of using breadcrumbs and milk,
some cooks prefer to use the soft white
part of bread soaked in dry Marsala.

Be sure not to pack the stuffing too
tightly into the body of the duck
as it expands during cooking.
Pine nuts may be added to the stuffing,
or sultana raisins, plumped in warm
water, and a pinch of cinnamon, lending
a pleasantly "oriental" flavour.
Modern cooks tend to replace the
traditional salami with dried mushrooms,
soaked in warm water to plump.

d i n d i o a ' l a s ' c i a v o n a

DALMATIAN-STYLE TURKEY

The S'ciavoni *were the people from Dalmatia, subjects of the Serenissima Republic of Venice. One of the many dishes inherited from this area is this delicious method of preparing turkey, whose origins are betrayed in the ingredients making up the stuffing. Free-range turkeys are still a traditional inhabitant of Venetian farmyards in Venice and the inland areas. This dish requires a female turkey or young male turkey with bright red wattles and light grey feet, signs of young birds, as older turkeys have stringy and dry meat.*

*Ingredients
for 8 servings*
1 young turkey, 2 ½ to 3 kg (6 lbs)
100 g (3 ½ oz.) unsmoked bacon, sliced
2 pitted prunes
8 raw shelled chestnuts
2 hearts of celery
salt and pepper

Preparation time
About 2 hours

Clean and singe the feathers off
the turkey as indicated for poultry
on page 116. Sprinkle with a little salt,
both inside and out.

——

Cut the celery hearts into pieces
and stuff them into the turkey cavity
with the prunes and chestnuts.

——

Bard the turkey with the
slices of bacon and truss it

carefully with kitchen string.

——

Thread the turkey onto a rotisserie
skewer and cook it, rotating slowly. Baste
it with the juices that collect in a roasting
pan underneath from time to time.

——

When the turkey is fully cooked, discard
the stuffing, cut the turkey into pieces
and serve it with oven roasted potatoes.

Variations
Turkey should always be seasoned
with highly flavoured herbs.
This Venetian recipe can also be easily
adapted to oven-roasting. Other methods
are used for cooking the turkey around
the Veneto (roast breast of turkey,
breaded cutlets, etc.) but there is yet
another very original method:

the *paéta al malgaragno* (or pomegranate). This recipe includes the juice of indigenous Vicentine pomegranates (grown in Marostica, Arzignano, Montebello, and the neighbouring zones) and dates back to the Middle Ages. The distinctive feature lies in cooking the turkey on a rotisserie or in the oven with a selection of herbs and basting repeatedly throughout cooking with the sweet and sour juice of pomegranates. The turkey is then cut into pieces and served with a sauce made from minced livers, tossed with oil and butter over high heat and moistened with pomegranate juice.

c o n i c i o   i n   t e c i a

STEWED RABBIT

*R*abbits are the most beloved animals in the farmyard to children because of their sweet and gentle ways and the charming way they hungrily eat fresh grass out of your hand. Years ago, children were given the early-morning and late-afternoon job of foraging in the fields, equipped with pruning shears to find soft grass for the rabbits to eat. Rabbits were raised cheaply as grass was collected along ditches and country roads (when cars were still a rarity) and thanks to their prolific reproduction, they constituted an excellent and economical source of nutrition. The lean white meat of rabbits is valued for its easy digestibility (ideal for the ill), provided it is appropriately seasoned to mask the slightly gamey aftertaste.

Butchers normally sell rabbits already cleaned and ready to cook. Otherwise, they have to be skinned and eviscerated. To skin a rabbit, tie its legs together and hang it upside down. Use a sharp knife to make a crosswise cut at the back feet. Lift up the skin and pull it down to reveal the thighs. Then make another cut at the tail and pull the skin down all the way to the neck. Cut off the head and feet and open up the belly. Spread apart the opening with the hands and remove the entrails, setting aside the giblets (liver, heart and kidney). Finally cut off the tips of the ribs. The rabbit is now ready for cooking, whole or cut into parts.

I n g r e d i e n t s
f o r   4   s e r v i n g s
1 rabbit weighing, about 1.2 kg
  (2 ½ lbs), with its giblets
a onion, a carrot
a stalk of celery
a clove of garlic
a sprig of rosemary
  80 g (5 ½ tablespoons) butter
    half a glass of extravirgin olive oil
      a glass and half of dry
        white wine
          salt and pepper

P r e p a r a t i o n   t i m e
2 hours

Cut the rabbit into parts, first cutting off the feet at the ankles, then the high part between the shoulders and neck and the lower part just above the tail.

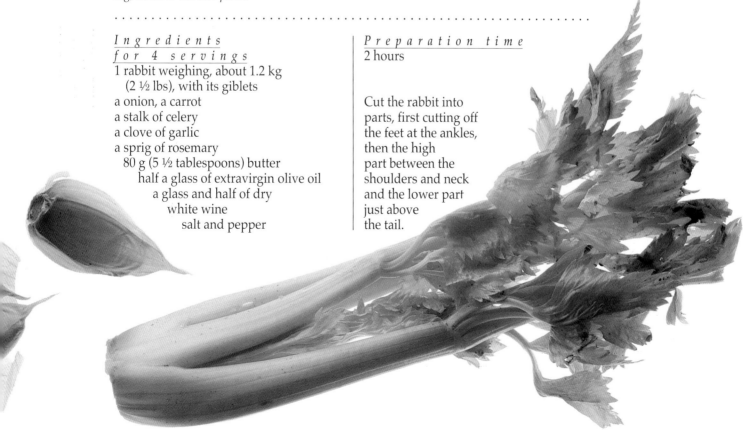

Cut the body into large pieces.

Melt 50 grams butter in a heavy pot with some of the olive oil. Add the clove of garlic, rosemary, and rabbit pieces and brown over high heat for a few minutes. Splash in the wine and then lower the heat. Remove the garlic and cover the pan. Cook slowly, stirring from time to time and adding water when necessary.

Chop the onion, the carrot and the celery, and chop up the giblets.

Heat up the rest of the butter and oil in another heavy pot. Add the mirepoix and the giblets, adding a bit of white wine. Cook over low heat for half an hour.

Pour the hot sauce into the pot where the rabbit is cooking.

Add salt and pepper and simmer for another hour, until tender.

Serve the rabbit with soft, steaming hot polenta and with a side dish of roasted potatoes.

R e c o m m e n d e d   w i n e
Bardolino superiore
or Merlot dei Colli Berici

V a r i a t i o n s
Some cooks in the Veneto add grated lemon rind to the giblet sauce and forego the white wine. Others let the rabbit marinate overnight in equal parts of water, vinegar and wine. Alternatively, the meat can stand for a few hours in the marinade before cooking to rid the meat of any excess liquid in the meat.

---

l i é v a r o   i n   s a l m ì

JUGGED HARE

T*he custom of using a particular marinade to "jug" a meat – which may be hare or any other kind of game meat from the Veneto Alps and foothills regions (pheasant, wild duck, wild rabbits, capercaillie, deer, goats, among others) – is a very ancient one. These days, it is still the most popular way to cook game meats throughout the region that was once part of the Serenissima Republic. Over the centuries, the flavour of the marinade was enriched with herbs brought over by spice merchants and has varied according to the tastes of the times. The only ingredient that has always remained a constant is wine (red or white). Once el salmì also included the addition of sultana raisins, pine nuts, chocolate, pieces of candied citron, or amaretto biscuits. Today, only herbs and spices are used. A peculiarly Venetian touch is adding pieces of minced giblets and some boiled blood to the hare at the end of cooking.*
When the hunter returned from a day's work with a hare, it was immediately skinned and cleaned as for rabbit (page 123). The giblets and a half a cup of the blood were set aside in grappa or other highly alcoholic distilled spirit. The hare was left to age for a couple of days in a covered container and was then immersed in the marinade, where it remained for at least a day.

. . . .

I n g r e d i e n t s
f o r   4   s e r v i n g s
1 hare weighing, about 1.2 kg (2 ½ lbs), with its giblets and blood set aside in grappa

80 g (3 oz.) unsmoked bacon
80 g (5 ½ tablespoons) butter
half a glass of extravirgin olive oil
a bit of white flour
salt

FOR THE MARINADE
1 litre (4 cups) of full bodied red whine
   (Amarone della Valpolicella
   is a good choice)
half a glass of vinegar
a onion, a carrot
a stalk of celery
a clove of garlic
a sprig of rosemary
a sprig of thyme
a few sage leaves
a few mint leaves or basil
a few juniper berries
a piece of cinnamon bark
a pinch of coarse salt
2 bay leaves
some peppercorns, some cloves

P r e p a r a t i o n   t i m e
3-4 hours, plus the marinating time

Cut the hare into pieces and let it marinate
all day and overnight in the red wine
mixed with the vinegar, the chopped
vegetables (carrot, onion and celery)
and the herbs and spices.

The next day, remove the pieces
of hare from the marinade, drain them
well and dust them with the flour.

Chop the bacon and fry it with 50 grams
of butter and a little oil. Add the floured
rabbit pieces and brown on all sides.

Add a little bit of the marinade with
the vegetables and herbs gradually.
As the liquid evaporates, keep adding
more until it is all gone. Let the rabbit
cook slowly for three hours.

Remove the giblets and blood from
the grappa. Chop the giblets finely
and sauté separately with a little broth.

When the cooking is almost finished,
remove the pieces of meat and strain
the sauce left in the pan through a sieve.

125

Put the gravy and the meat back into the pan, add the blood and giblets and finish cooking. Add salt if needed.

———

Serve the jugged hare with steaming hot yellow polenta.

Recommended wine
Cabernet Superiore dei Colli Euganei or Pinot Nero del Piave

Variations
Never overdo it with the spices in the marinade as too much will mask the natural flavour of the hare. Many cooks prefer to use only fragrant herbs with 5 or 6 peppercorns and a few juniper berries. White wine may be used in place of the red. The gravy from jugged hare is often served on top of wide egg noodles (*papare'le al salmì*).

màsori a'la va'lesana

VALLIGIANI-STYLE WILD DUCKS

To fully appreciate the flavour of this dish, we think it is important to explain all the nuances that have made it so traditional. Masori are wild ducks (mallards) and, by extension, any large birds that live in the fishing valleys of the Venetian lagoon and the delta of the Po River, such as ose'le salvadeghe (wild valley birds in general) and others.

In the autumn, the hunter wakes early in the morning and accompanied by the slow and steady rhythm of the lapping of the oars, reaches his destination.

All around him is only foggy silence, marsh waters and plants, and as the pungent air slowly clears, the muffled sounds of nature become sharper but the man is alone, and so he waits and waits. Some days, his gamebag remains empty, but the charm of the setting and the silence are gratifying just the same.

To have an idea of this milieu, picture Pietro Longhi's (1702-1785) portrayals of hunting in the valley. Late morning, the hunter heads toward a casone (a refuge for the valley rangers) where he will meet up with companions and might share a meal, cooked fireside and well-basted with laughter and hearty wine.

Selvadego de va'le used to be much more popular than it is today. Giuseppe Boerio (see bibliography) writes that «Ancient doges enjoyed the fruits of the Maremma valleys of Marano, a small fortress in lower Friuli, but by decree of the Great Council in 1275 they had to give their noblemen five swamp birds, commonly called ose'le selvadeghe dai pié rossi, each December. Afterwards, in order to avoid resentment and jealousy, it was decided that each councilman would be given one fat and one thin bird (as in a proverb still in use today, "Like the chickens at the market, one good, one bad"). Another decree issued on 28 June 1521, under Doge Antonio Grimani, established that the donation of the birds would be symbolic and replaced by coins. This remained tradition until the end of the Republic» (page 457).

Since the ducks are wild and the water they live in is salty, it is important to clean them as soon as possible. Pluck and singe the feathers, keeping the giblets in grappa or another highly alcoholic spirit. Leave them to tenderise for two or three days and then marinate them before cooking for at least 12 hours (or up to two days) in equal parts of dry white wine and white vinegar. Add a bit of thyme, marjoram and a few peppercorns for flavour. During cooking, the ducks may be seasoned with anchovies or salted sardines.

Ingredients
for 4 servings
2 wild ducks, 1 ½ kg (3 lbs)
100 g (3 ½ oz.) unsmoked bacon
80 g (5 ½ tablespoons) butter
a onion, chopped
3 salted anchovies
15 pickled capers
a glass of dry white wine
half a glass of extravirgin olive oil
salt and pepper

Preparation time
1 ½ hours

Marinate the ducks as described
above, rinse them, let them drain
and rub them inside and out with some
salt. Bard them with the bacon slices.

———

Put the ducks in a roasting pan
with half the butter and roast

them for about 20 minutes in
a hot oven (200 °C) being careful
not to burn them.

———

Clean the salted sardines (as indicated
on page 54) and chop them with
the onion and capers.

———

Heat the remaining butter with
the olive oil in a heavy pot.
Add the chopped onion, capers
and sardines. Sauté over low heat.

———

Remove the ducks from the oven,
cut them into quarters and add
them to the onion/sardine mixture
in the pot. Raise the heat and add
the white wine. Let the wine
evaporate, add salt and pepper,
and lower the heat. Simmer the
duck for about an hour.

———

Serve the duck quarters and
the cooking sauce on a serving
platter, garnished with slices
of grilled polenta.

Recommended wine
Cabernet del Piave
or Pinot Nero di Breganze

Variations
The capers may be eliminated,
however the salted sardines
(or anchovies) are a must in this
recipe. Some cooks add a bit of lemon
rind to the marinade. The livers
set aside in grappa can be used
to make a sauce for other game dishes,
as indicated in the recipe for jugged
hare (see page 125-128 for recipe).
The ducks may also be roasted
in the oven, in the rotisserie, or stewed,
but Valligiani-style is the most
typically Venetian method.
The roasting phase may be eliminated,
replacing it with cooking directly
over heat.

Fish, crustaceans and molluscs

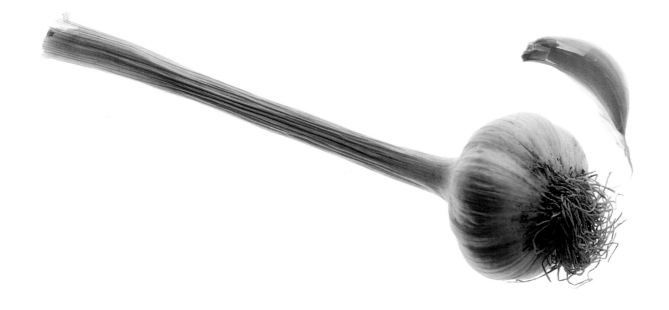

baca'là mantecato

BEATEN SALTED COD

*S*alted cod reached Venice in the centuries of the early Middle Ages, brought in by Venetian merchant ships that were sailing home from Northern European countries, where they had gone to sell their wares.

The new dish became an immediate success with the population, which delighted in the imaginative and original culinary delights it rendered. However, "baccalà" reached the height of its popularity after the Council of Thirty in the second half of the 16th century when the Catholic Church imposed on its followers days of fasting. Recipes for salted cod became so delicious that they were anything but the humble dishes intended for eating on those days of sacrifice.

The second half of the 16th century also marked the reigns of King Philip II of Spain and Elizabeth I of England and the wars fought for domination of the Atlantic, wars waged between Catholics and Protestants, and the definitive establishment of Spanish domination in Italy: all these events explain why the name of a dish so important to Venetian (and Italian) cuisine has a Spanish origin (bacalao, whose entomology is Nordic) and why the saying goes that "baccalà" was born Protestant, but died a Catholic. At that time, the Atlantic routes were abandoned by the Venetian sloops and supplies from the North continued to reach or cross Spain by overland routes.

131

BACA'LÀ MANTECATO

Plus, cod was fished in the seas of the Northern Lutheran countries, but the very best recipes are Venetian.
Baca'là is the generic Venetian name for cod fish (Gadus morrhua) *which is treated and sold either dried or salted.*

. . . .

Ingredients
for 4 servings
1 kg (2 lbs) stockfish, well-soaked
2 bunches of parsley
a clove of garlic
very fine extravirgin olive oil
salt and pepper

Preparation time
1 hour 15 minutes

Put the well-soaked stockfish in a heavy pot, cover it with cold water and bring it to a boil. Skim off any impurities that rise to the surface of the water, then turn off the heat, cover the pan and let the fish stand for 20 minutes.

——

Mince finely the garlic and parsley or crush well with a mortar and pestle.

——

Drain the fish, remove the skin, open it up and remove the bones.

——

Put the cleaned stockfish into a sturdy bowl and use a fork to break the flesh into a pulp. Whip the fish with a wooden spoon, while pouring in the olive oil in a stream. Continue to add the oil in a stream as the mixture absorbs it and becomes a whitish cream. The quantity of oil might vary according to the quality of fat in the flesh.

——

At this point, add a little salt, the garlic and parsley, and a dusting of ground pepper to the fish. Mix well and serve the "baccalà" on a serving plate whose colour contrasts the colour of the dish. It is best eaten cold, served with slices of grilled polenta.

Recommended wine
Soave classico or Gambellara Superiore, well chilled

Variations
Just two: the whipping can be made easier by putting the bowl on very low heat. A little sweet cream can be added at the end of whipping to make the "baccalà" even fluffier. Since this dish is strongly flavoured, it is best served as an appetiser or antipasto.

baca'là a'la visentina

SALTED COD
FROM VICENZA

*T*he popular Venetian dish of stewed salted cod (in tecia) *is prepared as per culinary tradition in Vicenza and has gained popularity all over Italy and around the world. This dish also requires well-soaked stockfish, since the original recipe did not use salted cod, as salt was prohibitively expensive in the northern countries that produced this fish. This was about two hundred years ago, when coal was still a commonly used source of heat: the lack of sun in the North and the calm ocean waters prevented those countries from generating salt with natural methods, which became an essential part of Venice's fortune.*

. . . .

Ingredients
for 6 servings
1 kg (2 lbs) stockfish, well-soaked
300 ml (1 ¼ cups) whole milk
200 ml (¾ cup) extravirgin olive oil
3 salted anchovies
3 large onions
2 cloves of garlic
2 bunches of parsley
3 spoonfuls of grated parmesan cheese
2 spoonfuls of flour
salt and pepper

Preparation time
5 hours

Cut the soaked salted cod into large
pieces (5 cm wide), then open each piece
out to remove the skin and bones.

———

Chop the onions, garlic, and parsley.
Remove the excess salt and bones,
from the anchovies and rinse well.
Add the anchovies to the onion,
garlic and parsley mixture.

———

Heat 100 ml of the olive oil in a large
heavy pot. Add the chopped onion
mixture and a bit of salt and pepper
and cook, stirring constantly, for 5-6
minutes. Turn off the heat, add the
grated parmesan and mix well.

———

Stuff each slice of "baccalà" with
a little of the onion and anchovy mixture,
but leave most of it in the bottom
of the pot. Dust the slices of "baccalà"
with flour and arrange them in the pot,
set closely together.

———

Add the rest of the olive oil, cover
with milk and put the pot on low heat.
Bring to a simmer and cook gently
for at least four hours, never stirring,
but shaking the pot every so often
so the "baccalà" doesn't stick to
the bottom of the pan.

———

Serve the "baccalà" piping hot with
slices of grilled polenta or with a side
dish of soft fresh yellow polenta.

Recommended wine
Durello superiore dei Lessini
or Tocai rosso dei Colli Berici

Variations
It might be said that every cook has
his or her own personal variation,
evolved after years of trial and error.
For example, some cooks don't add
the parmesan to the sauté but stir it into
the flour used for coating the pieces
of fish. Others don't stuff the fish slices
at all, leaving the vegetable mixture
at the bottom of the pot. Some
add nutmeg or cinnamon as flavouring.
However, the basic version always
remains the same. The dish can also
be cooked in the oven at low heat.

bisato in tecia

STEWED EEL In the Venetian dialect, bisato *is the word for an adult eel, fished not from fresh lake water, but
the salty waters of the lagoon. European eels* (Anguilla anguilla) *like their American
cousins, grow into adults in fresh river and lake waters and then swim down to the sea to per-
form the long and mysterious ritual of laying their eggs in the deep Sargasso sea.
The eggs hatch, from which larva emerge ("leptocephalus"), similar in appearance to small trans-
parent jagged leaves. It takes the larva three years to reach the European and Mediterranean shores*

135

(from Iceland to North Africa, from the Adriatic to the Black Sea), during which time they grow and develop. When they finally reach the coastal waters (shallow, colder and less salty than the open seas), they change shape, lengthening their bodies and becoming more adult (in this phase, they are inappropriately called "blind").

They swim against the river and stream currents, feeding on smaller animals, until they complete their growth cycle and make the return trip to the Sargasso sea. Here, they reproduce and remain for the rest of their days. This is the time when eels reach the peak of their physiological ability to face the long journey toward perpetuation of the species and inevitable death that they face in the salty water of the Venetian lagoon and the Comacchio valley. This is also when they are true eels, in the sense that they are fat and firm, at the peak of their flavour, especially for our kitchens. The Venetian word bisato is masculine, but most of the eels eaten are female, because the males are smaller.

However, no matter the gender, male or female, both eels are delicious.

- -

Ingredients
for 4 servings
1 kg (2 lbs) medium sized eels
100 ml (½ cup) tomato sauce
30 g (2 tablespoons) butter
2 cloves of garlic
2 bay leaves
1 bunch of parsley
a glass of dry Marsala
half a glass extravirgin olive oil
salt and pepper

FOR THE MARINADE
500 ml (2 ¼ cups) vinegar
100 ml (½ cup) water
3 bay leaves
salt and pepper

Preparation time
About 1 hour, plus time of marinating

Remove the entrails from the eels
and behead them. Remove the skin,
wash and cut them into 5-6 cm slices.

———

Marinate the eels in a half a litre
of vinegar, a little water, three bay leaves
and a pinch of salt and pepper for
a couple of hours in a large bowl.
Remove the eel slices and let them drain.

———

Heat the butter and oil in a large
pot and add the garlic cloves, green

shoot removed and slightly crushed.
When they begin to turn golden,
remove them and add the slices
of marinated eel. Brown these for
a few minutes over high heat.

———

Add the glass of Marsala and two
bay leaves and let the wine evaporate.
Add the tomato sauce and a bit of water
with the salt and pepper. Stir well
and simmer for a half an hour.

———

While the eel is simmering, chop
the parsley and add it to the stew two
minutes before turning off the heat.

———

Serve the stewed eel piping hot
with a side dish of thick white
corn polenta.

Recommended wine
Vespaiolo superiore di Breganze

Variations
Not all cooks marinate the eel before
cooking it. If marinating is eliminated,
add two spoonfuls of vinegar to
the cooking sauce.

b i s a t o   s u   l ' a r a

ROASTED EEL

This dish is a speciality of Murano, the island in the Venetian lagoon best known for the glass that its artisans have been producing since the 13th century. Ara is the Venetian dialect word for the stone lining the inside of glass furnaces where glass vases are left to temper (cool and season) after the glass blowers have shaped and decorated them. This recipe was made by placing the pot with the eel on the ara and letting it cook very slowly.

Ingredients
for 4 servings
1 large eel, about 1 kg (2 lbs)
plenty of bay leaves
salt
freshly ground pepper

Preparation time
About 2 hours

Rub a bit of wood ash on the skin
of the eel to remove some of the fat;
then remove the head and entrails
and cut it into 4-5 cm slices.

—

Place a thick layer of bay leaves
on the bottom of a casserole dish
and arrange layers of eel on top.
Sprinkle on some salt and a little
ground pepper and a splash of water.
Cover the whole thing with another
layer of bay leaves.

—

In the meantime, preheat the oven
to 170 °C then put the casserole
inside and leave the dish to cook
until the eel meat is white and tender
(about an hour and a half).
Fatty fish makes its own tasty sauce
when cooking.

—

Serve the eel in the heavy pot dish
where it was cooked, removing
the top layer of bay leaves first.
Serve with hot and firm yellow polenta.

Recommended wine
Tocai bianco or Pinot Bianco
dei Colli Berici or Euganei

Variations
There are no real variations to this recipe.
Cooks used to use a little sea water
mixed with a spoonful of vinegar
in place of the plain water.

sfogi al vin bianco

SOLE WITH WHITE WINE

Sole are considered by true gourmands to be the very finest fish because of the delicate flesh. They are bottom dwellers, and the sandy Adriatic provides a home for an abundant number of different species. The most common are sfogi, or authentic sole (Solea), flounder (Pleuronectes) *and the similar turbot* (Bothus). *The recipe given here is the most common in the Veneto and the one that preserves the fine flavour of these fish by grilling.*

Ingredients
for 4 servings
4 soles, about 250 g each (½ lb)
100 g (¼ lb) white flour
80 g (5 ½ tablespoons) butter
half a glass of dry white wine
juice of half a lemon
salt and freshly ground pepper

Preparation time
½ hour

Clean the soles, removing the entrails, and cutting off the heads, fins and tails with a scissors.

▬

Starting with the tail end, use the tip of a knife to remove the grey-brown skin. Grasp it with a kitchen towel and pull it off with a sharp jerk. Repeat the operation at the lower part.

▬

With a very sharp knife, detach the filets from the backbone. Wash the filets in the water and lemon juice. Dry them and dust with flour.

▬

Melt the butter in a frying pan and when it begins to foam, add the floured fish filets.

▬

When they are golden on one side, use a spatula to turn them over and fry for a few minutes. Add the wine and lemon juice.

▬

Cook the filets in the sauce for a few minutes to reduce the liquid. Add some salt and a little black pepper and serve the filets.

Recommended wine
Prosecco di Conegliano-Valdobbiadene

Variations
This recipe is also very delicious with dry Marsala in place of the white wine. Some like to add a sprinkling of minced parsley a minute or two before serving.

sievo'li ai feri

GRILLED MULLET

Sievo'li *and similar species of fish rub along quite happily in deep sea bottoms and therefore, are plentiful in the Venetian lagoon. The flesh is soft and white, albeit a little fatty, so the best method for cooking them is on the grill. Remember that the distance of the grill from the source of heat should be in proportion to the size of the pieces of fish. If they are small, they should be cooked at high heat and with the grill close to the flame. If they are large, the heat must be moderate, to gradually penetrate to the centre of the fish.*
Once, Venetians ate mullet without removing the entrails, which gave a more flavourful result. Some brave souls still eat the mullet this way, even though the seas aren't as clean as they used

to be. This method is fine as long as they are da bon, *that is, devoid of the unpleasant odour of* chum *and not* da rio.

. . . .

Ingredients
for 4 servings
4 small mullets, about 200 to 250 g
    each (½ lb)
or 1 large mullet, about 1 kg (2 lbs)
extravirgin olive oil
juice of a lemon
salt and freshly ground pepper

Preparation time
½ hour, plus marinating time

Clean the fish by removing the entrails, gills and scales. Then rinse in cold water and dry them well. Prepare a marinade with oil, lemon juice, salt and pepper. Spread this mixture onto the fish and let it stand to absorb the flavours for at least an hour.

Put the grill on the barbecue and wait until the grill gets very hot, otherwise the fish might stick to the metal break when turned over. Place the fish on the grill and watch the cooking carefully, turning it from time to time and basting with the marinade. Serve with lemon wedges.

Recommended wine
Prosecco del Montello e Colli Asolani

Variations
The mullet in this recipe can also be cooked in a frying pan or in the oven (ara) like eel (see page 137 for recipe). The method described here for grilling mullet works well with almost any other fish.

---

branzìn lesso

POACHED
SEA BASS

Branzìn *is a Lombard-Veneto dialect word and refers to the appearance of the fish to which it gives its name. The name means fish with exposed gills (*branchie*). Also known as* spigola (Morone labrax *or* Dicentrarchus labrax), *it lives in the Adriatic and Mediterranean, and in the eastern Atlantic. Its nickname also refers to the fact that it is full of bones (*spine*), a culinary defect that must be carefully remedied. But its white meat is exquisite and it is well suited to a myriad of different preparations. Amongst the numerous recipes popular in Venice (poached, grilled, roasted, in foil), we have selected the simplest, as well as the one that best preserves the flavour and reflects tradition.*

. . . .

Ingredients
for 6 servings
1 sea bass, weighing about 1 ½ kg (3 lbs)
2 bay leaves, 2 lemon halves
1 stalk of celery
extravirgin olive oil
black peppercorns
salt and freshly ground pepper

Preparation time
40 minutes

139

BRANZÌN LESSO

Since the most important quality of a fish is its freshness, look for signs that it has not been out of the water too long: clear eyes, pink gills, full and firm flesh, shiny scales and a good fresh aroma of the sea. Ask the fishmonger to remove the entrails, which will keep it fresher longer.

Once in the kitchen back home, clean the fish well, removing the residue in its belly, remove the scales and pull out the gills. Rinse well in cold water.

———

Place the bass in a fish steamer (a special covered pan with a grill inside for cooking fish). Cover with salted water, in the proportion of 10 g of salt for every litre of water. Add the lemon half with the skin, the celery and a few peppercorns.

———

Put the fish steamer on high heat and bring to a boil. Let the water boil for about 15 minutes (the rule is 10 minutes for fish weighing 1 kg (2 lbs), 15 minutes for 2 kg (4 lbs), 20 minutes for 3 kg (6 lbs) and so forth). Adjust the heat so that the water just simmers, letting the fish cook slowly and gently without breaking apart.

———

After cooking, remove the grill from the fish steamer with the fish on it.

Remove all the bones, head, fins and tail, etc.

———

Arrange the fish on a serving platter, garnishing as desired with slices of lemon and sprigs of parsley.

———

The poached sea bass is best served with boiled potatoes and with sauces depending on preferences. To avoid masking the delicious flavour of the fish, it is best to dress it simply with squirt of lemon juice, a drizzle of extra virgin olive oil, and some freshly ground pepper, tasting for salt.

Recommended wine
A dry and sparkling Prosecco di Conegliano-Valdobbiadene

Variations
Sauces to serve alongside the poached bass should not have such a strong flavour that they overwhelm the delicate taste of the fish. If lemon is eliminated from the poaching water, the resulting broth can be used in fish or seafood risottos. The other methods for preparing sea bass mentioned in the introduction can also be used for other types of fish.

go in broeto

STEWED GOBY

*T*he centuries-old story of the relationship between goby and Venetian fishermen is like a chivalrous poem which lacks only the poet to put it into verse. Gobies are the tiny little fish living in the Venetian lagoon that are much loved by the people because of their large heads, big bulging eyes and big fleshy lips (Konrad Lorenz, the prominent ethologist argued that these characteristics are emblematic of "baby" mammals and spark a protective and tender instinct in other adult mammals).
But gobies are also delicious. So, between gobies and man an unusual and conflicting a relationship was established, marked by injustice (because the fight is not between equals) but also mutual respect. As it happens, gobies live quite an active life, darting among the sea grasses, in mud-

dy and polluted seabeds: in the springtime, every male builds himself a little round nest amidst the underwater plants, with two openings. He then floats patiently beside one of these egresses, waiting for the female to arrive. Excitedly, the females enter the nest and lay their eggs, which the male hastens to fertilise. Then she departs. Up to ten females might visit a nest during a season. Once their lust has cooled, the males keep watch over the eggs until they hatch. Baby gobies grow rapidly: measuring just 10-15 mm in May, they will grow to 7-9 cm by August. Meantime, the male has taken himself off for a bit of rest and relaxation in the open sea, following winding courses that are never the same: he will return to the lagoon at the first sign of bad weather, when he builds his winter nest in between the deep grasses to protect against the cold and predators, patiently awaiting the wonderful season of love.

In this age-old perpetual cycle, the Venetians have intervened, some quite inconsiderately (capturing the gobies with their arms, small spears or even hoes – all methods now banned by law) and others with a bit more respect for the cycles and the environment, catching the gobies with traps or small fishpots or with large otter trawls that work the lagoon, called bragagne. *But even when the* palpadori *(bare-hand fishermen) went fishing for the gobies, touching the nests with their hands and capturing the fish as they exited, they were still careful not to completely uncover the nest, leaving a few gobies to stand guard and perpetuate the cycle.*

The species we are talking about bears the scientific name of Zosteriressor ophiocephalus or vene-tiarum. The Italian name "ghiozzo" derives from the large size of its head and is the most common name for this family of fish. In Venice, the goato de mar *or ghiozzo testone (Gobius cobitis or Ex-anthematosus gibbosus) is a popular and delicious species of goby. It is the largest type of goby living in the Mediterranean and Venetian lagoon and can reach up to 25 cm in length.*

The recipe given here for Go in broeto *is not a fish soup (see page 67-70), but rather, second course, since in the coastal regions of the gulf of Venice,* broeto *or* boreto *is a sauce that can be used to dress a variety of different types of fish (such as sardines, eels, mackerel, and mullet).*

. . . .

Ingredients
for 4 servings
700 g (1 ¾ lbs) of gobies
2 cloves of garlic
a glass of extravirgin olive oil
a glass of white wine and white
   wine vinegar, mixed together
in equal measure
salt and freshly ground pepper

Preparation time
40 minutes

Clean the fish and remove
the entrails. Wash them carefully
as their skin is full of mucus
and covered with tiny scales which
do not have to be removed.

Heat the oil in an earthenware
pot and add the cloves of garlic.

When the garlic begins to turn golden,
remove and discard it, and put
the gobies in the pot.

Add a pinch of salt, a dusting
of pepper and the glass of vinegar
and wine blended together.
Add enough water to cover.
Cover the pot, leaving the lid ajar
and let it simmer for 20 to 30 minutes,
depending on how big the fish are.
At the end of cooking, the sauce
should be quite concentrated and
golden in colour.

Serve the gobies in the sauce,
with slices of grilled yellow polenta
on the side.

Recommended wine
Vespaiolo di Breganze

143

Variations
Variations
When fishermen used to cook their
go in broeto while at sea, they would cook
the fish in sea water, acidulated with
a bit of vinegar (probably not a good idea
any longer). A bit of minced parsley

added at the end of cooking improves
the flavour of the dish, but it is not
necessary. However, it is never a good
idea to add tomato sauce to this recipe.
Small gobies are also very tasty fried.
Larger *goati* can be grilled or roasted.

---

marsioni friti

**FRIED
BULLHEADS**

Small bullheads or fresh water gobies (gudgeons, Cottus gobius) *that live in the gravelley bottoms of clear streams or inland rivers (the Piave, Brenta, Astico) are called* marsioni. *This dialect word derives from the fact that they are fished most abundantly in March (*marso*). Thanks to their unmistakable yet delicate flavour, they have become quite popular in Venice, where salt water fish still take up the lion's share of menus. An old Venetian proverb describes gratification as «bullheads fried and served with polenta, a piece of cheese and some wine just tapped from the barrel», putting into words the satisfaction that this fried dish delivers. It was originally a speciality of Vicenza, where the* marsioni *from the Astico River are particularly highly regarded.*

Ingredients
for 6 servings
1 kg (2 lbs) of bullheads
yellow cornmeal
plenty of olive oil for frying
salt
2 lemons cut into wedges

Preparation time
½ hour

Wash the bullheads thoroughly,
without removing their heads or
entrails. Dredge them in the cornmeal
on all sides.

Put a large cast iron frying pan
on the heat and heat the oil well.
Place the cornmeal coated bullheads
inside and fry them until they
are crispy and golden brown.

Remove the fried fish from the oil
with a slotted spoon and put them
on kitchen paper towels to drain.
Sprinkle generously with salt.

Serve them piping hot with lemon
wedges and a side dish of soft
and piping hot polenta.

Recommended wine
Soave classico or Garganega
dei Colli Berici, well chilled

Variations
Using yellow cornmeal for the coating
makes the bullheads pleasantly crunchy,
however, white wheat flour or a mixture
of wheat flour and cornmeal may be used
instead. This sort of frying technique
is also excellent for frying
small fish.

rane frite

FRIED FROGS

I f there is one dish that can be truly defined as peasant, invented with the ingenuity of folk of little means, then this has to be it. Nothing is more humble than frogs. Once, their joyful croaking filled the ponds and ditches all over the Padana plains.

Today, their song is much quieter: weed killer used on the fields has eliminated most of the frogs. The best thing about frogs was that they were absolutely free and all it took to catch them was a light placed nearby the water. They would approach the light in swarms and quickly filled up the game bag. These days, frogs they have become a delicacy for gourmets, to eat in small and exquisite bites. Frogs are excellent nutrition for sick people as their flesh has very little fibre, is rich in albumin and is easy to digest. No one catches frogs anymore: you can find them at the butcher, ready to cook.

. . . .

Ingredients
for 6 servings
32 medium sized frogs or 400 g
　frogs' legs
250 ml (1 cup) dry wine red or white
　(as desired)
2 eggs
300 g (¾ lb) white flour
500 ml (2 cups) olive oil for frying
50 g (3 ½ tablespoons) butter
salt, pepper (if desired)
a lemon

Preparation time
20 minutes, plus marinating time

Wash and dry the frogs or frogs'
legs and let them marinate for a while
in the wine.

———

Beat the egg with two pinches of salt.

Heat the oil and the butter in a frying
pan on high heat.

———

Remove the frogs from the wine and
let them drain. Coat them with the
egg and then dredge them in the flour.

———

Put them one by one in the boiling
oil and fry them. When they are golden
brown and crispy, remove them with
a fork and let them drain on kitchen
paper towels. Sprinkle on a bit of salt.

———

Serve the frogs with wedges of lemon.

Recommended wine
Tocai bianco dei Colli Berici

Variations
Old farmer's wives recommended
coating the frogs in egg before
dredging them in flour to plump
them up a little, otherwise the small
bites of frog would have really been
measly (a secret of poor cooks!).
Since frogs have a revolting appearance
and flavour for many people,
make sure that all the guests know
what they are being served.
If they have a strong odour at the time
of purchase, rinse them in vinegar
before marinating them in the wine.

m a s a n é t e

SOFT SHELL CRABS WITH SAUCE

Masanéte *are female shore crabs* (Carcinus maenas) *that are commonly found in the shallow bottoms of the Venetian lagoon. They have a short shell, slightly wider in the back (up to 4 cm) and their legs are attached in a semi-circle.*
In the fall, they shed their shells and fill up with eggs. At this point, males of the species carry them on their backs to fertilise them and protect them.
This is also the best time to eat them, as they are brimming with coral and their flesh is firm and flavourful.
They should be purchased live, sold by fishmongers at the fish market of Rialto, where they are as sight to be seen, scrabbling around boxes or jute bags.

Ingredients
for 4 servings
1 kg (2 lbs) live female shore crabs
extravirgin olive oil
a bunch of parsley
salt
freshly ground pepper

Preparation time
About 1 hour

Wash the crabs carefully in water, letting them soak and changing the water frequently.

Bring a large pot of a water to a boil. When the water is boiling, toss in the live crabs and boil them for 7-8 minutes.
Turn off the heat and let them cool down in the water.

Drain them and remove their legs and detach the hard shell from the abdomen.
The coral and flesh will remain attached to the upper shell.

Put the cleaned crabs in an earthenware dish. Add salt and a little pepper, some minced parsley and extra virgin olive oil.
Mix well and let them stand and absorb the flavours until it is time to serve them.

The crabs should be served cold with a side dish of soft and hot polenta.

Recommended wine
A dry and sparkling Prosecco di Conegliano-Valdobbiadene

Variations
A tiny bit of minced garlic can be added to the condiment or a splash of vinegar or lemon juice.
However, avoid using vinegar as it might make any leftover crab overly acidic and shore crabs are very delicious the next day.

146

mo'leche ripiene

**STUFFED
SOFT-SHELL CRABS**

M o'leche *is the dialect word for "soft" with the feminine ending, but the substantive designates male crabs during their moulting period (see the previous recipe), the time when they become soft and tender and their shells turn as soft as tissue paper. This happens twice during the year: in the spring and in the fall, whereas females moult just once, during the fall, after the males have finished moulting since the males have to be strong enough to protect and fertilise them.*

It is very rare to find a mo'leca *in the wild, but over the years, crab fishermen have perfected a way to raise them. They capture a large number of crabs, both the kind that can moult into* mo'leca *and those that cannot (*boni *and* mati*, respectively). They put the moulting crabs into special reed baskets, called* vieri*, and keep a close eye on them. The fisherman pick out the crabs one by one from the basket as they moult and bring them to market to the delight of the customers. Like the* masenéte*, mo'leche *must be live at the time of cooking, to avoid unpleasant consequences.*

· ·

I n g r e d i e n t s
f o r   4   s e r v i n g s
600 g (1 ½ lbs) live moulted male crabs
3 eggs
white flour
plenty of oil for frying
salt

P r e p a r a t i o n   t i m e
2 ½ hours

Beat the eggs in a bowl with a pinch
of salt.

Wash the live crabs repeatedly under
cold running water, then immerse
them in the bowl with the eggs, coating
them gently. Cover the bowl with
a tea towel for a couple of hours,
stirring the crabs from time to time.
After this time, the crabs will have
ingested most of the eggs and will have
smothered in it. Remove them from

the bowl, cut off the tips of their claws
and dust them with flour.

Heat up a large quantity of oil in
a heavy frying pan and fry the floured
crabs a few at a time, making them
golden and crispy on all sides.

Remove them from the oil one by
one as they are ready and put them
on kitchen paper towels to drain. Salt.

Serve them piping hot with a side
dish of yellow or white polenta.
The entire crab is edible.

R e c o m m e n d e d   w i n e
Pinot bianco di Lison-Pramaggiore

V a r i a t i o n s
The crabs may be cooked without
letting them stand in the eggs, simply by
dusting them with flour and cooking them
in hot oil. Another interesting variation
is using the crabs in a *fritata de mo'leche*:
here the crabs are fried, cut into pieces and
mixed with eggs beaten with parmesan
cheese. The egg mixture is cooked like
a normal omelette, served with a generous
sprinkle of minced parsley.

147

canocie conse

MANTIS SHRIMP

Mantis shrimp or squills are shellfish commonly found in the Adriatic. Although not as prized as scampi (see page 86-87 for recipe), they are still popular because of the delicate flavour of their flesh. Mantis shrimp can grow to 25 cm in length. The shell is a brownish grey colour and the best time to eat them is in the autumnl. An old Venetian proverb goes that on the feast day of Santa Caterina (25 November) «a mantis shrimp is worth a hen» because during that time, they are particularly firm and full of "coral", the golden-red coloured meat typical in females. Like other shellfish, they can be prepared in a variety of ways (fried, grilled, sauced and others still), but the simplest recipe is the one that best preserves the flavour of the meat, gently poached and dressed with good quality olive oil, lemon, salt and freshly ground pepper.

* *

Ingredients
for 4 servings
1 kg (2 lbs) very fresh mantis shrimp
a bunch of parsley, finely minced
juice from half a lemon
  and a whole half a lemon
extra fine extravirgin olive oil
black peppercorns
salt and freshly ground pepper

Preparation time
½ hour

Wash the mantis shrimp repeatedly
under cold running water.

―――

Bring a pot of light salted water
to a boil. Add a few peppercorns
and half a lemon.

―――

When the water is boiling, add the
shrimp and let them boil for 3 minutes.
Turn off the heat and let them cool
off in the water. Drain them.

―――

Remove the heads first and then
use a pair of scissors to cut the shells
length-wise along the edges of the body,
on the tail and under the head.
Pull out the meat and put it into a bowl.

―――

Add some salt and a bit of freshly
ground black pepper, lemon juice,

extra fine olive oil, and the minced
parsley. Mix well and serve.

Recommended wine
Prosecco di Conegliano-Valdobbiadene

Variations
A fumé can be prepared to use
as the basis of risottos and fish soups
by taking the discarded heads,
front legs and shells and crushing
them a little and then filtering the broth.
A tiny bit of minced garlic can be added
to the dressing given here.
The mantis shrimp may also be fried
by following the recipe given for
mixed fried platter (see page 157 for
the recipe). Grilling does not call
for any special preparations.
In Venice, the mantis shrimp are not
always prepared as described above,
but may also be served whole,
lined up belly-down along the plate.
Each guest dresses the shrimp at will
and must also take the time to remove
the shells, prolonging the time at
the table and enhancing the pleasure
of the dining experience.

148

g r a n s i p o r i a' l a v e n e s s i a n a

**EDIBLE CRAB,
VENETIAN STYLE**

Gransipori, *close cousins to the French tourteaux, are large crabs that live along the coast, at the mouth of ports and on the gravelley bottom of the lagoon, all places where the water is clear and not very deep. Today, they are captured by underwater fishermen using special tongs, because the tools used in the past (nets) didn't always ensure a successful catch considering the strong and sharp claws.*
The word gransipori *is used for two separate species:* Eriphia spinifrons *and* Cancer pagurus. *Both have delicate and tender flesh and are more frequently found in the fall, but the best time to eat them is in the spring. The* poressa *(female) is more flavourful than its male counterpart.*
They are both prepared in a way similar to granseo'le *(see page 36-40 for recipe) even though no one dares to handle them while alive due to the dangerousness of their claws. However, they still must be very fresh.*

. . . .

I n g r e d i e n t s
f o r   4   s e r v i n g s
4 large, very fresh crabs
2 bunches of parsley
a clove of garlic
juice of a lemon
extra fine extravirgin olive oil
salt and freshly ground pepper

P r e p a r a t i o n   t i m e
1 hour

Remove and discard the green shoot from inside the garlic. Mince it finely with the parsley.

Wash the crabs repeatedly under cold running water, brushing the shell vigorously with a small brush.

Bring a large pot of lightly salted water to a boil. Immerse the crabs and cook them for twenty minutes.

Remove the crabs, snap off the legs near the shell and remove the lower part of the shell. Use a fork,

a nut cracker and special tweezers to remove the firm and creamy coloured flesh from the legs, claws and inside the body, as described in the instructions for *granseo'le* (see page 37). Put the meat into a bowl. Drizzle the meat with olive oil and lemon juice and add the minced garlic and parsley, a pinch of salt and a few twists of the pepper grinder. Blend thoroughly.

Replace the dressed crab meat into the shells and serve.

R e c o m m e n d e d   w i n e
Soave classico superiore or Sauvignon dei Colli Berici

V a r i a t i o n s
Some very good olive oil, salt and pepper would suffice to simply dress the meat of this exquisite shellfish, but to each his own. Some cooks prefer hot melted butter, slightly redolent of garlic or with a sprinkle of vinegar in place of the lemon juice. Among friends, the crabs can be informally served straight out of the pot, allowing each diner to crack the shells and dress the meat to his heart's content.

149

GRANSIPORI A'LA VENESSIANA

s e p e   n e r e   c o ' l a   p o ' l e n t a   b i a n c a

**BLACK CUTTLEFISH
SERVED WITH
WHITE POLENTA**

Cuttlefish are caught in abundance in the Mediterranean and Adriatic in particular, where they live in the sandy sea bottom, swaying gently to and fro in the waves. If disturbed, they make their escape by emitting a cloud of black "ink", which fortunately does not occur when they caught unawares by the slow and steady nets of expert fishermen.

These are oval shaped cephalopod molluscs, of variable lengths (in all sizes, small, medium and large) and with tentacles and an internal bone that must be removed before cooking. Once dried, the bone is frequently hung in canary cages to allow the birds to clean their beaks. Venice is the only Mediterranean city where as far back as memory can recall, the cuttlefish ink – found in a special sac – has been used to flavour the famous risotto (see page 84-86 for recipe) and in stewed cuttlefish recipes such as this one. The reason for this custom probably stems from the fact that in times of hardship, cooks would not have expensive herbs and spices to season dishes and attempted to use as much as possible natural seasonings found in the animals themselves. Tradition also dictates that sepio'line (tiny cuttlefish) should be used, which are particularly excellent from September to October, before November rains.

*Ingredients
for 4 servings*
1 kg (2 lbs) of medium sized cuttlefish
a clove of garlic
a bunch of parsley
a glass of dry white wine
half a glass of extravirgin olive oil
juice of a lemon
salt and freshly ground pepper

Preparation time
About 45 minutes

Clean the cuttlefish, remove their skin, eyes, cartilaginous beak, bone and entrails, as described in the recipe for black risotto (see page 86), setting aside the ink sacs in a cup. Wash them thoroughly and cut them into strips, making a vertical cut and a series of diagonal cuts in each strip.

Heat up the olive oil in a heavy pot and add the garlic. Sauté the garlic until golden and then discard it.

152

Add the strips of cuttlefish to the pot and let them sauté for a few minutes, stirring well. Add the wine, let it evaporate, lower the flame, cover and let it cook slowly.

___

In the meantime, rupture a few of the sacs into a cup (the amount of ink used depends on personal taste), dissolve it in a little warm water. Filter the liquid through cheesecloth and add it to the cuttlefish. Simmer for about half an hour. Add salt and pepper at the end, after tasting.

___

Once the cuttlefish are cooked, turn off the heat and add the minced parsley and a squirt of lemon juice. Blend well.

___

Serve the stewed black cuttlefish with a side dish of soft white polenta, prepared according to the recipe given on page 50.

Recommended wine
Vespaiolo superiore di Breganze or Pinot bianco dei Colli Euganei

Variations
To give the black colour of the stewed cuttlefish a slightly golden hue, add a bit of tomato puree halfway through cooking. Cooks in Chioggia never use garlic in the cuttlefish. The ink can also be eliminated entirely and the dish will still be very delicious. Foregoing the ink and adding some tender tiny peas to the cuttlefish about halfway through cooking gives a famous Venetian dish called *sepe coi bisi*, cuttlefish and peas, also served with white polenta.

folpeti

TINY OCTOPUS

The Venetian word folpeti *describes tiny octopuses. However, these little creatures are not really octopus but eledone, a cephalopod mollusc of the* Ozaena moschata *(= Eledone) species. The name derives from the musky odour that emanates from their glands (eledoinis). When these little octopus family members are very large, they are still no bigger than 35 cm. while octopuses are usually at least twice as big.*
Octopuses imported from the coast of Istria and Southern Italy are also eaten in Venice, but the flavour of local folpeti *is more traditional. The molluscs live happily on the sandy or muddy bottoms of the Adriatic, feeding on small dead animals. They are best eaten young when about as big as a baby's hand and have a reddish violet colour. Since they are tiny, they need little preparation for cooking, and the females are so full of eggs they are called* folpeti da risi, *"full of rice". They are almost always available at popular Venetian informal restaurants, where they are traditionally served alongside other appetisers, plucked up with a toothpick and popped into the mouth in one bite, washed down with a glass of local wine to perk up the appetite before lunch. They also make a good, easy to prepare second course.*

. . . .

Ingredients
for 4 servings
12 medium sized octopus, about 1 kg (2 lbs)
extra fine extravirgin olive oil
half a lemon

2 bay leaves
a bunch of parsley, minced
black peppercorns
salt
freshly ground pepper

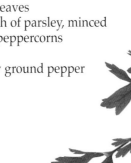

153

Preparation time
About 40 minutes

Use a very sharp knife to clean the octopuses, removing their eyes, cartilaginous beak and pulling out the bone inside (nowadays fishmongers generaly clean the octopuses before selling). Wash them thoroughly.

Bring a pot of lightly salted water to a boil. Add two bay leaves, half a lemon and a few peppercorns.

Take each octopus by the head and emerge it in the water slowly, lifting it up and down with its tentacles in the water until they curl up like ringlets. Then drop them all into the pot. Cover the pot almost all the way and boil the octopus for about 15 minutes.

Drain them, let them cool in a bowl and dress them with salt, freshly ground pepper, lemon juice, extra fine olive oil and minced parsley.

Arrange the octopus on a platter with the tentacles curled upwards and serve.

Recommended wine
Tocai bianco dei Colli Berici

Variations
If the octopuses are not very small, they can also be cut in half before arranging on the platter. If they are very tiny, they may be washed, dusted with flour and fried in hot oil. They make a pleasant addition to delicious fried platters.

ca'lamereti friti

FRIED SQUID

*S*quid (Loligo vulgaris) *are cephalopod molluscs, commonly found in the Adriatic where they play an important part in Venetian cooking as the main ingredient in several popular specialities and combination dishes (mixed fried platter) as well as excellent on their own (fried, roasted or stuffed squid).*
Their bodies are a pearly pinkish colour with brown spots, in the shape of an elongated sack with tentacles, and like cuttlefish, have a sac of bluish-black ink that they will expel if disturbed or threatened. Fishmongers sell a variety of different shapes and sizes of squid, from small, medium to large, whose tentacles can reach up to 50 cm. Similar to squid are the small tòtani *varieties (Ommatostrephes* sagittatus) *that are frequently called by housewives by the same name and used in the same recipes. Squid need to be cleaned thoroughly before use. If they are not very tiny, it is important to peel off the tough skin from the sac. Then, holding them by the tips of their body with the left hand, use the right hand to remove the tentacles and entrails. Discard the entrails. Use a sharp knife to remove the eyes and horny beak from the tentacles. Remove the cartilaginous bone and the two small lateral wings that are joined to the body from halfway down to the tip. Wash the body sacs and tentacles thoroughly. If the squid are small, they don't need to be cut after cleaning. It is best cut medium sized squid into 1 cm thick rings and leave the tentacles whole. Large squid are ideal when stuffed (the stuffing recipe often includes the minced tentacles) and roasted in the oven.*

Ingredients
for 4 servings
1 kg (2 lbs) of small to medium sized squid

a small amount of flour
olive oil (or sunflower seed oil) for frying

154

salt and freshly ground pepper
2 lemons, cut into wedges

Preparation time
About ½ hour

Clean and wash the squid
as described in the introduction.
Dust them with flour.

Heat the oil well in a large frying pan.
Add the squid.

Watch the frying carefully, turning
the squid often so they don't overcook
or burn. They will become tough
if overcooked.

When they are finished frying,
remove them from the oil with a slotted

spoon and drain them on kitchen
paper towels. Sprinkle with salt.

Serve them hot and crisp with
a bowl of lemon wedges.

Recommended wine
A dry and sparkling Prosecco
di Conegliano-Valdobbiadene

Variations
If the squid are very small, some
cooks don't even bother to clean them.
The rings and tentacles are fried in the
same way as whole squid. To prepare
stuffed squid, use the minced tentacles,
some bread crumbs, a couple of eggs,
a bit of minced garlic, parsley and
rosemary, some olive oil, and salt and
pepper to make a stuffing. Fill the squid
body sacs with the mixture and close
the top and bottom with toothpicks
or sew them up with kitchen string
to keep the stuffing inside. Finally, sauté
them in the oil, add some dry white
wine and let them cook slowly
in a covered pot until they
are tender, turning
them from time
to time.

canestrei friti

FRIED COCKLES

*C*ommon cockles (Chlamys opercularis) *are bivalve molluscs fished abundantly in the Adriatic and Mediterranean. The ones fished out of the lagoon have firmer meat than the ones found in the open sea. If they are truly fresh, they can also be eaten raw with little black pepper and lemon during the winter months. No matter how fresh sea cockles are, they should always be eaten cooked (delicious when fried or in risottos). Their scientific name* Chlamys *(= cloak) comes from the fact that their flesh inside the shell is covered with* barbato'le – *as the Venetians call it – the thin membrane that keeps the valves together and must be removed before eating as it is generally full of sand. The shell is similar to a scallop shell since both belong to the same family of molluscs (Pettinidi), but cockles are usually only half as big. Plus, since cockles are also less attractive than their cousins, they are almost always sold cleaned and without the shell. Their meat is firm and white with a small black pearl and a crescent of coral. Shelled or shell on, it is still important to rinse them well before cooking to remove all the sand trapped inside.*

Ingredients
for 4 servings
600 g (1 ½ lbs) of fresh cockles
a small amount of flour
100 g (½ cup) olive oil for frying
salt
a lemon, cut into wedges

Preparation time
About 20 minutes

Wash the cockles repeatedly under cold running water, mixing them around well with the hands. Drain them and dust with flour.

Heat up the oil in a frying pan and add the floured cockles, letting them fry until they "holler" – as the older Venetian housewives would say – describing the noise made during frying that indicates that they are done.

Remove them from the pan with a slotted spoon and drain them for a few minutes on kitchen paper towels. Sprinkle generously with salt and shake the paper.

Move the piping hot cockles to serving platter, garnish with some lemon wedges and serve.

Recommended wine
Tocai bianco dei Colli Berici

Variations
The cockles may be the basis of an excellent risotto if they are minced and sautéed with some chopped onion and garlic. Proceed according to the recipe given for seafood risottos on page 83-84.

frito misto de mar

FRIED SEAFOOD PLATTER

*L*ike fish soup, this dish is very popular along both coasts of the peninsula, but every area features characteristic regional variations depending on the types of local fish, seasonal availability, and traditions established over the centuries. In Naples, for example, no fried seafood platter would be complete without red mullet and squid because, Neapolitans argue, you*

only need these two varieties to reproduce the true flavour of the sea. In Venice, an authentic frito misto must include tiny cuttlefish or squid, scampi or prawn tails, and the rest of the fritura (small blue fish, tiny soles, whitebait, and others). Once upon a time in Venice, you could find fitro'lini at every street corner, basically shops or peddlers that offered portions of frito misto with polenta to passersby for a light snack or housewives who prefer to bring home a ready-to-eat meal rather than slave over a hot stove. These days, shops like this have practically vanished, but nearly every Venetian restaurant still includes a hot and crispy seafood platter on its menu.

Ingredients
for 6 servings
300 g (¾ lb) scampi tails or prawns
300 g (¾ lb) small mixed fish
   (whitebait and other varieties, to taste)
200 g (7 oz.) squid rings
200 g (7 oz.) cockles
a small amount of flour
100 g (½ cup) olive oil or sunflower seed
   oil for frying
salt
2 lemons, cut into wedges

Preparation time
About ½ hour

Remove the shells from the prawns or scampi tails as indicated in the recipe on page 87. Wash the mixed fish, shellfish and molluscs repeatedly under cold running water.

Drain them and dust with flour. Heat up the oil in a large frying pan and add the squid rings and scampi tails first,

then after five minutes add the remainder.

Remove them from the oil with a slotted spoon as soon as they are golden brown and crispy and drain them on kitchen paper towels. Sprinkle with salt.

Serve the fried seafood platter hot, garnishing with the lemon wedges.

Recommended wine
Prosecco di Conegliano-Valdobbiadene

Variations
If there are some larger varieties of fish among the mixed fish (*fritura*) it is best to clean them, removing the head and entrails. Otherwise, tiny fish can be eaten whole. Venetians sometimes make the mixed seafood platter with only whitebait, served with a soft white polenta.
For a more sophisticated seafood platter, use only prawns, scampi and squid and let it stand for an hour to marinate in oil, lemon, and salt before frying.

s'ciosi in salsa

SNAILS IN SAUCE

S' *ciosi is the Venetian word for the snails that are the larger cousins of the tiny sea snails (called bovo'leti, see page 48 for the recipe) and are frequently called bovo'loni. These are land gastropods molluscs, with a spiral-shaped shell, probably a member of the Elicidi family. They are highly prized in French cuisine (the snails from Burgundy are the most famous, also called "vineyard snails" and give the exquisite escargots à la bourguignonne). Nevertheless, the great cooks of the Serenissima have also been able to transform s'ciosi into a delicacy. Still, snails are the quintessential peasant dish, eaten for centuries by people who have had to be very creative in order to fill their bellies, using only what was available and offered spontaneously by the land.*

Snails are fairly bland food on their own and require a special preliminary preparation and a good dose of herbs to make them flavourful. Because s'ciosi eat various kinds of grasses, the first thing to do in preparing them is purge them. This entails leaving them without food for at least ten days inside a closed perforated wooden boxed with a bit of wheat bran on the bottom.

Or they may be kept in the dark, in a reed basket with a few bits of well-washed grape leaves and pieces of soft bread soaked with water. In this way, they rid themselves of excrement from past meals and acquire a more meaty and delicate tasting flesh. If they are not purged before cooking, they would have the bitter and metallic flavour of the grass they had eaten.

When purchasing snails, be sure to inquire whether they have already been purged or check whether the shell still has the operculum, the hard disc covering the opening of the shell, indicating that the snail is still hibernating and therefore does not require purging as most of the vital functions have slowed down. After being purged, wash the snails and their shells repeatedly under running water. Put them into a large pot of cold water and bring the water to a boil slowly for ten minutes.

This makes them come out of their shells and washes them again. Drain them and rinse them under cold water. Remove the snail from the shell and discard the black-coloured swollen part (the intestine) and the operculum, if present. At this point, the snails are ready for cooking.

. . . .

Ingredients
for 4 servings
1 kg (2 lbs) snails in the shell
4 cloves of garlic
2 bunches of parsley
2 bay leaves
a bunch of celery leaves
a handful of fennel seeds
2 glasses of dry white wine
250 ml (1 ¼ cups) water
half a glass of extravirgin olive oil
salt and pepper

Preparation time
About 5 hours

Clean, wash, cook and prepare the snails as indicated in the introduction.

—

Remove and discard the green shoot from the clove of garlic and mince the garlic finely. Coarsely chop the parsley and celery leaves.

—

Put the olive oil, garlic, parsley, celery, bay leaves, fennel seeds, wine and snails in a terracotta pot. Cover it and let the pot simmer very gently for 4 hours, stirring from time to time and adding a bit of water if necessary. Add salt and pepper halfway through cooking.

—

Serve the snails on a platter, with a side dish of piping hot polenta.

Recommended wine
Duello superiore dei Lessini

Variations
In Venice and around the Veneto, snails are generally served without the shells. However, some cooks prefer to serve them with the shell, following the recipe more or less as given above. After cooking, the shells are stuffed with the snails and a mixture of butter and herbs and are then placed in a baking pan with the open-side and baked for another 15 minutes. Other variations usually involve changes in the flavourings used: some like to add a spoonful of tomato sauce, others add minced sardines (rinsed of the excess salt), or a pinch of grated lemon rind, or rosemary and sage. The variations are endless.

S'CIOSI IN SALSA

Side dishes and eggs

tego'line in tecia

STEWED STRING BEANS

*T*ego'line *is the Venetian word for* mange-tout *legumes, because both the beans and pods can be eaten. These beans (Phaseolus vulgaris) are picked when very young and before the seeds have become firm and the pods are still tender and meaty. The plants may be dwarf or climbing varieties. In the second case, they need to grow on poles. The most popular variety grown in lagoon gardens is called the "wonder of Venice", wide, yellow, fleshy climbing beans.*

Ingredients
for 6 servings
800 g (2 lbs) beans
200 ml (1 cup) tomato sauce (see page 64)
100 ml (½ cup) extravirgin olive oil
a clove of garlic
a bunch of parsley
salt
pepper

Preparation time
About 1 hour

Remove both tips from the beans, being careful to remove the strings that run along both sides of the pod.

———

Wash the beans and let them stand in cold water for little while, to plump them.

———

Heat up some oil in a frying pan and add the clove of garlic after removing the green shoot and mincing. Add the beans, mix well, then add the salt and pepper.

———

Halfway through cooking, add a little of the tomato sauce.

Let the beans cook for about an hour with the pot closed and when the beans are done, add the parsley and blend well.

Recommended wine
Merlot del Piave

Variations
Many housewives save time by boiling the beans first and then sautéing them. To boil the beans, toss them into a pot of boiling water and cook, pot uncovered, for about 15 minutes. They should retain their brilliant colour. They are also delicious boiled, served cold dressed with good quality olive oil, vinegar, salt and freshly ground pepper.

fasioi sofegai

STEWED BEANS

B eans play a very special and highly regarded part in Venetian cooking. They are valued for their delicious flavour in traditional dishes (pasta e fasioi, *see page 64-65 for recipe) and be-cause they have always provided a good and economical source of vegetable proteins (poor people's meat). Beans were brought to Venice in the 1500s by merchants who traded with Spain, while the Spaniards in turn, brought this new vegetable eastward from the New World. The most prized beans around Venice come from Lamon, a little town in the province of Belluno, because they have a thin skin and floury texture.*

Ingredients
for 4 servings
500 g (1 lb) fresh beans or 250 g (½ lb) dried beans
100 g (½ cup) *peverada* sauce (see page 120)
half a glass of roast guinea hen drippings (see page 120) or extravirgin olive oil

Preparation time
About 1 ½ hours, plus the time to make the sauce

Boil the beans in plenty of water, salting them only at the end of cooking to keep them from hardening (if dried beans are used, they should be softened first in a large pot of cold water for eight hours or overnight, adding a spoonful of baking soda, which makes them plump more quickly).

Drain the beans and dress them with the *peverada* sauce along with the drippings from the roast guinea hen or olive oil. Taste and add salt, if necessary.

Mix well and let the beans stand covered for a little while to heighten the flavours. Serve hot.

Recommended wine
Cabernet Sauvignon di Lison-Pramaggiore

Variations
Beans can also be stewed with a mirepoix of onions, carrots, celery, and garlic, with parsley and tomato sauce, if desired. These beans make a splendid side dish to *muséti* (see page 114) or *'luganeghe* (see page 115).

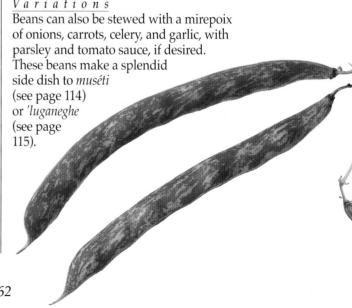

sego'lete agrodolse

WEET AND SOUR PEARL ONIONS

Onions are a mainstay in most of the dishes in Venetian cuisine, because almost no recipe is complete without their subtle yet distinctive flavour. Onions may even be the main ingredient in other dishes, such as saòr *(see recipe page 35)* or figà *(recipe page 111). In Venice, onions are also mixed with boiled beans to make a flavourful and hearty salad (fasioi co'le sego'le) or boiled and served up as a side dish in their own right. Among the many recipes, sweet and sour onions are one of the most popular. The best type of onion to use in this dish is the small, slightly flat pearl variety.*

. . . .

Ingredients
for 4 servings
400 g (1 lb) small, flat or pearl onions
a bay leaf
a clove
extravirgin olive oil
half a glass of dry white wine
half a glass of vinegar
salt

Preparation time
1 hour

Clean the onions, remove the roots and the even off the top side. Remove the first layer of papery skin.

Put the onions in a heavy pot with the oil, salt, bay leaf, clove, and half glass of white wine. Put the pot on high heat and cook for about five minutes. Then transfer the pot to a hot oven and cook the onions slowly until they are golden.

When the onions are just about done, add the vinegar and let it evaporate. Serve.

Recommended wine
Gambellara or Bianco di Custoza

Variations
Sweet and sour onions make a wonderful side dish with boiled meat platters or they are also delicious eaten with toothpicks as appetisers. To keep them on hand for last minute guests, make a batch of sweet and sour onions and keep them in glass jars, filled up with vinegar or oil. Blanch the small onions for a minute in lightly salted boiling water then drain well. Let them stand for 24 hours in herb flavoured vinegar. Remove them from the vinegar and put them in glass jars with a bay leaf, a few peppercorns, and a clove. Bring the vinegar used to marinate them to a boil and pour it over the top of the onions in the jars. Let the jars cool, cover the surface with oil and close the jars. Onions preserved this way are best when eaten within 2 months. If oil is used to cover the onions in place of the boiling vinegar, it is best to wait a few days before lidding the jars as the onions will absorb some of the oil. Top up the jars and then cover tightly.

163

fenoci col late

FENNEL KED IN MILK

This vegetable has been grown in the Mediterranean area for years. It is so ancient that its name was given to one of the cradles of Western civilisation: Marathon, near Athens, where the Greeks fought off invasions in 490 B.C. In ancient Greek, Márathon meant fennel.

Two species of fennel are used most commonly: the sweet kind, which is cultivated, and the wild kind which is mostly used for its aromatic seeds and medicinal qualities.

Old Veneto farmers tell a tale about a "savage worm" that lived in the large edible hearts of fennel that if inadvertently eaten, would cause serious stomach ache. Today's modern pesticides have practically eliminated this problem, although today, we have other more serious problems in agriculture.

Ingredients for 4 servings

500 g (1 lb) fennel
  (weighed after cleaning)
300 ml (1 ½ cup) milk
30 g (2 tablespoons) butter
extravirgin olive oil
salt and pepper

Preparation time
About 45 minutes

Remove the cores from the green upper parts and the outside parts that are damaged. Cut the fennel in half lengthwise.

Put the fennel into a pot, cover with lightly salted cold water and bring to a boil for a few minutes.

Drain the fennel and let it cool for a while. Then cut each half into three wedges.

Melt the butter with a little olive oil in a frying pan. Add the fennel wedges and sauté them on both sides, turning when necessary.

Cover with milk, add salt and pepper and let the fennel simmer for 10 to 15 minutes, until the milk has thickened.

Arrange the fennel wedges on a platter with cooking sauce.

Recommended wine
Bianco di Custoza

Variations
Fennel are delicious served just about any way: raw in mixed tossed salads or alone; boiled; gratinéed in the oven, and so forth.

Of all the recipes for fennel, fennel cooked in milk is probably the best-loved, because it is so traditional. If the fennel is very fresh and fairly small, there is no need to blanch it before sautéing with the butter. Some cooks add a dusting of parmesan cheese to the dish before serving to enhance the flavour.

s p à r e s i   l e s s i

BOILED ASPARAGUS

Asparagus eaten in the Veneto may be one of two varieties: the cultivated, garden variety and a flavourful wild variety plucked furtively and joyfully by hand in abandoned fields. Wild asparagus picking provides the same kind of thrill as wild mushroom hunting, only mushrooms are found hidden under layers of dead leaves in the wood and asparagus hide just under ground. Wild asparagus are really shoots of Asparagus officinalis that, generated from the underlying rhyzome, try to push up through the surface. As soon as asparagus pickers find them, they insert a special tool alongside the delicate stalk, turn it slowly and pull the tool up out of the ground, bringing the spear up with it. This operation is a full-fledged cruelty perpetrated against the plant which will then gather its strength to produce new offshoots in the desperate attempt to stay alive. This is why sparesère (asparagus growers) are a very productive and very lucrative bunch. The most popular of all the varieties grown in the Veneto is from Bassano del Grappa (VI), thanks to the particular silty composition of the earth produced by the Brenta River that intersects it.

Ingredients
for 4 servings
1 kg (2 lbs) asparagus from Bassano
3 eggs
extravirgin olive oil
a drizzling of vinegar
salt and freshly ground pepper

Preparation time
½ hour

Clean and trim the asparagus, cutting all the stalks to the same length and peeling them from top to bottom with a sharp knife to remove the tough and stringy parts (without touching the tips).

———

Tie them together in bunches of 5-6 asparagus.

Arrange them in a tall pot fill with lightly salted water. The tips should stick out of the water. Cover the pot and bring the water to a boil. Cook for 15-25 minutes, depending on how thick the asparagus is.

———

While the asparagus is cooking, prepare the sauce. Hard boil the eggs, cool them then chop them coarsely with the tines of a fork. Add some salt and pepper, a drizzling of vinegar and olive oil. Blend well.

———

Remove the asparagus from the water when cooked to taste. Untie the bundles and arrange them on a serving platter with the tips facing inward, like a flower. Garnish with the egg sauce and serve.

165

SPÀRESI LESSI

Recommended wine
Pinot grigio di Breganze or del Piave

Variations
Asparagus go very well with eggs, which can be used in the garnishing sauce and also to make a delicate second course. A celebrated Venetian dish is *spàresi coi vovi duri*, where boiled asparagus are served with hard-boiled eggs, giving each diner free hand to dress the asparagus as he or she sees fit. Other traditional ways to dress boiled asparagus include melted butter with a good dusting of grated parmesan cheese and some toasted bread crumbs or a sauce made up of salt, pepper, fresh herbs (parsley or basil), oil and vinegar (one spoonful of vinegar for every four of oil), emulsified well and serve on the side in a sauce boat.

me'lansane al fongheto

GARLIC EGGPLANT

Eggplant has been grown in lagoon gardens since the 15th and 16th centuries after the Jews in the Ghetto, faithful to their religious restrictions, gradually spread its popularity. Before this, the Venetians considered eggplant a mysterious and dangerous plant to eat. It would seem that the name "melanzane" derives from the Latin malum insanum, *meaning "poison apple". Luckily, nowadays people no longer harbour these suspicions and eggplants are eaten widely from spring time right up to late autumn.*

*Ingredients
for 4 servings*
1.2 kg (2 ½ lbs) eggplant
2 bunches of parsley
a clove of garlic
a glass of extravirgin olive oil
salt

Preparation time
About 1 hour

When buying eggplant, choose long eggplants over the rounded ones, with unblemished dark purple skin. Wash and dry them. Remove the stem and the green leaves and cut the eggplant lengthwise into four quarters and remove the seeds.

Cut the eggplant into cubes, salt the pieces and put them into a colander. Let the eggplant stand so that the salt can draw out the bitter liquid inside.

In the meantime, heat the oil and fry the garlic and chopped parsley. Add the cubed eggplant and cook it, uncovered. As the eggplant cooks, its skin will turn dark and shiny and the mixture will begin to resemble mushrooms.

Recommended wine
Raboso or Merlot del Piave

Variations
The eggplant can also be cut into slices and grilled or floured and fried. They are also a delicious addition to summertime *pevaronada* (see page 172-173 for recipe).

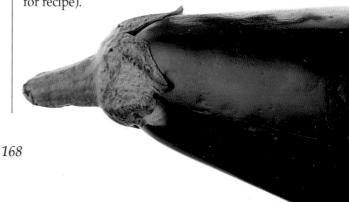

168

pissacani o roso'line in tecia

SAUTÉED
DANDELIONS
R CORN POPPIES

Pissacani *are young shoots of dandelions* (Taraxacum officinalis) *that are often called "soffione" in Venice because when they are mature, their heads become white and fluffy and children love to blow their seeds.* Roso'line *are young shoots of poppy* (Papaver rhoeas). *Both of these plants can be found wild around the world but their use in cooking is distinctly Veneto.*

Ingredients
for 4 servings
800 g (2 lbs) dandelions or corn poppies
100 g (¼ lb) lard
2 cloves of garlic
a drizzle of extravirgin olive oil
salt and pepper

Preparation time
About 1 ½ hours

Clean and trim the plants, discarding the outermost leaves and thinning out the roots but not eliminating them altogether. Wash the greens

repeatedly under running water.

Place them in a pot of slightly salted water, bring to a boil and cook for half an hour.

Drain them and let them cool. Squeeze out the excess water using the hands.

In the meantime, chop the lard and let it melt in a frying pan with some olive oil and the garlic, after removing the green shoots.

Add the boiled greens, a bit of salt and pepper and cook for about 20 minutes, mixing from time to time. Add salt if necessary.

Once cooking is completed, remove the garlic and serve the greens as a side dish to boiled and roasted meats.

Recommended wine
Valpolicella classico or Cabernet del Piave

Variations
The lard can be replaced with smoked or unsmoked bacon. The dandelions and corn poppies can also be mixed together instead of serving them separately. In the Veneto, the cooking water is not discarded, but saved and used as an early morning tonic. It is not particularly good tasting, but tradition has it that it purifies the system, improves digestion and eliminates toxins.

169

radicio rosso ai feri

**GRILLED
RED RADICCHIO**

Radicchio (Cichorium intybus) *was named because its leaves as well as its tiny roots ("radice") are edible. Various forcing methods are used to make the colour of the leaves either green or red and by the time the radicchio is ready for eating in autumn, it will present several shades of red.*

The four varieties grown in the Veneto vary in colour from the deep rich red of "Treviso Red" radicchio to the brilliant red "Verona" variety to the mottled "Castelfranco" type and finally the light pink radicchio "Chioggia".

The varieties also differ in their shape. Verona and Chioggia radicchio have tightly packed, rounded heads. Castlefranco radicchio is also round, but its leaves are wider and slightly ruffled, while the Treviso variety has an elongated head with spear-shaped leaves and a large white centre rib. Radicchio has a gently bitter but still delicate and pleasant flavour.

In the Veneto, a proverb goes that red radicchio is the gift that autumn gives to winter to liven it up with a bit of colour. In fact, there is something uplifting about gazing at otherwise desolate late autumn fields and seeing the sparkling bunches of red radicchio just about ready to harvest. The fairly recent habit of serving radicchio grilled or roasted drains it of its delicate flavour which would be enhanced by a simple drizzle of good quality olive oil.

....

*Ingredients
for 4 servings*
800 g (2 lbs) Treviso red radicchio
  (with an elongated head
  and spear-shaped leaves)
a glass of extravirgin olive oil
salt and freshly ground pepper

Preparation time
½ hour

Heat up the barbecue grill using wood for heat (even better if covered with a light layer of ash so that the heat is not overly intense).

When buying the radicchio, select firm and compact heads.
Trim off the roots and leave a small portion near to the leaves, keeping the head intact.

Starting at the root, cut the heads in half lengthwise.

Wash the radicchio repeatedly to remove the sand, then dry well and drain on a tea towel.

In a large bowl, prepare a marinade with the oil, a pinch of salt and fresh ground pepper. Toss in all the radicchio halves.

Arrange them on the hot grill and barbecue them for about five minutes. When the leaves begin to wilt, baste them with more of the marinade, turn them over and let them cook on the other side, being careful not to burn them.

Serve the radicchio piping hot off the barbecue as a side dish for grilled or roasted meat or game.

Recommended wine
Tocai rosso dei Colli Berici
or Refosco di Lison-Pramaggiore

Variations
Radicchio may also be roasted.
Prepare the radicchio for cooking

RADICIO ROSSO AI FERI

as in the recipe above, then arrange the halves in a baking pan and bake in a preheated oven.
Radicchio is also delicious cut into wedges and eaten raw. To dress raw radicchio, dissolve a pinch of salt in a spoonful of vinegar. Pour it over the radicchio with good quality extra virgin olive oil and blend well. Our forebears often dressed raw red radicchio with hot melted lard.

p e v a r o n a d a

PEPERONATA (FRIED PEPPERS)

This simple and satisfying dish is a triumph of mixed cooked vegetables where peppers lend the distinctive, succulent flavour. It is a quintessential late summer and early autumn dish, when local gardens being bearing their most flavourful fruits. It makes a perfect side dish for boiled or roasted meats.

*Ingredients
for 4/6 servings*
400 g (1 lb) seasonal peppers, green, red and yellow
400 g (1 lb) white onions
400 g (1 lb) tomato
eggplant (if desired)
carrots (if desired)
a few stalks of celery (if desired)
extravirgin olive oil
salt

Preparation time
Anywhere from 40 minutes to 2 hours, according to taste

Wash the vegetables well and cut

them into small pieces and strips. Before cutting the tomatoes, make sure to remove their skins. Do this by blanching them briefly in boiling water and then pulling off the outer membrane.

Pour some olive oil into a heavy pot. Add a layer of onions first, then peppers, then carrots, eggplant and celery (if used), and finally the tomatoes. Sprinkle on some salt and then put the pot on low heat.

When the mixture begins to come to a boil, mix well. Keep cooking, mixing from time to time, for about half an hour if the vegetables should be cooked and tender but still intact or longer

172

if a more amalgamated *peperonata* is desired. Add salt to taste.

———

Serve the *peperonata* cold or just warm on a serving platter.

Recommended wine
Pinot nero del Piave

Variations
There are countless variations to this recipe, considering the simplicity in preparation and the diversity of the ingredients. We have taken the advice of an older Treviso lady who recommended using peppers, tomatoes and onions in equal quantities and to be judicious with the eggplant, carrots, and celery so that the flavour does not become unbalanced. Some cooks like to add a bit of sautéed scallions to the bottom of the pot before adding the vegetables.

---

p e v a r o n i

PEPPERS

Peppers (Capsicum annuum) *were introduced to Europe only in the 16th century, arriving on our shores practically simultaneously from America (probably from Brazil) and the East. In the century of the Renaissance, Venice still dominated the trade of spices entering Europe, but Venice got its products mostly from the Asian territories. So, peppers and their smaller more piquant cousins, peperoncini (Capsicum frutescens) reached Venice from the East and in the process, gained much popularity in the Slavic countries. Nevertheless, the flavour of peppers – which ranged from the sweet large bell peppers to the strongly flavoured paprikas – did not catch on in Venice until at least a century later, after the Serenissima was conquered by Napoleon, and when it became part of the Austrian Empire (Lombard-Veneto Kingdom). Since then, more than two hundred years have passed and the lagoon tradition of growing peppers in back yard gardens and preparing them as a side dish for boiled, stewed and roasted meats has become very common.*

....

Ingredients
for 6 servings
400 g (1 lb) bell green, red and yellow
   peppers
3 stalks of celery, with or without
leaves (as desired)
2 carrots
2 salted sardines
extravirgin olive oil
a drizzling of vinegar, a clove of garlic
salt (to taste) and pepper (if desired)

Preparation time
About ½ hour

Wash the peppers well and remove the stems, seeds and white internal membranes. Cut them into 1 cm wide strips.

———

Wash and trim the celery and the carrots. Cut them into strips.

———

Bring some water to a boil with a little vinegar and salt and toss in the pepper strips. Let it boil for 5 minutes.

———

Remove the peppers with a slotted spoon and drain them in a colander. Put them into a bowl to dress them.

———

Bring the water and vinegar to a boil once again and add the celery and carrot strips. Let them boil for five minutes.

———

PEVARONI

Remove the carrots and celery with a slotted spoon and put them into a mortar. Remove the green shoot from inside the clove of garlic with the salted sardines, rinsed and cut into pieces.

——

Crush well and pour into the bowl with the peppers.

——

Add a bit of olive oil and mix. Taste for seasoning and add salt and pepper if necessary. Give the mixture one last stir before serving.

Variations

This recipe reflects the Venetian tradition of cherishing traditions and experiences borrowed from other regions of Italy. Therefore, it is easy to find peppers prepared in many other ways in Venice: raw as an addition to tossed salads; roasted over an open fire, peeled and served dressed with good quality olive oil, salt and pepper; fried in oil with a dash of vinegar (sweet and sour); or stuffed with meat, rice and other vegetables and baked in the oven.

Recommended wine
Refosco di Lison-Pramaggiore

patate a'la venessiana

VENETIAN-STYLE POTATOES

Potatoes were brought to Europe in the 16th century on Spanish galleons returning from the New World. They were not well-received at first on the continent and were even less popular in Venice where for a long time, potatoes were considered no more than food fit for peasants or mountain dwellers. But with the Treaty of Campoformio (1797), Napoleon ceded Venice to the Austrians and among the many gifts the Germans bequeathed to Venice was their love for these underground tubers. Nowadays, potatoes are enjoyed cooked in a myriad of ways (fried, baked, mashed, in casseroles and so forth) but the most traditional Venetian recipe calls for the combination of potatoes with onions, although French cuisine makes its own claim to the invention of this extraordinary dish.

Ingredients
for 6 servings
600 g (1 ¼ lbs) potatoes
a large onion
a bunch of parsley
40 g (2 ½ tablespoons) butter
half a glass of extravirgin olive oil
salt

Preparation time
About 1 hour

Peel the potatoes, wash and dry them
and cut them into cubes.

——

Chop the onion and fry it in the oil
and the butter. Add the potatoes
to the frying pan and cook over moderate
heat, mixing from time to time with
a wooden spoon.

——

When cooking is almost complete,
add the minced parsley and salt to taste.

Recommended wine
Bardolino or Tocai rosso dei Colli Berici

Variations
Some minced unsmoked bacon can
be added to the fried onions along with
a couple of rosemary leaves, to enhance
the richness of the dish.

castraure de Sant'Erasmo

NEW BAB ARTICHOKES

Castraùre *is the dialect name for the tiny first blooming artichokes that are removed from a plant that has produced too many blossoms. Venetian farmers usually leave only a few artichokes on the plants or sometimes just one, so that these vegetables can grow large and meaty. Tiny artichokes bear the distinction "di Sant'Erasmo" because they come from the eponymous lagoon island where there is a monastery and artichokes seem to grow in abundance. Sant'Erasmo is also the patron saint of sailors whose feast day is celebrated on 2 June. This saint, popularly called St. Elmo, is also associated with an unusual and fantastic weather condition called "St. Elmo's fire" made up a series of lightening flashes that appear at the top of the masts of ships during storms.*

Ingredients
for 4 servings
16 tiny artichokes
50 g (2 oz.) unsmoked bacon
a onion
a clove of garlic
a drizzle of extravirgin olive oil
salt and freshly ground pepper

Preparation time
About ½ hour

Clean the artichokes, by trimming
away the stem and removing
and discarding the tough outer
leaves; then cut them in half
lengthwise. Make a mirepoix of onion,
garlic and bacon.

Heat up a small amount of olive
oil in an oven-proof frying pan and
sauté the mirepoix.
Add the tiny artichokes and brown
them, stirring delicately so that they
don't break.

——

Add the salt, pepper, a splash of water,
and cook for 10 minutes uncovered.

——

177

Put the uncovered pan in the oven
for about ten more minutes or until
the artichokes become crunchy.

Recommended wine
Vespaiolo di Breganze

Variations
Tiny artichokes can also be eaten raw,
after coating the leaves into a dipping
sauce made with olive oil, salt, and
pepper. For a slightly richer dish, some
cooks add cream or white sauce and
grated armesan cheese at the end.

articiochi a'la venessiana

**ARTICHOKE
BOTTOMS**

In the City of St. Mark and the surrounding areas, artichokes are held in very high esteem because of their medicinal properties (hepatological, digestive, diuretic, anti-inflammatory and toning) as well as for their other special qualities. In late winter and early spring, the Rialto vegetable market and most of the peddlers in city squares proudly display their wares, with stands brimming with artichokes, most of which are "violets of Venice" grown in the lagoon gardens. Every vegetable seller worth his salt has a terracotta tub of water next to his stand, overflowing with artichoke bases already trimmed of the tough centre and leaves, floating lazily in water with lemon slices to keep them from darkening.

*Ingredients
for 4 servings*
12 artichoke bottoms
a clove of garlic
a bunch of parsley
20 g (1 ½ tablespoons) butter
half a glass of extravirgin olive oil
salt and freshly ground pepper

Preparation time
½ hour

Choose large and meaty artichoke
bottoms and keep them in water
mixed with a little lemon
juice until cooking so they
don't turn dark.

Chop the parsley and garlic and sauté
them in the olive oil.

Add the artichoke bases and cook
them slowly, adding a little water
if necessary to keep them from sticking.
Add salt and pepper to taste.

Recommended wine
Bardolino or Tocai rosso dei Colli Berici

Variations
A popular variation on the cooking
is whole artichokes cooked in a frying
pan, or boiled and eaten one leaf at a time
after dipping in a sauce of oil, vinegar,
salt and pepper. Artichoke bases can also
be baked in the oven (after flavouring
them as above and sprinkling bread
crumbs over the top). They may also be
stuffed with a mixture of chopped boiled
eggs, ham, parsley, basil, garlic, salt
and pepper, topped with a dusting
of bread crumbs and baked in the oven.

ARTICIOCHI A'LA VENESSIANA

cardi in tecia

STEWED THISTLES

Closely related to the artichoke family, thistles (Cynara cardunculus *var.* altilis) *are vegetables that are trained during the growing period to encourage growth of the ribbing in the leaves and the central leaf stalk and to enhance the organoleptic qualities thanks to the whitening process. This is why the outer leaves are discarded and the edible part is made up of the lower and central rib of the plant. They generally appear on the market in late autumn-early winter.*

Ingredients
for 4 servings
500 g (1 lb) thistles
a onion
a spoonful of white flour
2 spoonfuls of lemon juice
20 g (1 ½ tablespoons) butter
half a glass of extravirgin olive oil
salt and pepper
grated parmesan cheese

Preparation time
About 1 hour

To prepare the thistles, remove the ribs from the heart one by one, eliminating the tops. Then trim off the strings and the notched part on both sides of the ribs. Cut them into 8 cm pieces.

Put the thistles in a pot with plenty of salted water. Add a spoonful of white flour and the lemon juice to keep the thistles white. Bring to a boil and cook for half an hour.

Drain the thistles and then sauté them in the butter and oil with the finely chopped onion, salt and pepper. Sprinkle on a bit of grated parmesan before serving.

Recommended wine
Bardolino chiaretto

Variations
After boiling the thistles as given above, some cooks put them into a heavy pot with a few knobs of butter, salt and pepper. Blend with a litre of white sauce, 100 ml of sweet cream, some parmesan cheese, and two egg yolks, and then brown in a hot oven for about twenty minutes.

verze sofegae

SMOTHERED CABBAGE

Savoy cabbage is a variety of cabbage (Brassica oleracea *var.* bullata) *that owes its common Italian name to the intense green colour of the leaves (verde / verze). The leaves are large, ruffled and patterned, and grow one on top of the other to make the rounded and slightly flattened head, whose dimensions vary from small (in the early harvest, spring and summer varieties) to very large (in the late harvest, autumn and winter varieties). Savoy cabbage is the best loved member of the cabbage family (which also includes broccoli, cabbage, cauliflower, etc.) in Venetian cooking, especially when it is the extra sweet and tender variety grown in Padua. This variety ripens in late autumn and lasts the entire winter, when the fields are covered with early morning haze and their heads sparkle with dew.*

Ingredients
for 4 servings
a head of sweet Padua Savoy cabbage
a onion
a clove of garlic
a sprig of rosemary
100 ml (½ cup) extravirgin olive oil
salt
freshly ground pepper

Preparation time
2 ½ hours

Remove the tough outer leaves from the cabbage. Cut it into wide or narrow strips, to taste.

Chop the onion, the clove of garlic, and a few of the rosemary leaves. Heat the oil in a large pot and sauté the mirepoix. Add the cabbage and salt and pepper to taste.

Cook the cabbage on low heat for a couple of hours, keeping the pot covered for at least the first hour and a half. Remove the lid toward the end of cooking and make sure that there is not too much liquid to cook off. By the end, the cabbage will have reduced to about one-fourth its original volume. Stir gently from time to time.

Let the cabbage cool slightly before serving. Cabbage makes an excellent side dish to most meat dishes.

Recommended wine
Select the wine to go with whatever the cabbage is served with; a Gambellara or Gargenega are good choices.

Variations
It is common to add a piece of lard or unsmoked bacon (50-100 grams) to the oil (which is then reduced to 50 grams). Some cooks don't add garlic, others add a glass of dry white wine or broth, while others still enjoy the flavour lent by a spoonful of tomato sauce.

suca rosta

BAKED PUMPKIN

From the end of summer right up until winter, large Chioggia pumpkin (Cucurbita maxima) is found abundantly at fruit and vegetable stands across the city, either whole or sold in wedges. Venetians call these pumpkins suche baruche *because of the warty, greyish-green peel. The flesh is a pleasant yellow-gold and is used to make a very popular risotto (see page 80-81 for recipe).*

181

Ingredients
for 4 servings
1 kg (2 lbs) pumpkin
sugar or salt

Preparation time
About 2 hours

Cut the pumpkin into pieces,
leaving the skin on but removing
the seeds.

Put the pumpkin into a hot
oven (200 °C) and leave it in for
a couple of hours until the flesh
is soft and tender.

It is eaten straight from oven, dusted
with sugar or salt, depending
on preferences.

Recommended wine
Gambellara superiore (for salted pumpkin)
or Recioto spumante di Gambellara
(for sugared pumpkin)

Variations
Pumpkin is also delicious boiled in
lightly salted water. Years ago, country
folk gave it to children to eat as a
favourite after-school snack. It can also
be cut into small pieces (without the skin),
dipped into a batter and fried until crispy.
Pumpkin seeds are also edible:
clean them of the strings, salt them
and toast them in the oven.

sèleno rava

CELERIAC

Celeriac is a member of the rapaceum family of ordinary celery (Apium gravolens) *and its most popular cultivar is "di Verona". It is easily distinguishable because of its fat root which resembles a turnip. Unlike regular celery (var.* dulce) *of which only the stalks and leaves are eaten, celeriac has a delicious edible root.*

Ingredients
for 4 servings
2 celeriac
50 g (3 ½ tablespoons) butter
grated parmesan cheese
salt

Preparation time
About 40 minutes

Peel the celeriac carefully,
wash it and cut it into large wedges.

Blanch the pieces in salted water, cooking
them until tender but firm. Drain.
Melt the butter and sauté the celeriac
wedges over low heat until golden.

Add a good dusting of parmesan
during the last few minutes of cooking.
Turn off the heat once the cheese
has melted.

Recommended wine
Tocai rosso dei Colli Berici
or Bardolino chiaretto

Variations
Celeriac can be cut into dice and
sautéed in a pan, or it may be cut into
rounds, boiled and dressed with oil,
salt and pepper. It is also delicious,
albeit a bit heavier, cut into a julienne
and dressed with mayonnaise and
a bit of mustard.

erbete rave

BOILED RED BEETS

A round Venice, erbete rave are round red beets (Beta vulgaris var. rapa forma rubra) either of the "Chioggia" and "quarantina di Chioggia" varieties, selected by Venetian growers. They are not recommended for diabetics as they are rich in carbohydrates in the form of sugars.
Today, supermarkets and fruit and vegetable stands sell the beets already cooked and vacuum packed, making preparing them that much easier. Just peel, slice and dress to taste.

Ingredients for 4 servings
4 medium sized round beets
extravirgin olive oil
a drizzle of vinegar
salt and pepper

Preparation time
About 1 hour

Clean the beets thoroughly, washing off all the dirt. Let them stand in cool water for about an hour.

Cook the beets in the skin in lightly salted water. When tender, drain the beets and let them cool.

Peel them, cut into thin slices, and dress with oil, vinegar, salt and pepper. They are also delicious served cold as a side dish to omelettes, hard boiled eggs and boiled meats.

Recommended wine
Valpolicella classico

Variations
Beets may also be steamed or baked in the oven. To bake them, arrange them in a baking dish and cover halfway with water. Bake until tender and then proceed as given above.

vovi a'ocio (de bò)

FRIED EGGS

E ggs play a fundamental role in every culinary tradition, both as a basis to many recipes (pasta for first courses, sweets, etc.) and as binder in many others (in frying batters, stuffings, fillings, and so forth). But on their own, eggs also constitute a complete food and have always had an excellent reputation.

183

Nowadays, hens' eggs are what we eat most, but once, the range was much wider and included a variety of different birds' eggs (ducks, quails, guinea hens, etc). Venetian farmers hold on jealously to the eggs laid by their free-range hens, keeping them for family consumption and leaving the industrial-quality product to the others.

Our forebears knew innately much more about eggs than we do today: for example, a "glass" of fresh beaten eggs is an energetic and revitalising drink (it contains a high amount of protein). Since egg shells are porous, eggs should be kept away from air and odours which would affect the delicate flavour. They knew that springtime and summer eggs were the finest and in order to achieve a perfect hard boiled egg, it was best to make a tiny pin prick in the shell before boiling. Finally, eggs were often used as tender in exchange for other goods, when farmers were short of cash.

Venetian cooking includes countless recipes and methods of preparing eggs, but the most traditional are also the most simple. First we have vovi a l'ostrega *(oyster style) which entails placing the yolk onto a spoon, dressing with a pinch of salt (and pepper, if desired) and a drop of lemon juice and then eating it in one go. Then, there are* vovi suài *("sweaty" or eggs in the shell): put eggs in cold water, bring the water to a boil and as soon as it begins boiling, remove the egg. Put it into an egg cup and remove the top part of the shell with a knife, add a pinch of salt and eat with a spoon. Eggs in the shell become* vovi duri *(hard boiled) if the cooking time is extended to 8 minutes (or 6 minutes for soft-boiled, "uova barzotte").* Vovi sofegai *or* in camisa *(smothered or poached eggs) are prepared by cooking them in water without the shell: bring a pot of water to a boil with a spoonful of white vinegar (one spoonful for every litre of water), crack each egg into a saucer and slide the egg into the water where the bubbles are rising. After 3 minutes, remove the egg with a slotted spoon. Put it onto a cutting board and trim off and even out the sides. Serve on a bed of asparagus (or spinach or otherwise) or continue with more elaborate preparation in any number of ways (dusting the eggs with bread crumbs and sautéing in butter, serving on a bed of peppers or grilled bacon; dusting with bread crumbs and baking for a few minutes in a hot oven).* Vovi a l'ocio (de bò) *are eggs fried "sunny side up" in lard, oil or butter. For best results, they should be cooked one at a time and should be full and swelling in a golden crispy shell.*

. . . .

Ingredients
for 4 servings
8 eggs
100 g (3 ½ oz.) butter
salt

Preparation time
About 15 minutes

Melt the butter in a pan, letting it fry slightly.

——

Crack the eggs gently one at a time into a saucer. Sprinkle with salt and slide them into the frying pan.

——

With a spatula or a spoon, keep the white from spreading too far out beyond the yolk.

——

When the white is slightly solidified and golden at the edges, remove the eggs with a slotted spoon and arrange on a serving platter as they are cooked.

——

Serve with a side dish of seasonal vegetables.

Recommended wine
Tocai bianco dei Colli Berici

Variations
No variations come to mind except perhaps for variations in the "bed" on which the fried eggs are lain (for example, a bed of fontina cheese, zucchini, peas with ham…).

186

fritata co'le sego'le

ONION OMELETTE

*O*nce upon a time, Venetian housewives kept a farsòra *(special frying pan)* in the pantry which they used to cook only omelettes. This was the secret to obtaining a perfect result. The farsòra was a large, perfectly flat iron frying pan with low sides and a thick bottom. It was never washed, but after each use was simply wiped clean with a tea towel. If, in spite of this diligence, omelettes still dared to stick to the bottom of the pan, then the bottom of the pan had to be lubricated with a bit of lard, the greased pan was put on very high heat, sprinkled with fine salt and rubbed energetically with a cloth. These days, non-stick coating on frying pans has resolved these quandaries.

Omelettes are cooked at high heat so that the beaten eggs coagulate quickly and the result is dry and golden on the outside, soft and creamy within.

. . . .

Ingredients for 4 servings
8 eggs
2 onions
60 g (4 tablespoons) butter
salt and pepper

Preparation time
About 15 minutes

Beat the eggs with a bit of salt and pepper in a large bowl.

——

Slice the onion into thin rings and sauté the onion rings in a pan with the butter, being careful not to let them brown.

——

Pour in the beaten eggs and mix well. As soon as the eggs begin to coagulate on the underside, shake the pan to keep the omelette from sticking to the bottom.

——

When the upper edge begins to coagulate, flip the omelette over to cook it a bit on the other side, sliding it first onto a lid or a plate having the same dimensions.

——

Serve the omelette piping hot on a round serving platter.

Recommended wine
Tocai bianco dei Colli Euganei

Variations
Omelettes are prepared in any number of ways but the most traditional are: *fritata rognosa*, with onions and diced smoked or unsmoked bacon, or with sausage meat crumbled on top; with boiled prawns; with soft shelled crabs (see page 147 for recipe); with blanched hop shoots (see page 80 for recipe); with asparagus or with minced *erba mare*, atricaria *(Chrysanthemum parthenium)* or other wild and highly flavoured herbs; or finally with ricotta or other delicate cheese.

Dessert

baìco'li

VENETIAN BISCUITS

Before industry turned homemade biscuit baking into a superfluous and unnecessary caprice by filling the market with ready-made biscuits of all shapes and sizes, ladies of the Venetian household personally prepared biscuits which were kept on hand in the pantry for unexpected guests, children, snacks and to eat for breakfast with a cup of tea.

Despite the many different kinds of traditional biscuits available, the quintessentially Venetian biscuits were (and still are) baìco'li, named such in the 1700s by the baker who invented them due to the shape that vaguely resembled a crosswise slice of mullet (baico'lo).

These delicate biscuits were ordinarily served with coffee or zabaione, or sweet wine from Cyprus or Moscato from Istria, or even a cup of hot chocolate, flavoured with cinnamon or nutmeg.

Nowadays, hardly anyone makes baìco'li at home because the Colussi baking company in Vittorio Veneto prepares an excellent quality biscuit that has the same fragrance as times past and is still sold in the traditional metal tin. A little tune sings the praises of baìco'li which goes something like this: «There is no biscuit more beautiful in the world, nor finer, sweeter, lighter or tastier, to dip into the cup or glass, than our Venetian baìco'li».

You can believe it.

189

Housewives no longer have to toil over preparation of these sweet and crispy biscuits which, as can be seen from the recipe, require a fairly complicated two-step process.

. . . .

Ingredients
for 6 servings
400 g (1 lb) white flour
70 g (4 ½ tablespoons) butter
60 g (2 oz.) fine white sugar
15 g (½ oz.) yeast
1 egg white
1 ½ glasses of milk
half a spoonful of salt

Preparation time
3 hours (first step) plus 2 days of rest,
plus another hour (second step)

Crumble and dissolve the yeast
in half a glass of warm milk.

——

Make a mound with 100 grams flour.
Make a hole in the middle of the flour
mound and add the milk and yeast.
Mix well, kneading to form a fairly stiff
dough (if necessary, add a little more
flour). Cut a cross in the top of the
dough with a sharp knife and put it aside
in a bowl, covered with a tea towel.
Let the dough rise for half an hour
in a warm place. It should double
in volume by the end of rising.

——

While the dough is rising, beat the egg
white until stiff. Soften the butter and
knead it lightly with dampened hands.
Warm up the rest of the milk.

——

Take the rest of the flour and mix
it with the sugar and a pinch of salt
on a counter top. Mound the flour
mixture as before and make a hole
in the centre. Put the risen dough
in the middle of the mound of flour
with the beaten egg white and softened
butter. Knead with the hands for
about 10 minutes, gradually adding
the warm milk, adding just enough

to make a dough similar in consistency
to bread dough.

——

Divide the dough into four parts.
Using the hands, shape each portion
of dough into a loaf, 8-10 cm diameter.

——

Butter a baking sheet and put the
loaves on the sheet with sufficient
space in between. Press them
down with the hands to achieve
the slightly rounded, flattened shape
typical of *baìco'li*. Cover the baking
sheet with a tea towel and set
the loaves aside in a warm place
to rise for a couple of hours.

——

Preheat the oven for about 10 minutes
at medium heat (180 °C).
When the oven is hot, put in the
baking sheet with the loaves and bake
for 10-15 minutes. Watch carefully
so that the dough takes on a golden,
not brown colour.

——

Remove the baking pan from
the oven when the loaves are golden.
Let them cool and then cover again
with a tea towel and set the loaves
aside for a couple of days.

——

After two days, cut the loaves into
slices with a very sharp knife
(ideally, the slices should no thicker
than 2 mm and cut on the diagonal)
as you would cut a salami.

——

In the meantime, preheat the oven
to 180 °C with the baking sheet in the
oven. Remove the baking sheet quickly
from the oven (closing the oven
immediately to keep it hot). Arrange
the slices on the sheet and put it
back into the oven. Watch carefully
while the slices are cooking, as they

should toast, not brown or burn (about 10 minutes should be enough time).

—

The slices should now be light and crispy. Let them cool then store in a tin or a tightly closed glass container. They keep well for several months.

<u>*Recommended wine*</u>
A fortified Recioto di Soave

<u>*Variations*</u>
To make the preparation faster and less complicated, eliminate the two-day rest period and adding an egg yolk to the first batch of dough along with the yeast. Proceed as in the recipe. The amount sugar can be varied according to taste.
The quantities given in this recipe are for 6 servings: to make more *baìco'li* to keep for future consumption, just multiply the ingredients.

ossi da morto

BONE-SHAPED BISCUITS

The unusual name of these popular biscuits (they are called trandoti *in the area around Verona) comes from their rounded shape that is fatter at the ends, making them resemble* ossi, *bones. They are eaten all year round with morning coffee or as a quick dessert after an informal lunch, dipping them into a glass of sweet wine.*
In Venice, ossi da morto *can be found at the* pistòri *(bakeries) as well as the* sca'letèri *(small pastry shops). Time ago, the variety and sheer number of pastries eaten in Venice was so widespread that – as G. Boerio confirms in his dictionary (1856) – each shop specialised in one type of pastry. There were the* ciambellai *who made doughnuts, the* offellaro *that sold crunchy pastries, the* bericuocolaio, cialdonaio, cantucciaio, confortinaio, *all of whom sold a different type of sweet.*
According to Boerio: «... it would seem that scalete *was the term used to describe all sorts of sweets confected by the* ciambellaio, *but perhaps most particularly the kind of bread with sugar and butter whose shape resembled the Easter breads eaten by the Jews...».*

. . . .

191

BISCOTI VENESSIANI

TWICE-COOKED
DOUGHNUTS

Ingredients
for 6 servings
500 g (1 lb) white flour
150 g (5 ¼ oz.) white sugar
100 g (3 ½ oz.) butter
50 g (2 oz.) yeast
2 spoonfuls of extravirgin olive oil
3 whole eggs
a glass of milk
a small glass of anisette liqueur
  (a shot glass)
a pinch of salt

Preparation time
1 hour in total plus a rest time of 3 hours

Dissolve the yeast in the glass of warm milk. Melt the butter in a saucepan. Beat the eggs with a pinch of salt (keep one egg white aside).

——

Mound the flour on the counter top and pour the beaten eggs into the centre with the melted butter, oil, sugar, anisette liqueur, and milk and yeast and mix well working and kneading with the hands to form a smooth and uniform dough. Cover the dough with a towel and set it aside in a warm place for 3 hours.

——

Shape the dough into rolls 2 cm in diameter and cut them into 15 cm sections. Pressing and flattening the tips, shape the pieces into bone-shaped biscuits. Place them on a baking sheet.

——

Put them into a moderately hot oven (150 °C) and bake for 15 minutes.

——

Remove the baking sheet from the oven and brush the surfaces with the beaten egg white to make them shiny. Set them aside to firm up overnight.

——

But them back into the oven to finish cooking for 20 to 30 minutes. These are true "biscotti" because they have been baked twice.

Recommended wine
A fortified Recioto di Valpolicella

Variations
Around the Treviso area, the dough used is common risen bread dough, made with water instead of milk. The glass of anisette added as a flavouring ingredient is traditional but may be redundant. Some cooks like to add a bit of honey, consequently reducing the amount of sugar. Veronese *trandoti* are made with polenta that has not yet hardened with the addition of a handful of flour and other ingredients.

---

bigarani

*V*enetian *baìco'li and ossi da morto (see preceding recipes) are only two of the many varieties of Venetian biscuits. All have a common base of yeast-risen dough, made with milk instead of water. Countless other biscuits can be obtained with slight variations in the ingredients:* bigarani *are shaped to vaguely resemble the female genitalia (biga in the dialect of Venice means vulva). If they have a more or less phallic shape, they are then called* pando'li; *if they are rounded, they are called* busso'lai *(less sweet and more bread-like in texture); when they have an irregular form, then they are called* bruti ma boni *and so on and so forth.* Bigarani *were once a traditional gift presented to women who had just given birth, accompanied by a good bottle of sweet sipping wine, so that she might regain her strength all the sooner.*

Ingredients
for 5 servings
500 g (1 lb) white flour
100 g (3 ½ oz.) fine white sugar
100 g (3 ½ oz.) butter
50 g (2 oz.) yeast
3 whole eggs
a glass of milk
a pinch of salt

Preparation time
1 hour in total,
plus a rest time of 3 hours,
plus overnight

Dissolve the yeast in the glass of warm milk. Melt the butter in a saucepan. Beat the eggs with a pinch of salt (keep one egg white aside).

Mound the flour on the counter top and pour the beaten eggs into the centre with the melted butter, sugar, and milk and yeast and mix well working and kneading with the hands to form a smooth and uniform dough. Cover the dough with a towel and set it aside to rise in a warm place for 3 hours.

Shape the dough into rolls 15-20 cm long and 1.5 cm in diameter. Then shape them into twirls them into circles and place them on a baking sheet.

Put them into a moderately hot oven (150 °C) and bake for 15 minutes. Remove the baking sheet from the oven and brush the surfaces of the *bigarani* with the beaten egg white to make them shiny. Set them aside to firm up overnight.

But them back into the oven to finish cooking for about 20 minutes, watching carefully so that they don't burn or become too dark.

195

Recommended wine
Prosecco di Conegliano-Valdobbiadene
"superiore di Cartizze"

Variations
Bigarani mori are a dark version

of the biscuits, made by adding other ingredients, such as grated chocolate or cocoa powder to the dough (about 50-60 grams according to the quantities given above) or equal quantities of chopped toas ted almonds.

---

amareti venessiani

AMARETTI

These little sweet pastries owe their name to the bitter sweet taste given by a few bitter almonds (or the inner nut inside peach or apricot pits) offset by a large quantity of sweet almonds. Ideally, they will emerge from the oven crunchy on the outside and soft and tender within.

. . . .

Ingredients
for 8-10 servings
500 g (1 lb) shelled sweet almonds
(with the skin)
50 g (2 oz.) shelled bitter almonds
(with the skin)
500 g (1 lb) fine white sugar
4 egg whites
10 g (⅔ tablespoon) ground cinnamon
the grated rind of 2 lemons, a pinch of salt

Preparation time
About 40 minutes

Beat the egg whites until stiff peaks form.

———

Chop the sweet and bitter almonds very finely, add the sugar, the grated lemon rinds, cinnamon, a pinch of salt and the beaten egg whites. Blend well.

Butter a baking sheet. Use a spoon to make walnut sized balls out of the dough. Put the balls on the baking sheet and flatten them slightly. Bake in a medium oven (150-180 °C) for about 20 minutes making sure the biscuits don't become excessively brown.

Recommended wine
Moscato dei Colli Euganei

Variations
The spices and flavourings (cinnamon and grated lemon rind) can be changed depending on taste, for example, a glass of liqueur of choice can be added instead. If hazelnuts or toasted peanuts are used in place of the almonds, the result will be a deliciously different biscuit.

---

za'leti

SWEET CORNBREAD CAKES

The name of these sweets derives from "gialletti" – little yellow morsels – and refers to the colour of the dough due to the cornmeal used. As in frito'le (see page 199-202 for recipe), za'leti are also typical and traditional sweets eaten around carnival time and are believed to bring good luck.

Every authentic Venetian housewife has her own personal and closely guarded recipe for zal'eti, usually associated with local products, personal tastes or a particular flight of fancy.

. . . .

Ingredients
for 8-10 servings
400 g (1 lb) corn meal
300 g (¾ lb) white flour
150 g (5 ¼ oz.) fine white sugar
150 g (5 ¼ oz.) butter
100 g (3 ½ oz.) sultana raisins
100 g (3 ½ oz.) yeast
70 g (2 ½ oz.) pine nuts
3 whole eggs
a glass of milk
a pinch of salt
a pinch of vanilla
the grated rind of a lemon
powdered sugar
a little butter for the baking sheet

Preparation time
About 1 hour

Sift and blend together the flour
and the cornmeal. Dissolve the yeast
in the warm milk. Plump the raisins
in a little warm water. Melt the butter.

—

Beat the eggs with the sugar in a bowl
and add the flour, cornmeal, salt, milk
and yeast, the drained, plumped raisins,
pine nuts, lemon rind, melted butter and
vanilla gradually. Blend all the ingredients
together to make a smooth dough.

If it is too firm, add a little more milk.

—

Shape the dough into rolls of 3-5 cm
diameter. Cut them into pieces to make
7-8 cm long logs with rounded ends
or small oval shaped biscuits.

—

Butter a baking sheet. Put the shaped
biscuits on the baking sheet leaving some
space in between. Bake in a medium
oven (180 °C) for about 25-30 minutes,
depending on how big they are.

—

When the biscuits are done, let them
cool off, dust with powdered sugar
and serve either warm or cold.

Recommended wine
Bianco di Custoza
or Vespaiolo di Breganze

Variations
The amounts of flour and cornmeal
can vary by either using equal parts
of each or double the amount of cornmeal
(some cooks use white cornmeal instead
of yellow). The sultana raisins may also
be plumped in grappa or rum. The pine
nuts may be eliminated or replaced with
pieces of candied fruit. Finally, quite a few
cooks prefer to leave out the yeast.

crosto'li o ga'lani

**CRUNCHY
FRYCAKES**

V enetians are quite clear on the point: crosto'li or ga'lani *are their invention, or to make a
concession, are at least a speciality of the Veneto, born at the same time as Carnival. Mention of these delights can be found in cookbooks dating back to the 1500s. Giovàne de
Rosselli, for example, in his* Opera Nova chiamata Epulario *(Venice, 1518) defined them as follows: «Frycakes full of air: frycakes that appear to be full and yet are empty».
However, the Tuscans swear that they invented "frittele", and have called them "cenci" or "chiacchiere". In fact all the other regions of Italy raise their voices to the same song, changing the name
with the homeland: "lattughe" in Brescia, "bugie" in Piedmont and Liguria, "frappe" or "flappe" in
Umbria, "sfrappole" in Emilia-Romagna or "nastri" or "nastri delle suore" everywhere else.
Both Venetian names,* crosto'li *or* ga'lani, *stand for a sweet prepared in different shapes: the first a
diamond shapes with a fluted slit in the middle (like the Tuscan "cenci") and the second are braided
strips ("chiacchiere").*

. . . .

*I n g r e d i e n t s
f o r   6   s e r v i n g s*
300 g (¾ lb) white flour
60 g (4 tablespoons) fine white sugar
60 g (4 tablespoons) butter
2 whole eggs
a pinch of salt
a small glass of grappa
   (a shot glass is about right)
half a glass of milk
seed oil or lard for frying
50 g (2 oz.) powdered sugar
   or vanilla sugar

P r e p a r a t i o n   t i m e
About 1 hour

Soften or just melt the butter.

———

Put the flour in a mound on the counter
top and make a crater in the centre
for the eggs, melted butter, sugar, milk,
the grappa, and a little salt and mix well.
Knead the mixture until it becomes
soft and elastic and can be rolled
with a rolling pin.

———

Roll it out with a rolling pin as thin
as possible. Use a fluted rotary cutter
to make diamond shapes and rectangles

(crosto'li), making two slits in the
centre or make ribbons as wide as two
fingers to knot together *(ga'lani)*.

Heat the oil in a large pot and fry
he *crosto'li* or *ga'lani* making sure that
they don't brown excessively.

———

Remove them from the oil and let
them drain on kitchen paper towels.
Arrange them on a serving platter,
dusting with a little powdered sugar.

R e c o m m e n d e d   w i n e
Recioto della Valpolicella spumante

V a r i a t i o n s
According to tradition, the amount
of sugar and butter must be equal to
half the weight of the eggs, while
the amount of flour must be
measured according to the
consistency of the dough.
Use of grappa as a flavouring
is typically Veneto, but
Marsala or another sweet
fortified wine can be used in its
place. A little orange juice and/
or a bit of fresh grated lemon rind
makes a pleasant tangy addition.

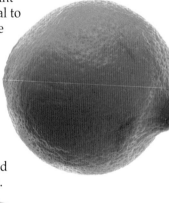

frito'le venessiane

VENETIAN FRYCAKES

Frito'le *and Carnival go hand-in-hand in Venice: you can't have one without the other, since these little cakes come sizzling and popping out of the oil, bursting with flavour like the joy that rings through the streets each year in February.*
Plus, they are best eaten right away, while fresh and hot as they only last as long as the masquerade festival. Finally, because they are rich and filling, they are ideal during the cold season that welcomes hearty foods.
The recipe can vary widely (with apples, semolina, cornmeal, rice, pumpkin, cream and so forth) but all share the same basic batter and the method of frying in boiling oil and lard, just like in ancient Chinese cooking, observed G. Maffioli (see bibliography). In fact, contact between the Serenissma Republic and China was frequent and friendly, especially during the period between Marco Polo's visit and the onset of Black Death in 1348.

. . . .

Ingredients
for 6 servings
500 g (1 lb) white flour
130 g (4 ½ oz.) sultana raisins
80 g (3 oz.) fine white sugar
40 g (1 ½ oz.) yeast
2 whole eggs
2 glasses of milk
2 small glasses of grappa
   (a shot glass is about right)
the grated rind of a lemon
   (only the yellow part)
a pinch of ground cinnamon
a pinch of salt
sunflower seed oil for frying
   (lard was used in the past)
vanilla sugar

Preparation time
½ hour (step one),
5 hours of rising, plus another
½ hour (step two)

Soak the sultana raisins in the grappa to soften and plump them.
Dissolve the yeast in half a glass of warm milk.

Mix the flour, eggs, milk, sugar, lemon rind, cinnamon and salt in a bowl. Mix well and add the dissolved yeast and raisins soaked in grappa. Blend the mixture well using a wooden spoon. The dough should be quite loose. Cover the bowl with a tea towel and let it rise for about 5 hours in a warm place.

When rising is complete, stir the dough again, add a little more milk or water if the dough seems too firm. It should be fairly liquid.

Heat the oil in a heavy pot for frying. Pour in the batter by the spoonful, keeping them well apart so they don't stick together.
Fry them until fairly dark (a nice hazelnut colour) then turn them over and fry on the other side. Remove with a slotted spoon and let them drain on kitchen paper towels.

Finally, while the frycakes are still hot, dip them in vanilla sugar

199

FRITO'LE VENESSIANE

and arrange them into a pyramid shape on a serving platter.

Recommended wine
Malvasia dolce

Variations
Frito'le made in the past were made with water instead of milk and anisette liqueur was used in place of the grappa. The grappa may also be left out in today's *frito'le* and pine nuts and candied citron can be added instead. The pinch of cinnamon is a clear throw back to the oriental influence on Venice, but it can be easily left out, as it is a spice that may not be to everyone's taste.

spumilie

MERINGUES

Simple but elegant desserts, very popular in Venetian households as desserts and decorative elements for fancy cakes. Made only with whipped egg whites and sugar and dried out rather than baked in the oven, these sweet bites can take on a variety of shapes and sizes (baskets, mushrooms, O-shapes) and colours (by adding cocoa powder or a few grains of coffee, etc).

Ingredients
for 6 servings
4 egg whites
200 g (1 ¼ cup) vanilla sugar
butter and flour for the baking sheet

Preparation time
About 1 hour plus cooling time

Beat the egg whites until stiff peaks form, using a whisk or electrical mixer.

——

Fold in the vanilla sugar, sifting it into the mixture and blending with an up and down motion to avoid deflating the egg whites.

——

Butter and flour the baking sheet. Use a pastry bag or a spoon to form little mounds of the egg white mixture, making sure to leave some space on the baking sheet.

——

Put the baking sheet into a warm oven (about 100 °C) and bake the meringues with the oven door ajar for 30 minutes, watching carefully as the *spumilie* must remain as pure white as possible.

——

Remove the baking sheet from the oven, let the meringues cool and remove them from the baking sheet.

——

Arrange on a serving platter.

Recommended wine
Prosecco di Conegliano-Valdobbiadene "superiore di Cartizze"

Variations
If the meringues are shaped fairly large, they can be filled with whipped cream or ice cream by making a hole in the bottom and removing some of the middle with a spoon. A sure way of baking is to warm up the oven, turn it off and then add the baking sheet with the meringues, leaving them inside until they are firm and dry.

r o s a d a

MILK PUDDING

This elegant and creamy spoon dessert is simple and yet delicate: simple ingredients (milk, sugar and eggs) with a very basic method of preparation (slow and rhythmic moving of the hand). It is a dense and creamy pudding that would ordinarily be poured but Venetians prefer to serve it by the spoonful directly from the pot. The name refers to the colour and echoes the strong Spanish influence in the Venetian dialect: this dessert used to be called "Catalan cream".

Ingredients
for 4 servings
500 ml (2 cups) fresh milk, a vanilla bean
5 egg yolks
80 g (3 oz.) fine sugar

Preparation time
About ½ hour, plus refrigeration time

Bring the milk to a boil with the vanilla bean. Let the milk cool and then remove the bean.

——

Pour the yolks and the sugar into a bowl and beat until fluffy with an electric mixer or whisk. The mixture should be soft and voluminous. Add the warm milk and stir

very carefully and gently with a wooden spoon, stirring in the same direction.

——

Pour the cream into a double boiler or into a pot set over another pot of simmering water, and cook, stirring constantly and always in the same direction.

Let the pudding cool and serve it directly from the pot used for cooking.

Variations
A sachet of vanilla powder or a bit of vanilla extract can be used in place of the vanilla bean.
Or eliminate the vanilla altogether and add the grated rind of one lemon.

creme frite

FRIED CREAM

A very popular dessert in the lagoon city, it can be eaten in any season and can be found for sale in the early hours of the morning at bakeries and in other small stores around the Veneto. Its delicate and distinctive flavour makes it perfect served as an original dessert for special occasion lunches.

Ingredients
for 5 servings
200 g (½ lb) white flour
180 g (¾ cup) fine sugar
100 ml (½ cup) fresh milk
5 egg yolks
grated rind of a lemon
fine bread crumbs
olive oil and butter for frying
vanilla sugar

Preparation time
About 1 ½ hours

Blend the egg yolks (setting aside
the whites) and the sugar well in a heavy
pot. Add the sifted flour, the grated
lemon rind, and add the milk a little
at a time, mixing well.

Put the pot on the heat and bring
to a boil, stirring the mixture constantly
and always in the same direction.
Cook for about ten minutes.

Sprinkle water over a marble
countertop and pour on the cream.
Spread it out well, making it
about a finger high and let it cool.

Beat some of the egg whites. Heat up
the oil and the butter in a frying pan.

Cut the cream into diamond shapes
or squares and dip them into the beaten
egg whites, then in the bread crumbs
and fry the shapes until golden brown.

Serve the fried cream piping hot,
dusted with a bit of vanilla sugar.

Recommended wine
Moscato dei Colli Euganei
or another dessert wine

Variations
The cream may also be poured into
a low-sided buttered baking sheet to
cool and even out before cutting.
A little vanilla can also be added to
flavour the cream, either a sachet or boil
a vanilla bean in the milk and then
let it cool in the milk. For a crunchier
coating, dredge the cream shapes
in flour, then beaten egg white and
finally bread crumbs before frying.

z a b a j ò n

ZABAIONE

G iven the fortifying virtues of this nutritious food, Venetian custom goes that it was always offered by the friends of the groom at the end of the nuptial banquet, in order to ensure success for the labours he would put through later on that evening.
It seems that the name has an Illyrian origin: in the 18th century, on the Venetian coasts of Yugoslavia, a dense mixture of barley water was called "zabaja" held to be a good source of energy and nutrition.
It is most likely that Venetians introduced this recipe, altering it slightly to suit local tastes. It is delicious as a dessert in its own right or as an ingredient in other pudding recipes.

Ingredients
for 5 servings
8 egg yolks, 12 spoonfuls of sugar

300 ml (1 ¼ cups) egg Marsala or other
   sweet fortified wine
2 pinches of cinnamon

ZABAJÒN

Preparation time
About ½ hour

Beat the egg yolks and the sugar with a wooden spoon in a heavy pot until foamy and pale yellow in colour.

Add the sweet wine and the cinnamon and mix well.

Put the pot on very low heat, mixing all the while in the same direction, until the mixture begins to swell in volume. Be very careful that it does not boil or the eggs will scramble. To prevent this from happening, some cooks prefer to beat the eggs in a double boiler.

Serve it hot in cups, accompanied by *baìco'li* (see page 189-191 for recipe).

Recommended wine
Vin santo di Gambellara

Variations
It is not a hard and fast rule to serve the "zabaione" hot: some people like it warm or even cold. It is a matter of personal taste. Others like a little whipped cream on top or the dessert can be made more "spirited" with a couple of spoonfuls of rum. A peasant variation eliminates the cooking and uses the egg whites: beat the egg whites until stiff and fold in the egg yolk and sugar mixture. Blend well and serve the "zabaione" as it is or with a little coffee or coffee and milk folded in. This version is then known as *sbatudìn* (beaten) and is offered to school age children at breakfast or as an after school snack.

budìn de cioco'lata

CHOCOLATE PUDDING

In the 18th century, Venetians would frequently go to the coffee shops (akin to contemporary coffee bars) and drink cups of hot chocolate or coffee or **cafè** cioco'lata *or other beverages (such as rose liqueur). Carlo Goldoni immortalised the gentile custom in his plays. Hot chocolate was prepared using grated bitter chocolate, sugar, milk and ground cinnamon, while coffee was made in the* cògome *(coffee maker) and was poured through a strainer. Customers would ask for either coffee as* **cafè** de co'lo *or* cioco'lato de cu'lo, *meaning the clear coffee poured from the coffee maker whereas the best and most delicious chocolate was the last one taken from the hot chocolate pot. Among the many ways of eating and drinking chocolate, this pudding is one of the most sublime, and is best when served with fragrant* baìco'li *(see page 189-191 for recipe).*

Ingredients
for 4 servings
500 (2 cups) ml of milk
100 g (3 ½ oz.) dark bitter chocolate, grated
100 g (3 ½ oz.) potato flour or white flour
100 g (3 ½ oz.) butter
100 g (3 ½ oz.) sugar
3 egg yolks

Preparation time
½ hour, plus chilling time

Sprinkle a little liqueur in a pudding mould.

Beat the butter and the sugar in a heavy pot with a wooden spoon. Add the egg yolks and mixing continuously, add the flour, milk a little at a time, and the grated chocolate.

Put the pot on the heat and cook the mixture until it thickens. Pour it into

the mould, cover and let it cool well.
Then place it in the refrigerator to chill.

———

Before serving, unmould the pudding
onto a serving platter.

Recommended wine
Recioto di Gambellara

Variations
The pudding mould can also be

dampened with cold water, or
buttered, or even brushed with a light
coating of almond oil. For a more
uniform mixture, cook the pudding
in a bain-marie in the oven at 150 °C.
Put the mould with the pudding
into a recipient with water to about
two-thirds the way up.
After about 20 minutes, cover the
pudding with a sheet of aluminium
foil and let it cook for about ten more
minutes.

f u g a s s a   d e   P a s q u a

EASTER BREAD

Every city in the Veneto has its own version of typical Easter bread to commemorate the res-
urrection of Christ the first Sunday after the first full moon of spring. They are all soft risen
pastries, light and kneaded and left to rise for a lengthy period.
Vicenza has fogasse *in several different sizes, that become* bussolà, *redolent with grappa or*
colombine *with coloured eggs.*
In Treviso, the cakes are flavoured with anise, while Verona has brassadèla, *a soft and aromatic doughnut, that becomes the everyday treat* brassadelòn *when made without a centre hole.
There is a saying that goes, «If it doesn't rain on Palm Sunday, it will rain on the* brassadela
(Easter day)».
*In the area around Padua, Easter breads closely resemble their Venetian cousins, but in Este, a
large town just 30 kilometres from the capital, a family of bakers has been handing down a secret
recipe for* fogassa pasquale *so delicious that it is sent as a gift each year to the Pope in Rome.
Venice's Easter bread is perhaps the most complex of all and its recipe is given below.*

*Ingredients
for 5 servings*
500 g (1 lb) white flour
150 g (5 ¼ oz.) butter
150 g (5 ¼ oz.)fine white sugar
25 g (1 oz.) yeast
6 whole eggs, a small glass of kirsch
  (a shot glass is about right)
half a glass of milk
the grated rind of a orange
a pinch of ground cinnamon
a pinch of salt
butter and flour for the cake pan
40 g (2 ½ tablespoons) almonds and sugar
  to sprinkle

Preparation time
1 hour of preparation time,
plus 9 hours of rising, plus another
hour for baking

Dissolve the yeast in the warm milk.
Sift 150 grams of flour in a bowl. Add the
milk and yeast and knead until the dough
becomes soft and elastic. Cover with
a kitchen towel and put it in a warm place
and let it rest for a few hours.

———

The dough should double in volume
after rising.

torta nicol'lota

BREAD CAKE

This cake is called nico'lata because it was created by the people living in a tiny island of Venice where the church of San Nico'lo dei Mendigo'li was erected. Legend has it that these people were from Padua who escaped to Venice in the 7th century to flee the persecution of the Longobards and eked out a living by fishing in the lagoon. There were so poor that the island itself was called Mendigo'la (from mendicare = to beg) and the cake that bears the name of their parish church is none other than a way to use up leftover bread. Years ago, it was also prepared in the convents of Venice and handed out to the poor every Friday morning. It is still a very popular cake and can still be found in Venetian bakeries, or in the more sophisticated version, in pastry shops.

Ingredients

for 4 servings

600 ml (2 ½ cups) milk
300 g (¾ lb) leftover bread (without the crust)
100 g (½ cup) flour
100 g (½ cup) fine white sugar
100 g (½ cup) sultana raisins
30 g (2 tablespoons) butter
2 whole eggs
a pinch of salt
some fennel seeds

Preparation time

About 2 hours

Beat together the remaining egg and the egg white. Toast the almonds and remove the skin. Chop them coarsely. Butter and flour a cake pan.

After the dough has risen, knead it some more and shape it into a rough dove shape. Brush it with beaten egg and sprinkle the surface

Knead in the other 150 grams of sifted flour, half the softened butter, two beaten whole eggs and one yolk (set the white aside), and 100 grams of sugar. Knead the dough, put it into the bowl, cover and let it rise for another few hours.

Add the rest of the flour, the softened butter, two whole eggs, the kirsch, orange rind, vanilla, ground cinnamon, and salt and knead with the hands until soft and elastic. Cover and let it rise for about 5 hours.

with the chopped almonds and bake at 180 °C for about an hour. It is done when a toothpick inserted into the cake comes out clean.

Remove the cake from the oven, sprinkle more sugar on the surface and serve the cake either warm or cool, after decorating with coloured eggs.

Recommended wine

Moscato dei Colli Euganei

Variations

There are more simple as well as more complicated recipes: the former shorten the preparation times but not the rising times and use fewer flavourings. The latter include a five-stage procedure and use a variety of different spices and flavourings according to whim.

Soften and plump the raisins in warm water and beat the eggs. Cut the bread into cubes, put it into a bowl and pour over the milk. Let it stand for at least half an hour.

Add the sifted flour, sugar, softened butter, drained and squeezed raisins, the beaten eggs and a pinch of salt. Blend the ingredients together well until the dough has a soft consistency.

Butter a high-sided cake pan and dust with bread crumbs. Pour in the batter, level it out and sprinkle the surface with fennel seeds. Bake in a hot oven (180 °C) for about an hour.

Let the cake cool in the pan, then unmould it and serve.

Recommended wine
Moscato or Vin santo di Gambellara

Variations
To make the cake richer, a small glass of grappa, pine nuts or pieces of candied fruit can be added to the batter. Some cooks like a softer and lighter cake and thus add a little baking powder. The fennel seeds can be mixed into the batter or can be sprinkled on the surface. Finally, if a little diced up apple is added to the batter with some grated lemon rind, a simple version of *macafame* is obtained, a cake whose name in dialect means "hunger quencher".

pinsa venessiana

CORN CAKE

The word pinsa is dialect distortion of the Italian "pizza", meaning a substantial and hearty food whose ingredients vary from region to region and according to personal preferences. What doesn't change, however, is the base of yellow corn meal, highly flavoured and enriched with an array of ingredients. In times of yore, the cake was basted with the broth from muséto (in other words, pork broth) and sweetened with honey and molasses, as sugar was very expensive. A soft yellow cornmeal polenta was made and it was stuffed into cabbage leaves and baked under the grill of the fireplace hearth.
Country folk treasured this cake on the feast day of the Befana, the Epiphany on 6 January, and it was baked under the bonfire lighted on the eve of that occasion, to burn off any evil spirits left roaming from the past year and marking the transition from winter to spring.
The people of Vicenza called it the putana soto'l fogo – the "whore" because anything and everything went in (ingredients-wise) and "under the fire" for the method of baking. It is still a sweet found widely around Venice and the hinterlands of the Veneto.

Ingredients for 8 servings
500 ml (2 cups) milk
300 g (¾ lb) yellow cornmeal
200 g (½ lb) white flour
half a sachet of baking powder
200 g (7 oz.) fine white sugar
200 g (7 oz.) butter or lard

100 g (½ cup) sultana raisins
50 g (2 oz.) candied fruit
30 g (2 tablespoons) pine nuts
5 dried figs
a apple
a small glass of grappa
a pinch of salt
butter and bread crumbs for the cake pan

Preparation time
About 2 hours

Soften the raisins in warm water.
Cut the dried figs into pieces.
Peel the apple and cut it into slices.

——

Sift the flour in a bowl, add the baking
powder and mix. Add the sugar
and mix some more.

——

Pour the milk, butter, a glass of water,
and a pinch of salt in a pot. Bring to a boil
and add the cornmeal. Cook the mixture
for 10 minutes, stirring constantly.

——

Add the white flour (with the baking
powder and sugar) and all the
other ingredients; mix well and let it
cook for another 20 minutes, stirring
continuously.

——

Butter the cake pan, dust it with bread
crumbs and pour in the mixture,
which should be about two fingers

high in the pan. Bake the cake in
a moderate oven (180 °C) for an hour.
The *pinsa* will be ready when the
surface has formed a golden brown
crust or when a toothpick inserted
into the cake comes out clean.

——

Serve the cake cool or warm.

Recommended wine
Recioto di Soave or Valpolicella

Variations
The ingredients can be changed according
to personal preferences: rum or anisette
liqueur can replace the grappa, fennel
seeds instead of the anise; a pear in
place of the apple (or both); other types
of dried and candied fruit and so on
and so forth. Another slightly different
cornmeal dessert is called *torta sabiosa*,
which is made with potato flour and
eggs (with the whites beaten until stiff)
and served with a cake server as it is
very tender.

t i r a m e   s u

TIRAMI SU

*T*he original name of this spoon dessert comes from the energy-giving qualities and the calories that it contributes to the diet. Since it is very easy to prepare and requires no cooking,
the secret to a perfect result lies in obtaining the freshest, most genuine ingredients. It is a
fairly recent invention and therefore is not part of the traditional Veneto repertory of recipes, but has
a great number of variations, among which we chose the one that seemed most delicious.

*Ingredients
for 4 servings*
6 eggs
400 g (1 lb) ladyfingers (about 25)
500 g (1 lb) fresh mascarpone cheese
50 g (2 oz.) sweet cream, whipped
300 g (¾ lb) fine white sugar
300 ml (1 ¼ cups) light coffee
a small glass of kirsch (or rum)
20 g (¾ oz.) powdered cocoa

Preparation time
½ hour

Separate the eggs, keeping the yolks aside
and beating the egg whites until stiff.

——

Blend the yolks with 100 grams of sugar
and beat them until light and fluffy.
Blend in the mascarpone with a wooden
spoon. Fold in the beaten egg whites,

whipped cream and the kirsch,
until the mixture is uniform and creamy.

Dissolve the remaining sugar with
300 ml of the coffee. Dip the ladyfingers
in the sweetened coffee and line them
up in a rectangular high-sided serving
dish. Spread a layer of mascarpone
cream over the top, then add another
layer of ladyfingers soaked in coffee
and then another layer of cream.
Continue until all the ladyfingers
are used and finish the dish with
a final layer of cream.

Cover the dish with plastic wrap
and put it into the refrigerator until

serving time. Just before serving, dust
the surface with a little cocoa powder.

Recommended wine
Fortified Recioto di Valpolicella

Variations
Sponge cake can be used in place
of the ladyfingers and brandy or other
aromatic liqueur can be used instead
of the kirsch. The amount of sugar
can also vary according to personal taste.
Some cooks add some diced candied
fruit (orange peel and citron) between
the layers and finish with a thick
layer of bitter cocoa.

mando'lato veneto

**MANDORLATO
(ALMOND CANDY)**

Ringing in the traditional New Year's celebrations in Venetian homes, there will invariably be a large mando'lato. It used to always be prepared at home, but nowadays it is hardly worth the effort, considering the excellent quality of commercially prepared products available. The confection is similar to torrone (white almond nougat) of Cremona and other regions of Italy, but the Veneto version was supposedly created around 1852 by a spezier (a chemist) in Cologna Veneta, a large town lying just at the boundary between Vicenza, Verona and Padua. Some cooks still enjoy making it at home and therefore, we are providing a recipe below.

Ingredients
for 12-15 servings
2 kg of sweet toasted and peeled almonds
1 kg (2 lbs) of honey
4 egg whites
a spoonful of cinnamon
white wafers

Preparation time
3 hours

Heat the honey for 30 minutes, stirring constantly. Then let it stand to cool for half an hour.

———

In the meantime, beat two of the egg whites until stiff.

———

Put the honey back on very low heat for thirty minutes and, mixing constantly, blend in the beaten egg whites.

———

Remove the honey mixture from heat and let it stand another half an hour. In the meantime, beat the remaining two egg whites until stiff and line a large and low baking dish with the wafers.

———

Put the honey back on the heat and fold in the remaining egg whites, stirring constantly. Add the almonds and the cinnamon, mixing delicately and pour the mixture into the baking dish lined with wafers.

———

Let it cool completely. Serve the *mando'lato* by breaking it into pieces.

Recommended wine
Vin santo di Gambellara

Variations
The use of cinnamon is like a flashing light attesting to the Venetian origins of this sweet. Many cooks in the region add candied fruit to the mixture. It is slightly darker than its cousin, *torrone*.

pomi coti

BAKED STUFFED APPLES

Apples were once the only fruit available in the winter in the Veneto. Today, they are still more popular than citrus fruits. They can be served in many ways, in addition to eating the whole fruit out of the hand: grated raw with crumbled biscuits for small children; in meringues; in cakes, pies and tarts; baked in the oven for the ill, and so forth. Our forebears sometimes put a piece of apple skin on the hot plate of the wood stove to release a pleasant fragrance in the room. Cooking stuffed apples is the method that has best survived the evolution of modern tastes.

Ingredients
for 6 servings
6 large apples (best if slightly sour)
60 g (4 tablespoons) fine sugar
50 g (2 oz.) amaretti
50 g (2 oz.) sultana raisins
30 g (2 tablespoons) butter
a glass of white wine
half a glass of aromatic liqueur
   (kirsch does nicely)

Preparation time
30-40 minutes

Wash the apples well and remove the core and stem with an apple corer.

———

Blend together the crumbled amaretti, the sultana raisins, and the half glass of liqueur.

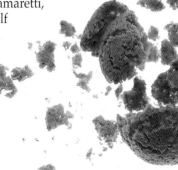

POMI COTI

Use the mixture to stuff the apples
and then place them in a baking dish.

———

Sprinkle the wine over the fruit.
Put a knob of butter on each apple
and dust with sugar.

———

Preheat the oven to 200 °C and bake
the apples until tender, between 20
and 30 minutes, depending on the size.

———

Serve the baked apples hot out of the oven.

Recommended wine
Malvasia dolce or Recioto di Soave

Variations
The filling may vary according to taste:
apples are delicious filled with apricot
preserves or orange marmalade;
candied citron or chopped walnuts
and Grand Marnier; or ladyfingers,
rum and sultana raisins.
Baked apples are also delectable
at room temperature or slightly warm.

persegada

**FIRM QUINCE
DESSERT**

Quinces are not fruit suitable for eating raw, but at one time, most farmers had at least one quince tree in their garden for the very distinctive and delicious flavour of the fruit. Their peels were added in the same quantities as other fruits to make ratafià, a sort of low-alcohol rose liqueur to sip with friends at the end of lunch or between meals. Persegada, rather, a unique dessert still eaten today, is a firm and highly nutritious marmalade, loved by children at breakfast time or for an after-school snack. When cut into cubes and dipped into sugar, it keeps well in tightly closed tins or glass jars, and once was a staple to have on hand to offer to friends on long winter evenings. The correct name would be cotognata, but time ago, the dessert was made with peaches and called persegada. Somewhere along the line it was decided that since peaches are delicious raw and quinces are not, quinces should replace the peaches. The fruit changed but the name remained the same. Venetian tradition dictates that the sweet is offered on the feast day of San Martino, formed in the shape of the saintly knight, sprinkled with sugar and decorated with silvered adornments.

· ·

Ingredients
quinces
lemons
fine white sugar

Preparation time
2 hours, plus cooling
and drying time

Wash the quinces, then cook them
in plenty of water until they are tender.
Remove the skin and core.

———

Put the quince pulp into a large pot,
bring to a boil and cook for
a long time to reduce the fruit

further, stirring constantly.

———

Pass the puree through a strainer.
Weigh the pulp and add sugar in an
amount equal to the weight of the puree.
Add lemon juice on one lemon for
each half-kilo of puree.

———

Put the puree back on the heat
and let it boil for 40 minutes.
Turn off the heat and let the mixture cool.

———

In the meantime, prepare the moulds
or use a rectangular baking
dish, lined with buttered
kitchen paper.

———

216

Pour in the *persegada*, let it cool
for 12 hours, then put it away
for a day to dry in the open air.
Turn it over and let the dessert dry
out on the other side.

——

Cut the dessert into cubes, large
or small or in any shape desired and
put it into dry and closed containers.
It can be kept this way for months.

Recommended   wine
A sweet fortified wine

Variations
Instead of the kitchen paper,
an innovative idea is to use a layer
of bay leaves to line the dish.
Persegada can also be prepared
with other types of fruit, adjusting
the amounts given in the recipe.

---

pe'ladèi

PEEL CHESTNUTS

Marroni *are a special variety of chestnuts, larger and more flavourful than the more commonly found variety. Unlike the oval-shaped common chestnuts, marroni are rounded, since only one chestnut generally grows inside the spiny hull. These nuts used to reach Venice in the fall from the inland areas and were either roasted on an open fire or sold hot by street peddlers. They can still be purchased this way today.*

. . . .

Ingredients
for 6 servings
1 kg (2 lbs) marron chesnuts
a sprig of sage
a pinch of salt

Preparation time
Peeling time,
plus about another
hour of cooking

Peel the chestnuts and put them
into a pot, covering with cold water.

——

Add the sage
and salt.

——

Put the pot on heat and bring the
water to a boil. Boil for 45 minutes.

——

Serve them hot as dessert
or as mid-afternoon snack.

Recommended   wine
Recioto di Valpolicella or Soave

Variations
In the play *Le Massere*, by Carlo
Goldoni, the author gave this recipe,
replacing the water with a mixture
of water and milk and suggesting
fennel seeds in place of the sage.
Fennel seeds are a traditional spice
in some parts of the Veneto.
In addition to *peladei* and *caldarroste*
(fire roasted) chestnuts can be eaten
boiled or dried. In the latter case,
they are called *stracagnasse*,
meaning "jaw breakers" because
they have to chewed at length
before swallowing.

217

Bibliography

ALBERINI, MASSIMO, *Pasta & Pizza*, Milano, Mondadori, 1974

BOCCI, ZEFFIRO, *I vini veneti*, Verona, ESAV/ESPRO, 1980

BOERIO, GIUSEPPE, *Dizionario del dialetto veneziano*, Milano, A. Martello, 1971

BONI, ADA, *Cucina regionale italiana*, Milano, Mondadori, 1988

CAPNIST, GIOVANNI, *I dolci del Veneto*, Padova, F. Muzzio, 1983

CIPRIANI, GIUSEPPE, *L'angolo dell'Harry's Bar*, Milano, Rizzoli, 1978

CARNACINA, LUIGI, La grande Cucina, Milano, Garzanti, 1960

COLTRO, DINO, *La cucina tradizionale veneta*, Roma, Newton Compton, 1983

CONTINI, MILA, *Veneto in bocca*, Palermo, La Nuova ED.RI.SI., 1988

CORTINE, ROBERT J., *Larousse Gastronomique*, Parigi, Larousse, 1984

DA MOSTO, RANIERI, *Il Veneto in cucina*, Firenze, A. Martello-Giunti, 1984

GIOCO, GIORGIO, *La cucina scaligera*, Milano, F. Angeli, 1982

GOSETTI DELLA SALDA, ANNA, *Le ricette regionali italiane*, Milano, Solares, 1967

MARTINI, ANNA, *Vecchia e nuova cucina regionale italiana*, Milano, Mondadori, 1982

MAFFIOLI, GIUSEPPE, *La cucina padovana*, Padova, F. Muzzio, 1981

MAFFIOLI, GIUSEPPE, *La cucina trevigiana*, Padova, F. Muzzio, 1983, 1988

MAFFIOLI, GIUSEPPE, *La cucina veneziana*, Padova, F. Muzzio, 1982

RIEDL, RUPERT, *Fauna und Flora der Adria*, Hamburg und Berlin, Verlag Paul Parey, 1970

SALVATORI DE ZULIANI, MARIÙ, *A tola con i nostri veci. La cucina veneziana*, Milano, F. Angeli, 1983

ZORZI, ALVISE, *La vita quotidiana a Venezia nel secolo di Tiziano*, Milano, Rizzoli, 1990

ZORZI, ELIO, *Gastronomia veneziana*, Venezia, s.d.

ZORZI, ELIO, *Osterie veneziane*, Bologna, Zanichelli, 1928; poi: Venezia, Filippi, 1967.

L'Accademia Italiana della Cucina, Milano, Ed. A.I.C.

Index of recipes

Antipasti

Marinated sardines (*sarde'le in saòr*) 35
Spider crab "alla veneziana" (*granseo'le a' la venessiana*) 36
Coquilles Saint-Jacques "alla veneziana" (*cape sante a'la venessiana*) 40
Razor clam "a scottadito" (*cape 'longhe a scotadeo*) 42
Sauteed mussels (*peoci saltài*) 43
Sea truffles (*caparosso'li*) 44
Sea snails (*garuso'li*) 46
Small land snails (*bovo'leti*) 48
Polenta and cooked salami (*po'lenta e sa'lame coto*) 49
Fried pumpkin or corgette flowers (*fiori de suca o de suchete friti*) 51

First courses

Spaghetti and sardines or anchovies (*bìgo'li in salsa*) 53
Bigoli with duck sauce "alla vicentina" (*bìgo'li co' l'anara*) 56
Spaghetti with clams (*spagheti a'le vongo'le*) 57
Tagliatelle and peas (*papare'le coi bisi*) 58
Potato gnocchi (*gnochi de patate*) 61
Pasta and beans (*pasta e fasioi*) 64
Vegetable minestrone (*minestròn*) 66
Fish soup (*sopa de pesse*) 67
Tripe soup (*tripe in brodo*) 71
Baked pigeon soup (*sopa coada*) 72
Pappardelle in broth with chicken livers (*papare'le coi figadini*) 74
Venetian bread soup (*panada venessiana*) 74
Risotto with peas (*risi e bisi*) 76
Asparagus risotto (*risi e spàresi*) 78
Risotto with potatoes (*risi e patate*), 79
Risotto with "hop sprouts" (*risoto coi bruscando'li*) 80
Risotto with yellow pumpkin (*risoto de suca za'la*) 80
Risotto with red radicchio (*risoto al radicio rosso*) 81
Rice and cabbage (*risi e verze*) 82
Seafood risotto (*risoto de mar*) 83
Squid ink risotto (*risoto nero*) 84
Risotto with prawns (*risi e scampi*) 86
Eel risotto (*risoto de bisato*) 87
Risotto with frog (*risoto de rane*) 90
Risotto with sausages (*risi e 'luganeghe*) 92
Rice cooked in milk (*risi col late*) 93

Meat and game

Boiled meat platter *(carne lessa)* 95
Pepper sauce *(pearà)* 98
Stewed beef *(carne in tecia)* 99
Marinated and braised horsemeat *(pastissada de cavàl)* 100
Dalmatian mutton *(castradina s'ciavona)* 102
Skewered meat shish kebabs *(ose'leti scampai)* 103
Carpaccio *(carpaccio)* 106
Corned beef tongue *(lengua salmistrada)* 107
Stewed tripe *(tripe a'la trevisana)* 110
Venetian style liver *(figà a'la venessiana)* 111
Pork cooked in milk *(porsè'lo al late)* 113
Pork sausage *(cotechino)* 114
Treviso sausage with polenta *('luganeghe co'la polenta)* 115
Pig's trotter *(or veal foot)* 116
Stewed chicken *(po'lastro in tecia)* 116
Guinea fowl in pepper sauce *(faraona co'la peverada)* 117
Stuffed duck *(anara co'l pien)* 121
Dalmatian-style turkey *(dindio a'la s'ciavona)* 122
Stewed rabbit *(conicio in tecia)* 123
Jugged hare *(liévaro in salmì)* 124
Valligiani-style wild ducks *(màsori a'la va'lesana)* 128

Fish, crustaceans and molluscs

Beaten salted cod *(baca'là mantecato)* 131
Salted cod from Vicenza *(baca'là a'la visentina)* 134
Stewed eel *(bisato in tecia)* 135
Roasted eel *(bisato su l'ara)* 137
Sole with white wine *(sfogi al vin bianco)* 138
Poached sea bass *(branzìn lesso)* 139
Stewed goby *(go in broeto)* 142
Fried bullheads *(marsioni friti)* 144
Fried frogs *(rane frite)* 145
Soft shell crabs with sauce *(masanéte)* 146
Stuffed soft-shell crabs *(mo'leche ripiene)* 147
Mantis shrimp *(canocie conse)* 148
Edible crab venetian style *(gransipori a'la venessiana)* 149
Black cuttlefish served with white polenta *(sepe nere co'la po'lenta bianca)* 152
Tiny octopus *(folpeti)* 153
Fried squid *(ca'lamereti friti)* 154
Fired cockles *(canestrei friti)* 156
Fried seafood platter *(frito misto de mar)* 156
Snails in sauce *(s'ciosi in salsa)* 157

Side dishes and eggs

Stewed string beans (*tego'line in tecia*) 161
Stewed beans (*fasiosi sofegai*) 162
Sweet and sour pearl onions (*sego'lete agrodolse*) 163
Fennel cooked in milk (*fenoci col late*) 164
Boiled asparagus (*spàresi lessi*) 165
Garlic eggplant (*me'lansane al fongheto*) 168
Sautéed dandelions or corn poppies (*pissacani o roso'line in tecia*) 169
Grilled red radicchio (*radicio rosso ai ferri*) 170
Peperonata-fried peppers (*pevaronada*) 172
Peppers (*pevaroni*) 173
Venetian-style potatoes (*patate a'la venessiana*) 176
New baby artichokes (*castraure de Sant'Erasmo*) 177
Artichoke bottoms (*articiochi a' la venessiana*) 178
Smothered cabbage (*verze sofegae*) 180
Stewed thistles (*cardi in tecia*) 180
Baked pumpkin (*suca rosta*) 181
Celeriac (*sèleno rava*) 182
Boiled red beets (*erbete rave*) 183
Fried eggs (*vovi a'ocio de bò*) 183
Onion omelette (*fritata co'le sego'le*) 187

Desserts

Venetian biscuits (*baìco'li*) 189
Bone-shaped biscuits (*ossi da morto*) 191
Twice-cooked doughnuts (*bigarani*) 194
Amaretti (*amareti venessiani*) 196
Sweet corn-bread cakes (*za'leti*) 196
Crunchy frycakes (*crosto'li o ga'lani*) 198
Venetian frycakes (*frito'le venessiane*) 199
Meringues (*spumilie*) 202
Fried cream (*creme frite*) 203
Milk pudding (*rosada*) 203
Zabaione (*zabajòn*) 204
Chocolate pudding (*budìn de cioco'lata*) 206
Easter bread (*fugassa de pasqua*) 207
Bread cake (*torta nicol'lota*) 210
Corn cake (*pinsa venessiana*) 211
Tirami su (*tirame su*) 212
Mandorlato-almond candy (*mando'lato veneto*) 213
Baked stuffed apples (*pomi coti*) 214
Firm quince dessert (*persegada*) 216
Peel chestnuts (*pe'ladèi*) 217